MW01283997

Murder on the Teche

Murder on the Teche

A True Story of Money
and a Flawed Investigation

By
Tom Aswell

DVille Press

Murder on the Teche

Cover artwork by Jeanette Herren

Layout and design by Write2Grow, LLC

ISBN: 978-1-7368172-0-9

DVille Press

Published by:
DVille Press, LLC
618 Mississippi Street
Donaldsonville, Louisiana 70346 USA
(225) 473-9319
www.dvillepress.com

Dedicated to Betty who has kept me focused
and deeply in love for more than half-a-century
and to my grandparents, who were my strength,
my inspiration and my guiding light until
Betty could take over the job.

Acknowledgements

No book like this would ever be possible without the able assistance of a number of peopled whose identities would otherwise go unheralded. I cannot let their contributions go unmentioned.

First, there is Paul Chastant, the brother of the slain subject of this book. He called me one day to suggest that I look into the circumstances and ensuing investigation of the murder of his brother, Dr. Robert Chastant, in New Iberia on December 13, 2010. He referred me to James Daniels of nearby Lafayette, the attorney who handled Robert Chastant's estate. Mr. Daniels opened his voluminous files to me and even allowed me to take about half of his documents home so that I could digest them more fully. For that, there simply is no really sufficient way to express my gratitude.

I also would like to thank my volunteer editors Steve Winham and wife Betty who has served as my moral and professional conscience for more than half-a-century. Also, there is Mary Gehman of DVille Press who displayed more patience with me than she must have felt – and certainly more than I deserved. Some might call her attention to minute detail nit-picking; I prefer to think of it as the perfectionist's perfectionist and for that, I am grateful. Besides, from my experience editing books for two other authors, I know her job was anything but enjoyable. Editing is difficult work that requires a tremendous amount of attention to detail and the stamina to endure resistance from temperamental authors.

Thanks to Jeanette Herren for the wonderful design work she did on the cover of this book.

I would be remiss if I did not include a group of Ruston High teachers who saw something in an indigent kid who had no outward signs of motivation or potential and decided as a group to take him under their collective wings, to nurture his limited ability and to make him better than even he thought he was. Mr. Ryland, Coach Perkins, Mr. Barnes, Mrs. Garrett, Miss Hinton, Miss Lewis, and Mr. Peoples, you will never know what your influence meant to me. I only wish you were around for me to tell you personally.

i

The late Dr. F. Jay Taylor, then-president of Louisiana Tech University and Journalism Department Head Wiley Hilburn were strong influences on my decision to reenroll in college after ignominiously flunking out on my first try.

I have worked for three outstanding newspaper editors who taught me the important lesson than writing about people and events can be a most rewarding way to earn a living. Thanks to Tom Kelly, the one who gave me my first job in newspaper at the *Ruston Daily Leader* and then brought me back three more times; to Jimmy Hatten of the *Monroe Morning World* and Jim Hughes, a quick-tempered, demanding managing editor at *the Baton Rouge State-Times* who probably should've fired me but who stayed with me and made me a pretty decent reporter, my sincere and heartfelt thanks.

And to my grandparents, who raised me from the age of eighteen months, I can never express my eternal appreciation. They were poor in finances, but oh, so rich in love and nurturing. God only knows what would've become of me without their decision to take me into their home. My grandmother shielded me from my grandfather's discipline more times than I can count, and my grandfather taught me that everyone I meet is a friend until they show they don't want to be. My grandfather died fifty years ago this year and my grandmother passed away in 1992. I still miss them terribly.

Table of Contents

Foreword

In 2016, I had written several stories about the beleaguered Iberia Parish Sheriff's Office which had been forced to settle several lawsuits over wrongful deaths and abuse of prisoners in the parish jail. Sheriff Louis Ackal seemed to have lost control over this department which was guilty of a multitude of civil rights violations against prisoners.

The most outrageous story to emanate from the Iberia Sheriff's Office concerned the shooting death of 22-year-old Victor White, III, as he sat in the rear seat of a sheriff's department's patrol car. Authorities claimed that White somehow got hold of a gun and shot himself in the chest – while his hands were cuffed behind his back. The parish coroner ruled the death a suicide.

That, and a virtual epidemic of assaults on other African American prisoners at the Iberia Parish jail that included turning vicious dogs loose on defenseless inmates and the mysterious deaths of several other black prisoners prompted a lengthy letter from then-U.S. Rep. Cedric Richmond to U.S. Attorney General Loretta Lynch seeking a "full investigation" of the facility.

Ackal, a retired Louisiana State Trooper first elected sheriff in 2007, would eventually be indicted by a federal grand jury in 2016 for civil rights violations. Ten of his deputies admitted to wrongdoing and several of those took the stand to testify against their boss. In all, seven deputies received prison terms ranging from six months to more than four years as the presiding judge dressed down Ackal for his "lousy leadership." Ackal, to the surprise of many observers, was acquitted of all charges. Deputies Jason Comeaux, who received a sentence of forty months, and Gerald Savoy, who at eighty-seven months, received the stiffest sentence, had figured prominently in the investigation of the murder this book is about.

One day during my coverage of Ackal and his department, my cellphone rang and the display showed an unfamiliar number. Normally, because of so many solicitations, push polls and outright scams, I do not answer calls from unknown numbers. For some reason I took this one and the caller identified himself as Paul Chastant of Fort Worth, Texas. "I've been reading your stuff about Iberia Parish and I think you should do an investigation of my brother's murder," he said.

We talked for several minutes about the death of his brother, New Iberia orthodontist Robert Chastant. When convinced of my interest in the story, he suggested that I visit the attorney who handled his brother's estate, James Daniels of Lafayette. "I can give him a call and tell him to expect to hear from you if you'd like," he offered.

I accepted, feeling that an introductory call would be far better than a cold call from me to the attorney. When I did call Daniels, he invited me to his office where he said I could have full access to his files. When I walked into his conference room, I was immediately overwhelmed at the volumes of files stacked in at least a dozen cardboard filing boxes. As I noted aloud that it would take me weeks to review the files, he made an interesting offer. "Take them with you. I don't need them anymore. Quickly taking him up on his officer, I loaded as many boxes as I could cram into the back seat of my crew cab pickup truck.

As fate would have it, the boxes were on the floor of my home when the devastating flood of August 2016 filled my house with thirty-three inches of muddy river water. I figured the files were lost along with the two thousand phonograph record albums that were also on the floor in preparation for having them transferred to digital compact discs. But my wife Betty and I spread every single page on plywood sheets in the hot sun that came out after the flood and we were able to save every page. Thus, were my research materials, in less than pristine condition, preserved for this book, thanks to the unselfish assistance of Betty who has been my rock of inspiration for more than half-a-century of marriage.

Glossary of Key Names in
Murder on the Teche

Acadiana Crime Lab: Where truck floor mat and other evidence sent but which provided no report on that evidence.

Louis Ackal: Sheriff of Iberia Parish

Liz Breaux: employee in Dr. Ritter's office

Tamara Chaplin: Friend of Laurie Chastant who wrote her a long letter

Bradley Chastant: Brother of Dr. Robert Chastant

Laurie Chastant: Wife of Robert Chastant

Paul Chastant: brother of Robert Chastant

Robert Chastant: New Iberia orthodontist, murder victim

Robert Chastant Jr.: Dr. Robert Chastant's son

William Chastant: Dr. Robert Chastant's son

Agt. Jason Comeaux: Iberia Parish sheriff's deputy who found Dr. Chastant's body

Ada Credeur: Receptionist in Dr. Ritter's office

James L. Daniels: attorney for Robert Chastant's estate

Donita Densmore: woman who had previous affair with Dr. Chastant

Nancy Dunning: Ismael Viera's court-appointed public defender

Steven "Buzz" Durio: Laurie Chastant's attorney from the firm Durio, McGoffin, Stagg & Ackerman

Richard Fleming: Iberia Parish Sheriff's Detective and former State Trooper.

Robert Futral: Laurie Chastant's father – St. Landry Parish sheriff's deputy

Sgt. Carmen Garcia: Iberia Parish sheriff's deputy

State Trooper Frank Garcia: Interpreter who interviewed Ismael Viera in Spanish

Nayeli Gutierrez: girlfriend of Ismael Viera

Federal Magistrate Richard T. Haik: federal judge who presided over Laurie Chastant's lawsuit against Prudential and Lincoln National insurance companies
Susan Hall: Robert Chastant's ex-wife
Tim Hanks: State Police investigator who interviewed Laurie Chastant on night of the murder
Pam Harris: Friend of Laurie Chastant who attended Dr. Chastant's funeral
Toby Hebert: Iberia Parish sheriff chief of detectives whom Ismael Viera first told he was paid to kill Dr. Chastant
James C. Ingram, III: Laurie Chastant's third husband, married April 12, 2014.
Sgt. Jeremy Landry: Iberia Parish sheriff's deputy
Dep. John McBride: Iberia Parish deputy sheriff who located Dr. Chastant's truck at Walmart
Kristen McClain: Woman in Fort Worth with whom Dr. Chastant may have been having an affair
David Moore: Laurie Chastant's first husband
Det. Emayla Papion: Iberia Parish sheriff's deputy
Daniel Phillips: Steven Durio's partner in the firm representing Laurie Chastant
Nancy Picard: Attorney with expertise in ERISA matters consulted about using funds from Dr. Robert Chastant's trust for legal fees
Megan Qualls: Robert Chastant's daughter
Jason Ramsey: Contractor remodeling rental house for Robert Chastant who was owed $2889
Donna Riley: friend of Laurie Chastant who stayed in motor home with Pam Harris for Dr. Chastant's funeral
Dr. Kenneth A. Ritter Jr: Dr with whom Laurie Chastant had appointment day of murder
Jan Romero: Nayeli's friend who picked up Ismael Viera at Walmart
Terry Romero: Jan Romero's husband for whom Ismael Viera once worked
Lori Roszczynialski: Pension consultant for Administrative Retirement Services (ARS)
Capt. Gerald Savoy: Iberia Parish sheriff's deputy
Michele Chastant Stark: Robert Chastant's daughter

Donovan Gutierrez Tovar: Infant son of Ismael Viera and Nayeli Gutierrez

Ismael Viera Tovar: Killer of Robert Chastant, (went by surname Viera)

Det. Dusty Vallot: Iberia Parish sheriff's deputy

Judith Vaughn: Notary Public who notarized spousal consent forms for Dr. Chastant to close out retirement account

Det. Adrienne Wells: Iberia Parish sheriff's deputy who headed murder investigation

Tom Aswell

Intrigue Worthy of James Lee Burke

The year 2010 began with the January 4 opening of the Burj Khalifa in Dubai, the tallest man-made structure ever built and the world's latest monument to ostentatious wealth and extravagant opulence. On July 25 and again on November 28, Wikileaks released nearly 350,000 covert and classified documents relating to America's war in Afghanistan and other diplomatic cables, including 100,000 marked "secret" or "confidential." Wikileaks founder Julian Assange was arrested on December 7 but was granted asylum by Ecuador.

On November 28, actor Leslie Nielson and former New York Yankee infielder Gil McDougald died. Ron Santo, who played for both the Chicago Cubs and White Sox, died four days later, on December 2. Only three days after that, former Dallas Cowboy quarterback Don Meredith died. On December 11, Mark Madoff, eldest son of Bernie Madoff, architect of a $65 billion Ponzi scheme, committed suicide by hanging himself with a dog leash from a pipe in the ceiling of his New York apartment.

As these human dramas were being played out on the world stage, a more obscure Shakespearian-like tragedy, the murder of a prominent orthodontist, was unfolding in New Iberia, Louisiana, far from the aforementioned events but a scant ten miles down the Teche Bayou from the majestic Evangeline Oak immortalized in Longfellow's epic 1847 poem.

Located thirty miles south of Lafayette, New Iberia, population 30,000, is a city of starkly contrasting images, picturesque on the one hand and beset by crushing poverty on the other. With a median household income of $26,000, nearly 30 percent of the population lives below the poverty line. Iberia Parish is a demographic mixture typical of most South Louisiana towns. Whites make up 65 percent of the population with African Americans accounting for 31 percent. Native Americans (2 percent), Asian and Pacific Islanders (.65 percent), two or more races (1.25 percent) and Hispanic (1.5 percent).

The "two or more races" designation generally refers to the Creoles, common to South Louisiana. Creoles are a mixture of French, Spanish and African American (with a smattering of Native American blood), a unique mix that resulted from the settlement of this part of the state by French, Spanish and refugees from the Haitian Revolution of the early 19th century.

About 12 percent of the parish's 68,000 citizens (Iberia lost population of about 1.5 percent per year from 2016 to 2021) still speak Cajun French and do the Cajun two-step at the local *fais-do-do*. The city was originally settled by five hundred Spanish Malagueño colonists who made their way up Bayou Teche and settled around Spanish Lake in 1779. The area was occupied by Union forces under General Nathaniel P. Banks during the Civil War and a few years later, in 1868, Iberia parish (county) was established and New Iberia became the parish seat.

Besides the historic antebellum residence Shadows-on-the-Teche, New Iberia is also home to the fictional detective Dave Robicheaux, the creation of local author James Lee Burke who wrote several murder novels set in Iberia Parish. *In the Electric Mist*, a 2009 movie based on one of Burke's novels starring actor Tommy Lee Jones, was filmed in New Iberia.

But on December 13, 2010, a murder that was not part of a Burke storyline but one all too real to local residents, occurred in the early morning hours on a horse ranch owned by Dr. Robert Brown Chastant, the murder victim. The crime, along with the accompanying violence and gore, offered all the ingredients of a plot worthy of *Othello* or *Hamlet*, including the age-old love triangle, a cunning, murderous servant, an aggrieved, jealous wife, and a bumbling sheriff's department, soon to be preoccupied with its own problems, that botched the investigation in every way imaginable. Three of the deputies who participated in the investigation would be convicted and would receive prison sentences on unrelated charges within several years.

Dr. Chastant fifty-four, married twenty-nine-year-old former waitress Laurie Futral on May 24, 2004. It was his third marriage, her second. Laurie's first husband, David Moore, was in the Navy and was deployed when she filed for divorce. Laurie and Robert Chastant met in

November 2002 while she was waiting tables at Nash's Restaurant in Broussard, a suburb of Lafayette. Prior to that, she worked from 1998 to 2002 as a waitress-bartender at the Hilton Hotel in Lafayette. In one of her depositions, taken on October 6, 2011, she said she quit her job at Nash's Restaurant to attend the University of Louisiana Lafayette but instead, worked for two more restaurants, Shannon's and Graham Central Station in Lafayette.

In August or September 2003, the year after meeting Chastant, the two moved into his camper until the divorce from his second wife was finalized and they could move into his home. She eventually did attend ULL, pursuing a teaching certificate to go with the bachelor's degree she already had. She began teaching in Jeanerette in September 2004, about three months after her marriage to Chastant.

Chastant had attended ULL and the LSU School of Dentistry before setting up his practice in New Iberia. He also had satellite offices in Morgan City and Abbeville. Already having experienced two failed marriages, Chastant was likely in no frame of mind to receive a third financial hit from a potential divorce settlement. Accordingly, he and Futral entered into a pre-nuptial agreement on May 14, just ten days before their marriage (See Appendix A). That agreement would be entered into evidence in federal district court in May 22, 2012, just two days shy of what would have been their eighth wedding anniversary, as legal wrangling over Chastant's estate and life insurance policies kicked into high gear.

Paragraph seven of the agreement stipulated that "All monies earned as salary, commissions, as well as all revenues, products and natural and civil fruits of each Appearer's property shall be his/her respective separate property." That sentence would explain why the third Mrs. Chastant had no access to her husband's checking accounts other than a modest account set up to run his nearby horse farm, Sonriente (*smiling*, in Spanish) Stables. But it did little to explain two checks, written for cash, in the amounts of $600 and $400 on that account just six and three days, respectively, before Dr. Chastant's murder.

Among other particulars commonly found in the verbiage of such legal documents, the agreement also stipulated that if the couple divorced within a period of five years of their marriage, then Laurie Futral "shall be entitled to receive the vehicle in which she is driving at that time free of any encumbrance on the vehicle and $10,000 per year for each full year that they were married. The amount due is payable three months after the date the divorce becomes final. The amount due is calculated as of the day the divorce is filed and not the day the divorce becomes final. No interest is payable on any of the above amounts.

If they were divorced *after* the fifth anniversary of their marriage, the terms were identical concerning her vehicle (emphasis added). But the terms of cash payout were radically different in that she would receive $50,000 cash, plus $30,000 for each full year after the fifth anniversary of the marriage, up to a maximum total cash payment of $200,000, inclusive of the first five years. As an example, if Appearers are divorced after the seventh year, then the total amount received by Futral will be $110,000."

In December 2010, as evidence would eventually demonstrate, the two were well on their way to divorce court—a third time for him and a second time for her—as he appeared to be involved in a relationship with another woman in Grand Prairie, Texas, named Kristen McClain. McClain initially denied knowing Dr. Chastant but when confronted with records of telephone calls and emails between the two, was forced to acknowledge their relationship.

Had divorce proceedings been initiated prior to May 24, 2011, the stipulations of the pre-marital agreement would have meant that Laurie would likely have received only eighty thousand dollars as her settlement, and nothing from his multi-million-dollar life insurance policies, retirement and profit-sharing funds. Thus, the timing of Dr. Chastant's murder hung heavy in the winter air during that fateful 2010 Christmas season on the moss-draped banks of Bayou Teche.

A Family of Achievers

Robert Chastant was born in New Orleans on December 23, 1950. He completed his undergraduate studies in 1972 at what was then called the University of Southwestern Louisiana (USL), now known as the University of Louisiana-Lafayette (ULL). He earned his dental degree from the Louisiana State University School of Dentistry in Baton Rouge in 1976 and two years later, he received his degree in orthodontics from the University of Pennsylvania Orthodontic Program in Philadelphia.

Residence of Dr. Robert Chastant and Laurie
at the time of his murder.
Photo by Tom Aswell

He returned to the Acadiana area of Louisiana, setting up his practice in New Iberia where he focused on orthodontics. He practiced for more than three decades, expanding his practice to offices in nearby Abbeville and Morgan City. He routinely attended continuing education courses, learning the latest techniques and new developments and procedures of his profession. He was named a diplomat to the American Board of Orthodontics and was appointed as an associate delegate to the board, representing the Southwestern Division. He also served as a member of the Committee on Scientific Affairs for the Southwest Society of the American Association of Orthodontists and in 2010, received the Better Business Bureau Integrity Award.

Described as an accomplished author, lecturer and inventor, he also was active in sharing information on dental health, for donating bicycles to local students and for creating Kid ID, a program in which children's fingerprints and digital images are filed for use in case a child should go missing.

Robert Chastant was not the only one of his family to distinguish himself professionally. Brother Bradley, two years younger than Robert, is an otolaryngologist. He continues to practice head and neck surgery in nearby Lafayette.

Another brother, Paul, is an architect who specializes in the design of public and private prisons. He resides in Plano, Texas. Four years younger than Robert, the two shared a passion for raising Paso Fino show horses. Paul raised Colombian Paso horses while Robert was awarded several championships for showing his Peruvian Paso horses. Robert, along with his wife, ran their horse farm located a short distance south of their residence.

Ismael Viera Tovar (alternately spelled Tobar), a twenty-one-year-old Mexican, was hired to work on the farm through Jan Romero, a mutual acquaintance. In Spanish-speaking countries, the individual, the child, takes both parents' surname, the father's first and the mother's maiden name second and is known informally by the father's surname – by which he was legally known in the U.S. He is most often identified simply as Viera or as Ismael throughout this book by detectives, attorneys and judges.

Viera's girlfriend, Nayeli Gutierrez, met Jan Romero when she and her father Felipe worked for Romero's husband Terry at the Romero's

Vinton, Louisiana, thoroughbred horse farm. Nayeli, called Natalie by Mrs. Romero, was hired to help Viera clean the stables and was later hired to perform occasional housework for the Chastants.

Ismael and Nayeli, both illegal immigrants, were already living together when Jan Romero met them. Their son, Donovan, was born while he was working at the Romero farm. Ismael was functionally illiterate and spoke only a little English. He and Nayeli were introduced to the Chastants by Mrs. Romero's husband Terry. After they started working for the Chastants, they were allowed to live in a pool house on their property. In addition to free housing and utilities, they were each also paid three hundred dollars per week—in cash. Both were quiet and said little unless spoken to and by all accounts, Ismael was a reliable worker and was also performing carpentry work on a rental house owned by Dr. Chastant.

Robert Chastant's commitment to his thirteen horses and the farm, coupled with an economic downturn that adversely impacted his orthodontic practice, and rumored marital problems would lead to financial decisions that likely contributed, at least indirectly, to his death just ten days before his sixtieth birthday. Jan Romero, though inadvertently, would play a role in the investigation of his murder.

Tom Aswell

Timeline Contradictions Surface Early

On the morning of December 13, 2010, Dr. Chastant left his 4,700-square-foot colonial-style home at 2607 Bayou Bend Road and drove the short distance to his barn at Sonriente Stables at 3214 Sugar Oaks Road. At the Stables, Ismael Viera picked up a claw hammer and bludgeoned his boss to death.

Little is known about Viera's background other than he was twenty-one years old at the time of the murder, spoke little English and had entered this country illegally from Mexico. Like many others who crossed the border into the U.S. illegally, he was seeking a better life where he might find employment to support his family and even from time-to-time, send a little money back home to relatives in Mexico.

He worked hard, first on a horse farm in the Calcasieu Parish town of Vinton in Southwest Louisiana, where he was employed by Terry Romero who befriended him and who first introduced him to Dr. Chastant. Chastant would hire him to work at his own horse farm in New Iberia until that fateful December 10 morning.

Details about the purpose of Chastant's drive to the barn and inconsistences in the time sequence of events both before and after the murder added confusion to an already amateurish investigation by the Iberia Parish Sheriff's Department that would only produce more questions than answers.

It should be noted that in the sheriff's deputies' reports, there are numerous grammatical and spelling errors. These are signified by [sic] where cited.

Laurie Chastant told Detective Emayla Papion on the morning of December 13 that she last saw her husband at "around 7:40 a.m." that morning as he was leaving for work, according to a three-page report of Papion's recorded interview with Laurie. Laurie told Papion that when she awoke that morning, Dr. Chastant was already outside "either emailing or texting someone on his cell phone and smoking a cigarette."

She said he then came inside, kissed her goodbye, exited the residence and got into his truck which was already running.

Papion had worked in law enforcement a little more than four years total—one year as a parole officer with the State of Louisiana before being hired as a patrolman for the Iberia Parish Sheriff's Office in September 2009. She remained on patrol only ten months before being promoted to detective, a position she had held for only fifteen months before Dr. Chastant's murder.

Detective Papion wrote in her four-page report that Laurie "assumed" Dr. Chastant left at that point. "Ms. Chastant then advises that Dr. Chastant follows pretty much the same routine each morning on his way to work, he either goes straight to his office or he stops for coffee or gas at one of two gas stations. If he is working in his New Iberia office, he will stop at the Food-N-Fun or if he is going to one of his satellite offices, located in Morgan City or Abbeville, he will stop at Valero."

But in her deposition taken on October 6, 2011, ten months after her husband's death, her story was at variance with what she told Detective Papion. The deposition was taken in connection with her civil lawsuit against Prudential Insurance Co., which carried a $600,000 life insurance policy on Dr. Chastant.

She was questioned by James L. Daniels of Lafayette, attorney for Dr. Chastant's brother, Paul Chastant, who was executor of his brother's estate. "That morning, you made breakfast for Dr. Chastant? Daniels asked."

"I made him coffee. He didn't eat breakfast," she said. That contradicted her statement given to Detective Papion in which she said Dr. Chastant was already outside, either texting or emailing someone on his cell phone when she awoke and that he subsequently came inside, kissed her goodbye and left.

Moreover, she told Detective Papion that she last saw her husband "around 7:40 a.m. on the morning he was killed. But Ada Credeur, officer manager for Dr. Kenneth A. Ritter, Jr., testified in her March 12, 2012, deposition taken in the same civil lawsuit against Prudential, that she opened the doctor's office at 7:30 a.m. and Laurie Chastant was already in the waiting room as a walk-in patient. Laurie Chastant had experienced flu-like symptoms over the weekend and was waiting to see Dr. Ritter, Ms. Credeur said.

When attorney Daniels tried to pin her down on the time of her arrival, Ms. Credeur continued to insist that Laurie arrived at "about 7:30." She said her computer indicated she logged on at 7:45 a.m. after "dilly-dallying in the back." When informed by the secretary for another doctor in the same building that she had a patient waiting, she testified, "I put everything down [and] went to see who registered. I looked only at the register. I saw it was Ms. Chastant. She said she then "went back, finished what I was doing [and] brought all the computers up, normal routine, and by the time I walked to the front of the office, it was about 7:45."

Laurie Chastant never saw the doctor, who was running late. She was shown into an examination room where a nurse weighed her and took her blood pressure. Around 9:00 a.m., she exited the examination room after receiving a call on her cell phone, telling another worker in the office she had to leave because of an "emergency situation," Ms. Credeur testified. She then asserted, "And she also said the same thing to me, 'Ms. Ada, I've got to go. Ms. Ada, I've got to go. Something's not right. Bob's never late for work. This is very out of the ordinary. I have to go.'"

In her deposition of October 6, 2011, Laurie Chastant put the call even later. She said Liz Breaux or Liz Wolfe called from her husband's office "and told me that he hadn't made it to work yet."

"What time was that?" asked attorney Daniels.

"Around 9:15, 9:30, something like that."

She also told Detective Papion on December 13, 2010, that she received the call from her husband's office "sometime between 9:00 a.m. and 9:20 a.m.," according to Papion's report.

There is no official record that Laurie, as the wife, was ever questioned as a suspect or even a person of interest from the day of Robert Chastant's death until Viera eventually pled guilty to the murder. Her only legal testimony was in civil litigation, not criminal.

Another Iberia Parish sheriff's deputy, Sergeant Carmen Garcia, who spoke Spanish, conducted separate interviews at the sheriff's office with Ismael Viera and Nayeli Gutierrez on December 13 but it was the interview with Nayeli that proved most significant. Usually employed to help Ismael at the horse farm, she was summoned to the Chastant house to work on the morning of December 13. When she arrived shortly after Ismael had left for the barn, she told Garcia, Laurie Chastant was crying "cause she could not reach or make contact with Dr. Chastant," Garcia wrote in his undated report. "Nayeli said Lori [sic] said that Dr. Chastant was missing and that she could not find him. Nayeli said Lori [sic] walked out and said she had to leave because she had a 0900 o'clock appointment with her Dr's appointment." (Author's note: investigators employed military time designations in their reports)

Garcia wrote that Nayeli said when she arrived at Dr. Chastant's residence, Ismael was already at work. "She said she always went to work after Viera (Ismael) because he always left before her. Garcia wrote that Nayeli arrived at the Chastant house at "approximately 0830 hrs. [8:30 a.m.]"

There was a discrepancy in the time Dr. Chastant left his house that morning. Sergeant Garcia was apparently incorrect in typing the time as "approximately 0830." It should have been 0730 if Laurie was correct in what she told Papion. On two different occasions (in her interview with sheriff's detectives and later, in her deposition), she put the time of Dr. Chastant's departure as being much earlier at "around 7:40 a.m.," and Ada Credeur also testified in her deposition that when she arrived at work at Dr. Ritter's office at 7:30 a.m., Laurie had already signed in. The time would become a factor later.

That should have raised an obvious question that detectives apparently never asked: if Laurie first received word that her husband was missing in a phone call at "around 9:15, 9:30" as she sat in a examination room in Dr. Ritter's office, how could she have known-- and told—Nayeli Gutierrez as much as two hours earlier that he was missing?

And was that visit to the doctor's office to establish her whereabouts at the critical time that her husband was being murdered? Was her statement to the staff at the doctor's office that her husband was missing a deliberate attempt to deflect suspicion away from her? In time, as additional facts emerged, those questions would take on more significance and seem less like the fertile imagination of a conspiracy theorist.

Many Investigators but no Crime Lab Report

The Iberia Parish Sheriff's Office received the first word that Dr. Chastant was missing when Sergeant Jeremy Landry was advised around 10:30 a.m. on December 13 that he had not shown up for work that morning, according to the undated supplemental report written by Detective Dusty Vallot.

What followed were investigations by no fewer than six deputies and a confusing hodgepodge of reports. Because only the reports generated by the deputies are available, there is no indication of a chain of command or the manner in which they were assigned to various aspects of the investigation. Their reports, only one of which was dated, and which were written over a period of several days and in some cases, weeks, after the murder, were devoid of any continuity and raised as many questions as they answered. That confusion would only be intensified by the depositions of the six deputies in, each of whom would display remarkable lapses of memory on key aspects of the investigation.

Incredibly, long after everything was settled and all principals had gone their separate ways, the crime lab on whose board the sheriff served and which had received important evidence immediately following the murder, still had not processed that evidence or submitted a report to the sheriff's office.

Adrienne Wells was the only investigator in the sheriff's office when the call came in that Dr. Chastant was missing so she became the lead detective on the case by default. She had all of six years' experience in law enforcement. She had worked three years in communications, two years on patrol and had been a detective only since July, less than six months.

"On December 13, 2010, at approximately 1200 hours, Detective Adrienne Wells responded to 1205 E Admiral Doyle Drive in reference to a report of a missing person," her undated written report began. She alternated between referring to herself in both the third person and first person. "Upon my arrival, Detective Wells spoke with Deputy [John] McBride who advised Dr. Robert Chastant did not show up at his office…"

McBride had located Chastant's truck in the parking lot of the New Iberia Walmart. "Deputy John McBride advised he had contacted OnStar and they provided the located [sic] of the truck.

"Detective Wells then observed the surveillance provided by Walmart which observed [sic] a Hispanic male subject later identified as Ismael Viera drove Dr. Chastant's white Cheverolet [sic] truck to the Walmart parking lot and left the vehicle. Ismael was seen a few minutes later getting into a white Ford Expedition Eddie Bauer model…"

That Ford Expedition was driven by Jan Romero, the woman who had first introduced Viera and Nayeli Gutierrez to the Chastants.

Meanwhile, Viera was already being questioned by Sergeant Carmen Garcia. The sheriff's deputy located Viera at a construction site where he was employed and Viera said that he and Dr. Chastant were at the horse barn at Sonriente Stables but "a lady" driving a black Ford Explorer drove up and Chastant got into her vehicle. He said Dr. Chastant instructed him to drive his truck to Walmart. He then said Dr. Chastant and the unidentified woman followed him to Walmart in her vehicle. Once at Walmart, Viera said he contacted Mrs. Romero to come pick him up and give him a ride home, according to Detective Wells's report.

Wells said in her report she later recorded a telephone interview with Romero and was advised that it was Nayeli, not Ismael, who called her asking if she could pick up Ismael.

Ismael's story of the mystery woman in the black Ford Explorer wouldn't hold up long. At approximately 9:30 p.m. Detective Wells was advised that a body, possibly that of Dr. Robert Chastant, had been discovered on the property of Sonriente Stables at 3214 Sugar Oaks Road, near the barn.

As evidence of the sloppiness exhibited in reports turned in by investigators, Deputy Dusty Vallot, in his report, put the time that Dr. Chastant's body was found as "approximately 0900 hours on December 13, 2010." That would have been 9:00 a.m., more than a full twelve hours before the actual discovery.

At the barn, Wells was advised by Sergeant Jason Comeaux of the sheriff's office that while searching the property at Sonriente Stables, he had observed a brown penny loafer sticking out of a wood pile. That led to the discovery of a human body partially covered by plywood. "Detective Wells observed the body to be laying [sic] mostly on the right side against the trash that was in the wood pile," Wells said in her report. "The body appeared to be in a fetal position, Upper body was sitting on its knees. Detective Wells observed the upper body to be covered with a black trash bag from his head to his waist area." Two thousand dollars in cash, consisting of one-hundred-dollar bills, was found in Dr. Chastant's front left jacket pocket.

Investigators who found the money were unable to locate his wallet at the scene but Wells wrote that she "observed tire tracks extending from the trash pile towards the rear of the barn. The tire tracks appeared to possibly belong to a smaller type size vehicle."

Orthodontist Chastant found murdered in NI

Dr. Robert Chastant was discovered murdered this morning at his horse stable in New Iberia, Lt. Ryan Turner of the Iberia Parish Sheriff's Office confirmed.

Chastant, an orthodontist, had practices in New Iberia, Morgan City and Abbeville.

Ismael Viera, 21, of New Iberia has been charged with the murder.

Police officers conducted a search for Chastant at the stable on Sugarmill Road and recovered the body of a male matching Chastant's description.

(Continued on Page 14)

Robert Chastant

Ismael Viera

The Daily Review (Morgan City, Louisiana) 14 Dec 2010

Then, Wells said in her report that Viera, who at some undetermined point had been brought into the jail for questioning, abruptly admitted to a Spanish-speaking interpreter, Louisiana State Trooper Frank Garcia (no relation to Sgt. Carmen Garcia), that he killed Dr. Robert Chastant. Garcia said Viera "was willing to come out to the barn and react [sic] the incident on video." Remarkably, no documents accurately pinpoint the time this occurred.

At the scene, Viera told investigators that he and Chastant got into an argument because of Viera's habit of consistently leaving tools lying around when he was finished using them instead of putting them up as Dr. Chastant had instructed him on repeated occasions. He said Dr. Chastant struck him twice with an open hand on the left side of his face. "Ismael said Dr. Chastant began to turn around and walk away." It was at that point, Ismael said, that he picked up a hammer from the ground and struck Dr. Chastant once on the back of the head. When Chastant fell to the ground, Viera said he struck him three times more in the back of the head. He put the time of Dr. Chastant's death at about 8:30 a.m.

Viera, who stood five-feet, six-inches in height, weighed one hundred sixty pounds. He told investigators that he rolled the doctor onto his back and felt for a heartbeat. When he was certain that Dr. Chastant was dead, he placed him in the black trash bags and carried him to the trash pile. Dr. Chastant was six-feet, five-inches tall, nearly a full foot taller than his killer and at one hundred ninety-five pounds, outweighed him by thirty-five pounds. As muscular as Viera was, it would have been a chore to physically carry the much heavier dead man some two hundred feet to the trash pile.

Detective Wells asked him to show the route he took through the barn as he carried Dr. Chastant to the trash pile. "Ismael advised that he carried Dr. Chastant the whole time. He said the doctor was heavy, so [he] had to take two breaks from carrying the doctor." Continuing to refer to herself in the third person, she wrote, "Detective Wells then asked if, at any point, did he [Viera] drag Dr. Chastant's feet on the ground. Ismael advise [sic] no in response to Detective Wells [sic] question. Trooper Garcia advised [that] Ismael said that tire marks towards the trash pile were from trucks bringing the wood to the trash pile from the barn.

"...Trooper Garcia asked Ismael if there was anybody else present when the murder took place. Ismael advised that it was only him and Dr. Chastant at the barn."

Detective Wells wrote, "After Ismael disposing [sic] of the body, he returned to where the blood splatter was located. He grabbed a post hole digger to cover up the blood. After he covered the blood, he then took his red car back to his residence. He then asked his girlfriend [Nayeli] to bring him back to the barn due to his car battery had died. While she was bringing Ismael back, Ismael told her what he did to Dr. Chastant. Ismael said he did not tell his girlfriend Dr. Chastant was dead, he only told her that he hit Dr. Chastant and beat Dr. Chastant.

"Ismael advised the vehicle that he and Natalie (she is alternately identified as Nayeli and Natalie throughout the investigation) were in was the grey Suzuki mini-truck. (The mini-truck would alternately be referred to as Suzuki or Isuzu in depositions that later ensued. It remains uncertain as to which is correct.) Ismael advised [that] Natalie dropped him off where the driveway [to the barn] meets Sugar Oaks Road. He then got into Dr. Chastant [sic] truck and brought the truck to Walmart. Ismael advised once he arrived at Walmart, he called his girlfriend to go pick him up. Ismael advised [that] his girlfriend was with Jan Romero, who drives a white Ford Expedition, when they picked him up at Walmart."

Viera, who was taken back to the jail, was booked on a charge of second-degree murder at 2:30 p.m. on December 14, the day following the murder. Meanwhile, Dr. Chastant's body was transported to Lafayette for an autopsy (See Appendix B).

The barn at Sonriente Stables.
Photo by Tom Aswell

After Mrs. Romero dropped Ismael off at the rental property where he was working, Wells's report continued, Nayeli asked to be taken to the local Winn Dixie store. There, she wired $850 to her mother in Mexico. The store charged her $9.99 for the money order. Nayeli gave the store $880 and received $20.01 in change. She later told Sergeant Carmen Garcia that she had saved the money from what she had been paid for working for the Chastants. That amount would prove significant in the investigation.

Who Was Ismael Protecting?

During State Police Trooper Frank Garcia's questioning of Nayeli at the jail the day following the murder, more discrepancies between her version of events and that of Ismael quickly surfaced, an indication that Ismael was trying to protect someone. But whom?

Garcia, speaking in Spanish, asked Nayeli, "Why did Viera call you to pick him up at Walmart?"

"I don't know, he just said he needed a ride back to work," she said, also in her native tongue.

Garcia then asked if she drove a vehicle and she replied that she did not.

"So, why would he call you for a ride?" Garcia's undated report said. "She said because he knows I have a friend, Ms. Jan Romero, who drives me and I could get a ride to pick him up."

Trooper Garcia then asked, "Why did you tell me you do not drive and Viera is telling me that you drove the Isuzu to the barn? He told me you drove him to the barn, stopped on the side of the road, but that you did not go to the barn, [but] you returned to the house."

"I do not know why he is saying that," Nayeli said, again asserting that she did not drive.

"Nayeli said, 'Bring him here to me. I will ask him why he is saying I drove him when I did not drive anywhere,'" Garcia wrote.

Nayeli was allowed to speak with Viera and their conversation—in Spanish—was monitored by investigators. "From the information viewed and received about what Viera had said Nayeli had drove [sic] him, it sounded like Viera wanted Nayeli to say that she had drove [sic] him and that she would not have to stay any longer than what she had already been if she just told the stupid people what they wanted to hear," Sgt. Garcia wrote. "Nayeli told Viera to stop saying that she drove because he knew she never drove him anywhere and that she was not going to say something she did not do or have any part in."

The exchange between Viera and a distraught Nayeli was marked by frequent emotional outbursts and impassioned denials of any involvement from Nayeli despite determined instructions from Ismael for her to say she drove him to the barn the morning of the murder. Judging from the exchange, it's likely they were unaware authorities were listening.

"You are telling them that I brought you to the barn and I didn't bring you," she said. "I was in the bedroom with Donovan [their son]. The thing is, I was over at the house."

For the first time, Ismael revealed that he was accused by authorities of having a sexual relationship with Laurie. "Right now, they are telling me that I slept with the lady and that's why I had to kill her husband – that I slept with her."

But Nayeli, also for the first time, indicated that investigators had been told that she had driven him to the scene of Dr. Chastant's brutal slaying. "But they are insisting that I took you to the barn," she said, "that I brought you there and left you outside the barn, and that you went inside the barn and that I was…driving."

"Well, that's the way they are," Ismael responded.

"It is not true, Ismael!"

Still, he insisted that she say what he was telling her, only now, he altered the story slightly. "Even so, only tell them that you brought me to the side of the highway and that's it, okay? That you left me on the side of the highway, on the way to the barn."

"I only say this just because you are telling me to?" she challenged him, again denying that she participated in any way. "That is not true."

"I know that," Ismael admitted while continuing to plea for her cooperation while seeming to protect the person who actually abetted him. "Only tell them that you took me over to the barn, and that you returned right back and now that's all they need to know, okay?"

She again challenged his authority to insist that she lie. "Just because you are saying this, I have to say it as well? But I did not do it. I did not take you over and did not bring you back and did not bring the Suzuki. I was with Donovan," she said, slapping her hand for emphasis.

"Nayeli, let us not have to use force," Ismael replied cryptically.

That appeared to throw Nayeli off-guard somewhat as she replied, "What force? Tell me. What force?"

"I know it is not by force," he said. "Only tell them what happened, that you brought me to the side of the highway. You just say that. Afterwards, you came back for me at the Walmart and you brought me back, back to work. And now, yes, that's all you know."

The pressure from Ismael was beginning to overwhelm her emotionally as she again protested, "I haven't done anything wrong and on top of that, they are going to take away my son and my other baby..." as she began to cry. This was the first indication that she was pregnant with the couple's second child. "I am saying the fucking truth," she said, pronouncing "fucking" in perfect English as she again slapped one hand with the other for emphasis. "I am not able to say something that I did not do, Ismael."

That exchange is significant because it was candid; the two did not know officers, especially Trooper Garcia, who was fluent in Spanish, were hearing every word they spoke

Once investigators monitoring the conversation determined that Ismael was not being truthful about Nayeli's having driven him to the farm in the Isuzu Garcia had him removed from the room.

A Money Order and $2880

On December 15, two days after the murder, Detective Wells contacted Jason Ramsey, the contractor who was overseeing the work on the Chastant's rental house at 311 Caroline Street in New Iberia where Ismael had been working. Ramsey said he and his crew had been remodeling the rental house for about two weeks and that Dr. Chastant was scheduled to have paid Ramsey for his work on the morning he was killed. Ramsey said Dr. Chastant owed him $2,880 but that he never collected the money.

To reiterate, when Dr. Chastant's body was discovered, there was $2,000 in cash in one-hundred-dollar bills found in his front left jacket pocket by investigators. Immediately after Nayeli and Jan Romero picked Ismael up at Walmart and delivered him to 311 Caroline Street, Nayeli had Romero drive her to Winn Dixie where she paid $880—an $850 money order she sent to her mother in Mexico and $9.99 for the money transfer, receiving $20.01 in change. That $880, along with the $2,000 recovered from Dr. Chastant's coat pocket, matched to the penny the money Ramsey said Dr. Chastant owed him for his work on the property.

During the course of her interview with Ramsey and one of Ismael's co-workers on the Caroline Street house, Detective Wells was summoned to the sheriff's office. Once there, she learned that Ismael had dropped a bombshell that instantly altered the focus of the investigation, would lead to litigation, produce a lingering suspicion and distrust of Laurie Chastant, and cast a cloud of doubt over the capability—or willingness—of the Iberia Parish Sheriff's Office to conduct a murder investigation in a competent or professional manner—especially when it involved the daughter of a fellow law enforcement official.

First, Ismael denied that he took the $880 from Dr. Chastant's person and that the $880 Nayeli spent at Winn Dixie came from another source that was, if true, just as illegal as if it had been taken off the dead man's body.

That source, he said, was the one thousand dollars Laurie Chastant paid him to kill her husband.

The new version of events was a radical departure from his previous confession that he acted alone but he would steadfastly stick to this newest scenario throughout the remainder of the investigation, his sentencing and his incarceration at Louisiana State Penitentiary at Angola, even with the knowledge that the legal consequences for him could be far worse than a mere prison sentence—worse even than a life sentence.

Upon her arrival at the sheriff's office, Detective Wells listened to a recording of a conversation between Chief of Detectives Toby Hebert and Ismael during which Ismael told Hebert in Spanish "that Laurie Chastant paid him $1,000 to kill her husband, Dr. Chastant," Wells's report said. Wells, in her report, said she was unable to understand Spanish.

Ismael was then transported to the sheriff's Bureau of Investigations to be re-interviewed. Trooper Frank Garcia, who was fluent in Spanish was again contacted and asked to assist in the interview.

Meanwhile, as everyone waited for the arrival of Trooper Garcia, Wells received a phone call on her personal cell phone from Laurie Chastant at 7:19 p.m. She told Wells that Nayeli had twice lied to her, telling her that Terry Romero, Jan Romero's husband, was the one who picked up Ismael from the pool house but was now changing her story.

That was in reference to the morning of December 13, right after Ismael had killed Dr. Chastant. Following the murder, Ismael had driven his truck to the pool house where he and Nayeli resided. Nayeli then returned to the Chastant house to do laundry work and when she returned, Ismael was gone but his truck was still there. She told investigators she was puzzled as to how he left because he never walked to the barn. She said the Isuzu mini-truck was still at the Chastant residence at that time. She next heard from him around 9:00 a.m. when he called from Walmart, asking to be picked up and taken to Caroline Street.

Then, during the phone call to Detective Wells, Laurie abruptly – and curiously – began asking questions about the investigation. Wells, who had Laurie on speaker phone so others could hear, told her the case was still under investigation. "There was a male subject in the background guiding her," Wells wrote, adding that she terminated the conversation with Laurie Chastant at that point.

"Trooper Garcia then arrived to reinterview Ismael," Wells's report reads. She said Garcia read Ismael his rights as per the Miranda card in Spanish. Ismael also signed the rights form and proceeded to speak with Trooper Garcia and Detective Wells. Garcia spoke to him during the first part of the interview in Spanish.

During the second part of the interview, Trooper Garcia translated in English. He advised that he had asked Ismael, why he wrapped the body in the trash bags. "Ismael responded Laurie told him to do it when she arrived at the barn," Wells wrote. Ismael told Garcia that Laurie showed up at the barn suddenly after seeing the doctor's truck at the barn. Ismael had already killed Dr. Chastant at that point and he now said that Laurie instructed him to get the bags to cover him.

Trooper Garcia's was the only report that was dated. In it, he said Ismael returned to his residence for lunch on December 7. As he was leaving to return to work, he was approached by Laurie Chastant. He told Trooper Garcia that he and Laurie Chastant conversed about marital problems she and Dr. Chastant were having. During the conversation, Laurie Chastant asked Viera if he would be willing to kill Dr. Chastant, but Viera refused. Laurie did not speak Spanish and Viera spoke only broken English, thus creating something of a language barrier.

Finally, he said Laurie offered him a thousand dollars to kill her husband and he accepted the offer. Laurie Chastant removed the cash in one hundred dollar-bill denominations from her front pants pocket and gave it to Viera. Viera put the money in his pants pocket and returned to work. After Laurie Chastant gave him the money, he said, they did not converse any more between December 7, 2010, and December 13, 2010, the day of the murder.

Viera said that Laurie Chastant wanted to pay him (and not another worker) because Viera happened to be exiting his pool house residence at the same time as Laurie Chastant was leaving the Chastant residence. Viera was adamant that he was never involved in any type of relationship with Laurie Chastant. He added that he was scared to tell the truth about being paid to kill Dr. Chastant because he felt threatened by Dr. Chastant's sons. Viera had seen one of Dr. Chastant's sons target practicing with a weapon and Viera was scared that the son would harm him if he told the truth.

Was he telling the truth now or was this story an elaborate ploy that he thought might somehow mitigate the gravity of his own complicity?

Key Checks for $600 and $400

Continuing to refer to herself in the third person, Wells wrote in her report, "Detective Wells then asked Ismael what was her reaction after she observed the doctor being dead? Ismael advised her reaction appeared like she wanted to cry, she had tears in her eyes but never cried. She told him to get the bags to cover his upper body."

Ismael told Garcia that Laurie originally arrived at the barn in her black Avalanche but left and returned in the grey Suzuki mini-truck. They loaded the body onto the mini-truck and Ismael drove it to the woodpile while Laurie stayed back to cover the blood.

He explained to the state trooper that he lifted Dr. Chastant's upper body and Laurie grabbed his ankles and together they placed his body in the bed of the grey Suzuki Truck. Ismael explained that after he covered the body in the trash pile, he returned to find that the blood which had been at the scene of the murder was already covered with fresh dirt and that Laurie was still inside the barn.

He said it was unnecessary to clean the Suzuki because the trash bags prevented any blood from getting onto the mini-truck. Laurie had instructed him to cover the upper body with the trash bags, he said, so that she would not have to see the blood. Ismael told Garcia that the only conversation between him and Laurie after he returned from concealing the body in the trash pile was when she instructed him to drive Dr. Chastant's truck to Walmart.

Wells wrote in her report that Garcia asked Ismael what he did with the remainder of the thousand dollars after Nayeli used $880 on the money order and the money transfer fee. He replied that there should be a blue box beside the bed (in the pool house) that contained "approximately two hundred dollars to two hundred thirty dollars."

Ismael said Laurie's instructions to him were to take the body to the back and place it in the trash pile and cover the body. Wells then asked what they planned to do with the body and Ismael said there was no plan and that they never considered setting the trash pile on fire.

Ismael told Garcia that Laurie came up with the initial story about Dr. Chastant leaving the farm with an unidentified woman in her black Ford Explorer. "Ismael said they discussed the story the same day she paid him to kill Dr. Chastant," Wells's report indicated.

"...Ismael advised they [he and Nayeli] did not deposit the money [that Laurie paid him] into a bank," Wells wrote. "They completed a Western Union money transfer to his girlfriend [sic] mother. Detective Wells will note [that] Natalie [Nayeli] did a Western Union money transfer of $859.99 to Mexico. The receipt indicated that she paid $880 and received twenty dollars and one penny in change. The money transfer was sent through the Western Union at Winn Dixie located at 1105 East Main Street in New Iberia within the city limits of New Iberia on December 13, 2010 at approximately 0934 hours," the report says.

In a subsequent search of the pool house, Detective Wells noted that she located $224 at the bottom of a blue plastic container just as Ismael had said. Wells also said $2,200 in cash was found "inside a jacket pocket in the bathroom closet. This was not the same $2,000 found earlier on Dr. Chastant's body, however. Dr. Chastant's wallet containing several credit cards was also found inside a shoe stored in a plastic container.

By applying simple mathematics, If the $880 used to purchase the money order at Winn Dixie was not part of the $2,880 that contractor Jason Ramsey said he was owed that Dr. Chastant was supposed to be delivering to the Caroline Street worksite the day he was killed, where did Ismael get the money? He told detectives the $880 was part of the thousand dollars paid him by Laurie Chastant to kill her husband.

If Ismael was being truthful with his revised story, which by now was becoming more and more convoluted, investigators ordinarily might have had a problem trying to trace the thousand dollars back to Mrs. Chastant. But in this case, they had the advantage of the prenuptial agreement between Robert and Laurie Chastant—and two interesting checks for cash totaling one thousand dollars—to facilitate their search.

Under terms of that agreement, Laurie Chastant had no access to her husband's personal or business checking accounts. The only checking account on which she could write checks was the account of Sonriente Stables. Attorney Daniels, representing Dr. Chastant's brother, Paul Chastant in his capacity as executor of his brother's trust, obtained copies of eight checks drawn on the Sonriente Stables account between November 29 and December 10. Six of those checks were made out to LAWCO (Louisiana Water Co., $90.00), Boudreaux, Henderson & Co. (a New Iberia CPA firm, $500.00), and Vermilion Shell & Limestone, $580.49, all on November 29; Louisiana Solar Works, $11,963.50, Iberia Rental, $1,500.00, and Teche Lumber & Building Supply, $197.18, all on December 3.

The remaining two checks were made out to cash, for $600.00 on December 6, and $400 on December 10, seven and three days, respectively, before Dr. Chastant was murdered at his beloved horse farm.

In her October 6, 2011, deposition in connection with her lawsuit against Prudential, she claimed to have no recollection of writing the checks for cash but her memory lapse could be attributed to the incorrect amount having been quoted when she was asked during her deposition. That was an important point on which she could hang her denial.

"Detective Wells learned [that] Laurie Chastant only had access to one account which is listed under Sonriente Stables," Wells wrote in an undated supplemental report. Her report listed ten other checks dating back to September 17. Each of those checks was for $600 but her report provided no information as to whom they were written. The final two were the checks written on December 6 and December 10. If Laurie Chastant did pay Ismael Viera a thousand dollars to kill her husband, authorities would have to turn next to her possible motivation. (Appendix C)

Tom Aswell

"A Million and One Reasons"

On January 13, 2012, a bitter Paul Chastant, in a deposition in the matter of Laurie Chastant v. Prudential Insurance Company of America, quoted Sheriff Louis Ackal as telling Ms. Chastant, "I have a million and one reasons to believe you were involved." Paul Chastant testified to that exchange right after testifying that Ackal had told him Laurie was a suspect in the murder.

Those "million and one reasons" included two life insurance policies totaling $1.1 million and Dr. Chastant's defined benefits (retirement) and profit-sharing plans. Another reason thrown into the mix could have been strong indications of infidelity on Dr. Chastant's part shortly before his death. And just for additional flavor, claims of forgery were looming on the horizon, creating additional information overload on an inexperienced and befuddled sheriff's department already satisfied that they had the killer in custody.

The first insurance policy was for $600,000 with Lincoln National Life Insurance while the Prudential policy was for $700,000. The defined benefits plan was for another $700,000, according to Paul Chastant's deposition testimony.

Attorney James Daniels, representing Paul Chastant, as executor of Robert Chastant's estate, later asked Laurie Chastant during her deposition how she would she describe her marital relationship, with Dr. Chastant.

"Were you happily married?" Daniels asked.

"Yes."

"You all were faithful to one another?" Daniels inquired, pressing on.

"I was faithful to him. He had had some sort of—not necessarily an affair, but he had something with a girl."

"When was this in your relationship?"

"There were two girls. One was in 2009 and the other was in 2010."

"Do you know who these individuals are?"

"I know the names of the girls," she said without elaborating at first.

"Okay," Daniels said. "In 2009."

"Donita Densmore."

"And where does Ms. Densmore live?"

"Somewhere in Texas."

When Daniels delved into more detail of Robert Chastant's relationship with Densmore, Laurie said that her understanding was that "she pursued him. He was receptive at first, and then he—they did not sleep together, however, they exchanged pictures and emails and then he broke it off."

"What about the 2010? What is the name of that individual?" Daniels asked.

"Kristen McClain."

"Had you ever spoken to Ms. McClain?"

"I did speak to her."

"When was that?"

"I don't know exactly. Sometime in October."

"Was that—in fact, wasn't it around Thanksgiving, 2010? What did Ms. McClain tell you?"

"She told me that it was my fault that my husband looked elsewhere."

Later in the deposition, Laurie said that she confronted her husband. "He told me that he had never slept with her, that he had planned to, but that he didn't."

"And when was it that Dr. Chastant told you that?" Daniels asked.

"Around the same time."

"October, November?"

"Yes. It was approximately October, November."

"Isn't it true, Ms. Chastant, that Dr. Chastant told you that he planned on spending Christmas 2010 with Ms. McClain?"

"No, that's not true," Laurie responded.

But Laurie's denial was only technically accurate. A travel itinerary prepared for her husband by online travel agency Travelocity indicates that Robert Chastant was booked on American Airlines Flight 1989 from New Orleans Louis Armstrong International Airport at 7:00 p.m. on Thursday, December 16, 2010, just before his sixtieth birthday and only three days after he was killed. He was scheduled to arrive in

Dallas/Fort Worth International Airport at 8:35 p.m. and was scheduled to return on American Flight 1292 at 2:45 p.m. on Saturday, December 18 with arrival in New Orleans at 4:00 p.m. The confirmation code of the itinerary, confirmed on November 11 at 2:50 p.m. was given as KMTTUZ.

Travelocity also had arranged for a rental car from Alamo and had booked Dr. Chastant to stay at the Magnolia Dallas Hotel on Commerce Street in Dallas. The combined cost of the flight, hotel, car rental and a travel protection plan was $609.

So, while Dr. Chastant was not planning on actually spending Christmas with Ms. McClain, it would have been accurate to say he planned on spending two full days and part of a third with her the *week before* Christmas.

Later in her deposition, Daniels asked, "In connection with your relationship with Natalie (Nayeli), was it such that you would confide in her concerning personal matters?"

"Not regularly, but I did confide in her one time."

"Isn't it true that you confided in Natalie concerning your relationship with Dr. Chastant?"

"I confided in her one time."

"What did you tell her?"

"I had told her that he had a girlfriend."

"Without recalling any specific date, can you give me an idea of when that may have been in relation to December 13?"

"It was before that."

"And this was the Ms. McClain that you were talking—had a conversation with her about?"

"Yes."

"And Ms. McClain, she resides in Dallas?"

"I believe it's somewhere outside of Dallas."

That exchange was on page 47 of her deposition transcript. On page 115, Daniels broached the subject of how Laurie learned of her husband's relationship with McClain.

"He had asked me to put some packets together [for his orthodontics office], some different paperwork, and some of the paperwork I was going to need to get off of his computer and print it out. And when I hit 'enter' on the computer [to activate the screen], there was an email that he had left up that he was sending to Kristen McClain."

"What did the email say?"

"It was of a personal nature and I don't remember the exact words to it."

"Give me the gist if you could, please."

"That she was pretty and sexy and that they would have fun together."

Laurie, upon further questioning by Daniels said when she contacted McClain by email, "I was angry and I told her to leave my husband alone and I called her some names."

"What names?"

"Home wrecker, whore, those kinds of things."

Christmas with Kristen?

Laurie denied her husband had planned to spend Christmas with Kristie McClain, but she was not completely forthcoming. Detective Wells had executed a search warrant to access the Yahoo email accounts of Dr. Chastant, Laurie, and Kristie McClain and received three CDs from Yahoo. Wells said in her undated supplemental report that Laurie had accessed her husband's emails and forwarded messages between him and McClain to Laurie's own email account. Among those messages she forwarded to herself was one that detailed Dr. Chastant's plans to travel to Dallas on December 16.

Moreover, at 8:30 p.m. on the night of Dr. Chastant's murder, Laurie was interviewed by State Police investigator Tim Hanks and when he asked about their marriage, Ms. Chastant told him that her husband was having an affair, but was unsure if it was sexual. She also told Hanks that she and Dr. Chastant had had an argument just the week before about McClain and that "Dr. Chastant was suppose [sic] to be flying to Texas to spend the following weekend with [her]."

Detective Adrienne Wells was instructed by Captain Gerald Savoy to begin searching for the girlfriend in Grand Prairie, Texas. "Detective Wells," she wrote, again referring to herself in the third person, "finally made contact with Ms. McClain's mother and advised her to have Kristin contact Detective Wells. Kristin later returned the phone call and Detective Wells spoke briefly with her. Kristin advised she does not know who Doctor Chastant is and has never spoken to anyone by that name. Kristin advised she had never been to Louisiana."

It would take nearly a year before it was learned that McClain had lied. In her deposition given on December 8, 2011, Detective Wells told attorney Daniels she had a subsequent conversation with McClain who at that time admitted the two knew each other but were only exchanging emails.

"Did you review the text messaging and emails back and forth between this woman and Dr. Chastant?" Daniels asked.

"Yes. Basically, from what I got out [of] the whole thing is a lot of cold reading that I had to do. Dr. Chastant would email her saying, 'I want you to wear this lingerie,' and stuff."

"Does Laurie Chastant's email to this woman indicate whether or not she thought Dr. Chastant was having an affair with this woman?"

"It says, 'Leave my husband alone.'"

"What was the date of that?"

November the 16th, 2010. It says, 'Leave him alone, get your own man. I found your emails and know about the affair.'"

"Did you ever personally meet with her? Did anybody go to Dallas and meet with her?"

"No."

"Was she brought in?"

"No."

"Did she know anything about the murder?"

"No. Actually, I made contact with her and then they had to actually research it on the Internet to make sure I was who I said I was and make sure, you, it was—he was dead. She freaked out on the phone."

Laurie Chastant told Detective Papion that when she was first notified that her husband had not shown up at work, she began calling him but his phone would go straight to voicemail. She then began texting him with messages such as "Are you okay?" She told Papion she soon began receiving answers in broken English, such as "I okay," or "Go home." She said she knew they were not from her husband "because he always speaks and writes in proper English and the person texting her was not." She then told Papion that she texted him again asking him to call her "because several people were looking for him and he had patients waiting for him at his office." Instead, she received a message saying, "I busy, go home."

She repeated that claim in her October 6, 2011, deposition, quoting the text messages as "I okay," and "Go home now."

Whether it was a simple mistake or a critical one is impossible to determine but when attorney Daniels asked Laurie when she received the messages, she responded, "as I was driving from the house *to the barn*, I mean, to the office, I got the text messages." (emphasis author's)

She had earlier denied that she ever went to the barn that morning.

When State Trooper Frank Garcia asked Ismael about the text messages that were received and sent on Dr. Chastant's cell phone, "Viera stated that Laurie Chastant and he were conversing. I went over each of the texts," Garcia said, "and Viera stated that all the outgoing texts after 0830 hours until 1200 hours were from him. All the incoming texts during that same time were from Laurie Chastant."

But if, indeed, she was involved at all, fury over her husband's apparent extramarital relationships may not have been the only motive in any decision by Laurie to have Robert Chastant pay Ismael Viera to murder Robert Chastant.

The prenuptial agreement alluded to earlier was hanging over her head like the mythical Sword of Damocles. As her marriage was disintegrating before her eyes, she was in peril of receiving a final settlement of only $80,000 as opposed to life insurance policies and Dr. Chastant's defined benefit and profit-sharing plans totaling more than two million dollars. It was those factors that prompted Sheriff Louis Ackal to tell her, "I have a million and one reasons to believe that you were involved" in her husband's murder, according to Paul Chastant's deposition testimony of January 13, 2012. But if she was indeed a suspect, that was as far as records of any thorough investigation of her possible involvement in her husband's murder went.

One of the clues, other than the insurance policies and defined benefit and profit-sharing plans that may have led Ackal to believe that was a black rubber floor mat that turned up in an exterior storage compartment of the motor home owned by Robert Chastant and which was parked at his New Iberia clinic. In the deposition given by Detective Wells, that one mat would become two but, in her report, she noted that it "appeared to belong to a pick up [sic] truck." Apparently, Ackal, for whatever reason, never followed up on the floor mat discovery.

She also testified in her deposition of December 8, 2011, that the Avalanche driven by Laurie Chastant "was the only vehicle without any floor mats."

Incredibly, however, it seemingly never occurred to her to attempt to match the floor mat to the Avalanche, a procedure any novice investigator would have performed immediately upon finding the mat.

Tom Aswell

Reports Rambling, Fragmented and Disorganized

Detective Emayla Papion dealt with Laurie Chastant's appearance at the Iberia Parish Sheriff's Office "to speak with someone about her husband, Dr. Robert Chastant, being missing." Papion at first suggested that perhaps Dr. Chastant simply needed a day to himself and did not wish to be located, but Laurie insisted that he was dedicated to his patients and would not miss a day of work or leave patients waiting.

Like Wells, Detective Papion referred to herself in the third person when she wrote, "At this time Detective Papion conducted a recorded interview with Laurie Chastant. During the interview Ms. Chastant advised the last time she saw Dr. Chastant was around 7:40 a.m. as he was leaving for work."

After searching places where he might have been, Laurie told Papion, she was en route to his dental office when she received a call from one of her husband's employees who suggested that OnStar be called to locate Dr. Chastant's truck and an OnStar representative subsequently advised that the vehicle was located at the New Iberia Walmart.

"Detective Papion then asked Ms. Chastant had anything out of the ordinary happened in her or Dr. Chastant's life during the past few weeks," the detective wrote. "Ms. Chastant advised that she and Dr. Chastant had been arguing because she [Laurie] found out that Dr. Chastant had been exchanging emails and phone calls with another female named Kristen McClain. Ms. Chastant advised she found out about this because she was doing some work for Dr. Chastant and she needed to get on his computer. When she pressed the enter key to make the screen saver go away, she observed an open email message that Dr. Chastant was planning on sending Ms. McClain. Ms. Chastant then advised that she does not know if Dr. Chastant had a physical affair with Ms. McClain but they were planning on it.

"Ms. Chastant advised she and Dr. Chastant had a fight about Ms. McClain a few nights ago," Papion wrote.

Sheriff's department Detective Richard Fleming had little to add in his report following his December 13 interview of Laurie Chastant or his interview with Nayeli on the next day. The report on his interview with Nayeli was date-stamped December 28, a full two weeks after she was interviewed.

Fleming merely reiterated that Laurie had said she had learned her husband was having an affair with McClain and that he previously had an affair with a woman named Donita Densmore. She also said that Chastant and his first wife had not spoken to each other in several years, according to his three-page report which also noted that Laurie claimed that Chastant "has hit her in the past."

When Dr. Chastant's body was discovered and positively identified that night, Fleming was assigned the task of accompanying another deputy to the Chastant home to notify Laurie.

As with his interview of Laurie, his session with Nayeli produced little information in addition to what investigators had already been told.

Fleming's only other involvement appeared to be when, on December 17, he was assigned to retrieve Chastant's DNA from the coroner's office and forward it to the Acadiana Crime Lab in New Iberia—and on December 20 when he was assigned to view the Walmart surveillance tape. "While viewing the video, I took notes on the suspect's [Ismael's] actions," was all he wrote in his sketchy report.

Sergeant Carmen Garcia interviewed Ismael Viera, also on December 13, identifying him in the opening paragraph of her report as the "suspect who was thought to be involved in the disappearance of Dr. Chastant." Ismael was advised of his Miranda rights by a Spanish interpreter and signed the Miranda rights form as well as a form authorizing authorities to take his DNA.

Viera told Garcia that he and Dr. Chastant had argued over Viera's failure to put tools away when he finished with them and that Chastant "talked to him like a dog and slapped him twice in the face and walked off." He told Garcia that he worked hard and would do whatever Chastant asked but that it was never enough.

Ismael said a few moments later that a "dark-colored SUV" drove (up) and parked behind his vehicle and that a dark-haired woman was driving. Chastant's mood quickly changed for the better, he said, adding that Dr. Chastant instructed him to drive his (Dr. Chastant's) truck to Walmart and leave it there. He then said that Chastant and the unidentified woman, whom he said appeared to be in her thirties, followed him to the Walmart parking lot so that Chastant would know where it was parked when he returned to pick it up later. Chastant and the woman then drove away.

From Walmart, he called Nayeli to pick him up and she later appeared with Ms. Romero in Romero's vehicle. He directed Romero to take him (Ismael) to the job he was working at the Caroline Street rental property, he said.

Throughout his questioning, Ismael denied any involvement in Dr. Chastant's disappearance, but that story fell apart before the day was over and he would try to say that Nayeli had driven him back to the barn in the Isuzu mini-truck and dropped him off at the entrance to the property. That too, would appear to prove untrue and Ismael would subsequently implicate Laurie in the crime as the story grew more and more bizarre and ladened with intrigue and bungled investigative work by sheriff's deputies.

The sketchiest investigative report of all was that of Detective Dusty Vallot. It consisted of fewer than two full pages. He reported that he went to Walmart "and viewed survailance [sic] near the truck and the front entrance" where he and Sergeant Jeremy Landry observed "a white male" exit wearing a gray hood, a red shirt, jeans and work boots. The man, later identified as Ismael, entered the store and several minutes later exited and got into a white Ford Expedition later identified as Mrs. Romero's vehicle.

Landry and Vallot drove to Sonriente Stables in an attempt to locate Dr. Chastant. While there, Landry received a call advising him that crime scene detectives had found what was thought to be blood on Ismael's boots. No results of DNA testing could be found among the thousands of pages of documents that would have determined whether or not the boots had the blood of Dr. Chastant on them.

Detectives executed a search warrant for the pool house residence of Ismael and Nayeli. There they found $2,000 in a coat pocket and $224 in cash in a can. "Dr. Chastants [sic] credit cards and wallet was [sic] also found inside of Ismael [sic] residence along with Dr. Chastants [sic] phone, which was located under the bathroom sink," Vallot wrote in his report.

"At approximately 0900 hours [sic] on December 13, 2010, Agent Jason Comeaux called and advised that he had found a body at 3214 Sugar Oaks Road (Dr. Chastants [sic] barn) under a wood pile in the back of the barn wrapped in a balck [sic] trash bag from the head to the waist."

The next day, Vallot and several other investigators returned to the barn where they found a hammer with what appeared to be blood on it in a trash bag inside the barn. Ismael admitted using the hammer to kill Chastant. "Detective Vallot has no further information to report in reference to this incident," his report concluded.

One would be hard-pressed to find a more disjointed collection of investigation reports than those written by the five detectives. But those paled in comparison with the uncertainties, lapses of memory and general unfamiliarity with the case exhibited later in their depositions— along with that of a sixth detective, Captain Gerald Savoy, who would experience his own criminal problems only a few years down the road. The depositions of the six deputies, along with those of other principals, will be discussed in more detail later. Suffice it to say they proved that the Iberia Parish Sheriff's Office was in over its head. In addition to being unprofessional and incompetent, Sheriff Ackal's office was simply not up to the task of solving any serious crime where the facts were not clearly established or were not in dispute. In essence, a gaggle of local political appointees with little or no qualifications was being asked to solve what Dr. Chastant's family still believes was a murder for hire plot.

In the meantime, even as detectives were duplicating each other's efforts, Laurie would soon learn of other secrets her husband had been withholding from her, secrets that had nothing to do with other women.

Horses and Hard Times

It's easy to ride a horse into the poorhouse and the Chastants had thirteen of them. The costs of caring for horses can be staggering, particularly if they are horses bred for show like the Peruvian Paso horses Robert and Laurie Chastant kept at Sonriente Stables.

The Peruvian Paso is a breed of medium-sized saddle horse noted for its smooth ride and its natural, four-beat, lateral gait called the *paso llano*. Described as "the Rolls Royce of riding horses, the breed is protected by a decree of the Peruvian government. They were brought to Peru during the Spanish Conquest, beginning with the arrival of Pizarro in 1531 and the breed remained virtually isolated for four centuries which allowed the bloodlines to remain pure.

There was a resurgence of the breed some thirty years ago and today, the annual National Show in Lima is a major event. Laws were enacted to restrict the export of national champion horses. There are fewer than 50,000 of the horses in the world.

Devoted to his horses, Dr. Chastant was obsessed with providing only the finest facilities for their care. He submerged himself in the construction of an elaborate building at Sonriente Stables that would double as a barn for the horses and a residence for the Chastants, who planned to sell their home on Bayou Bend Road. Brother Paul Chastant, an architect, was asked to design the building but refused, convinced that Robert was taking on too much expense. He was correct but by the time Robert realized the magnitude of his problems, the financial screws were tightening.

Unbeknownst to Laurie Chastant (or so she would claim in her depositions), her husband was deep in debt and desperate by late 2010. A downturn in the economy had resulted in patients opting for fewer orthodontic procedures and that was putting a financial squeeze on him. Only ten days before his death, Dr. Chastant had initiated proceedings to liquidate his defined benefits plan in order to pay down the mortgage on his house and the debt on his two-million-dollar, two-hundred-foot-long barn. Facts that emerged after his death indicated that Laurie could have been telling the truth when she denied any knowledge of his intent to liquidate his retirement plan. Because he died before he could complete the transaction, however, Dr. Chastant's family would have one more reason to question her innocence.

Typical of a tragedy that combined violence with money and infidelity, it didn't take long for a rift to develop between Laurie and her husband's siblings and children. The discord would immediately make its way into the legal system via a spate of lawsuits filed in state and federal courts.

It began during the initial stages of the murder investigation, continued during preparations for Robert Chastant's funeral and escalated from that point to district court in New Iberia and the federal courthouse in nearby Lafayette.

The dispute between Paul Chastant and his brother's wife erupted almost immediately when she suggested the day after Robert's death that he wanted to be cremated, which Paul said he knew was not the case.

"The first thing out of her mouth was, 'Don't you think we should cremate him? Bobby would have wanted to be cremated,'" Paul said. "I told her that we are Catholic, that was not something that we typically consider. Bobby and I were very, very close and I had never heard him refer to anything except a Catholic burial. And unless she had some kind of documentation to prove it, that we would not cremate him."

When Steven "Buzz" Durio of the firm Durio, McGoffin, Stagg & Ackermann, asked if there was any other discussion about cremation, Paul said, "No. I stopped it. It wasn't going to happen." (While Laurie may have acquiesced, Louisiana law gives the final say-so to the widow so had she insisted on cremation, there would have been no legal recourse for Paul and the rest of the Chastant family.)

Paul said Laurie also "made big objections," asserting that her husband's estate should pay for the funeral. "I thought the way it was handled was very, very impersonal and very indignant [sic] based upon her husband dying, especially since the money came from him anyway," he said.

"Her father also piped in at the same time and it got to the point where it was pretty much—I had to ask him to leave, to either be quiet or leave, because it was not his concern. I told him I was going to walk him out of the room if he got involved again, but he got very indignant to a level where it was—she made a comment that, 'This is my money, this is mine. I shouldn't have to pay for it.' We're talking about a man's funeral. I was taken aback by that."

In his deposition of January 13, 2012, given in the matter of Laurie Chastant's federal lawsuit against Prudential Insurance, Paul Chastant said he had "every reason to believe Laurie was involved" in his brother's murder.

Attorney Durio, represented Laurie Chastant at Paul Chastant's deposition and he was the first to question him. Dr. Chastant's brother told the attorney that as late as September 2011, nine months following his brother's murder, he still had not been given access to the investigation file by the Iberia Parish Sheriff's Office. He had, however, communicated regularly with Captain Gerald Savoy and Detective Adrienne Wells as well as other personnel in the sheriff's office.

Asked by Durio what his reasons were for suspecting Laurie in the murder, he responded, "There are instances before …the death and after the death which made me believe that she's involved."

He said it was apparent to him around November "they were having relationship problems." He said it was also apparent to him that Laurie was having "medication problems stemming from her Crohn's disease and also from psychotropic medication she was taking.

Even more significant, however, was his testimony that Robert was moving much of his defined benefit assets into his personal account in order to retire some of his outstanding debts. "I also saw documents— have seen documents—that Laurie signed releasing her rights to those [benefits]." Laurie would later claim that those documents were forgeries.

Paul Chastant also acknowledged in that deposition that he had become aware of a "potential relationship going on, and Bobby was getting much more involved with a lady and apparently going to travel to see her during the Christmas holidays."

Then came his most damning testimony against Laurie:

"…Laurie had spent or cashed some checks at some times that relate to the knowledge I have now with the testimony of the convicted murderer that relate to the movement of money to pay him off for his participation." Paul was referring, of course, to the $600 check for cash dated December 6 and the $400 check for cash dated December 10, just seven and three days before Robert Chastant's murder. The total of the two checks equaled what Ismael Tovar said he was paid by Laurie to kill her husband.

Durio asked Paul Chastant, "You've told me today that you think Laurie was involved—or you believe she was involved in Bobby's killing, is that right?"

"Yes, I do," Paul replied.

"Has anybody else ever told you that?"

"Yes."

"Who?"

"Sheriff [Louis] Ackal, Captain [Gerald] Savoy, Detective [Adrienne] Wells, [Assistant District Attorney] Bo Duhé, Robert Chevalier, Captain Hebert, and a couple of other people within the sheriff's department."

"Okay, who is the first person that told you this?"

"Sheriff Ackal."

"And when was that?" asked Durio.

"The 15th of December."

"He told you that he, Sheriff Ackal, felt that Laurie was involved in killing Bobby?"

"Exactly."

"Did he tell you why?"

"Some of the events that occurred the day of the murder when she was in the sheriff's office. That she cried for six hours and never shed a tear."

"Have you spoken to him about that feeling since?"

"Yes…it was in the time frame when Viera was…sentenced. He said he felt she was involved based on the information…He went through all the evidence…that we knew about…with Captain Savoy and Detective Wells…and he told us that it was still an open case and that he felt she was involved."

Durio, in that January 13, 2012, deposition, asked Paul about his claim that his brother was experiencing financial stress. "What did he tell you was causing him stress?" he asked. "What financial issues…"

"He had put a lot of money into the new barn he was building and also his practice was down because of the financial stress in the nation. People—orthodontia is a—it's not a practice that people go to when things are down, so his practice was down in all locations. He was also trying to close his Morgan City practice. And it was—he had an issue where they had filed the documents for closure too late and the [landlord] extended the lease three years or something—a five-year lease, automatically. So, he was all upset about that. Beyond that, we just talked about business. He sunk [sic] a heck of a lot of money into the barn and I was not in favor of the barn, period. I thought it was a bad investment. I refused to do the [architectural] drawings."

"Did he ever tell you why he was so driven to build this elaborate barn?" Durio asked.

"He was building it for Laurie so she could have the horses. And breed—they could do something together and breed the horses together…I stayed away from it. I refused to get involved with it."

Asked by Durio what other information he had learned about Robert's financial plight, Paul said, "I learned he was financially pretty well strapped, that he had about $2.5 million worth of debt."

Laurie's attorney then asked about Robert Chastant's attempt shortly before his death to move certain assets to pay off some of his debts. "What assets did you learn that he was moving?" he asked.

"I talked to the guy, I don't think he's even alive anymore, the gentleman from Edward Jones, and asked him if he [Robert] was closing out the defined benefit plan and what his intent for the defined benefit plan was. He specifically told me that his intent was to pay off his debts relative to the barn."

"You don't remember the fellow at Edward Jones's name?"

"He passed away. I mean, he was a manager, and he committed suicide. I don't know his name."

"Yeah," Durio said. "I think I know who you're talking about. He left Edward Jones and then he committed suicide since."

"He was a manager for Bobby's account," Paul said, "and I talked to him right after [Robert's] death and that's when I asked him."

Paul said he was aware of only one of his brother's life insurance policies, a $600,000 policy "that Bobby gave her [Laurie]…for her signing off on a prenuptial agreement. Bobby and I discussed it when Laurie made objection, when they were getting married, to her signing the prenup."

In that deposition, Paul Chastant said when Laurie learned about Kristie McClain, she called Robert's daughter Megan Qualls and said, "He's doing it again, he has a relationship with a woman. She was excited, she was upset. She had a potential of going through a divorce and she was going to get $110,000--$50,000 to $110,000 and a car. She had a potential to get $1.2 million that she was aware of, or $1.3 million." Paul then said that Laurie "also told her that she felt that Christmas was going to be canceled that year because Bobby had made arrangements to fly to Dallas on the 16th to be with the woman." He said within a couple of weeks of learning about Kristen McClain, Laurie had to sign a release on the defined benefits package "which said she had no rights to the money."

"From what I understand, that was a very—a bad time for she [sic] and Bobby. But she signed off on a document releasing her rights to the $750,000 he had in the defined benefits plan.

"It seemed very circumstantial that there was a potential that she might be going through a divorce, that they had a prenuptial agreement that stated that she was only going to get…either $50,000 or $110,000 and a vehicle, or an opportunity for $750,000. I see that as a motive," Paul concluded.

Durio tried pressing Paul Chastant. "So, you believe that her knowledge of his moving assets such as the defined benefit plan was a motive for her to kill him?"

"Most certainly. An opportunity for her to get more money, plus she was aware of the $600,000 insurance policy."

"The next thing you had mentioned," Durio said as he continued with his questioning, "was the signature on documents, but I think you've told me about them, at least insofar as it was a defined benefit plan. Anything else in terms of signed documents?" he asked.

"Checks for cash. She had not written many checks for cash…and they coincided with the time frame of when Viera was paid apparently—said he was paid for killing my brother."

"You're concluding that those checks were for that purpose because they don't have a notation, is that what you're saying?"

"Bobby didn't allow her to write checks except on one account. Bobby didn't allow any of his wives to have credit cards or checks. He was a cash person. I don't think she would be inclined to write a check for cash unless she had something, some specific reason."

Durio was attempting to lay a trap for Paul Chastant. His claim about the signatures on the form to liquidate the defined benefit plan would later become a major point of contention. Laurie had earlier given a deposition in which she challenged the authenticity of signatures on the document. Revelations, claims and omissions would unfold in a plot that had more twists and turns than a dangerous mountain road. And those twists and turns could be just as treacherous.

Tom Aswell

Allegations of Forgery

The trap being set by Durio for Paul Chastant dealt with signatures purported to be those of Laurie Chastant on Robert's application papers to close out his defined benefit program.

Laurie, under questioning from attorney James Daniels during her deposition taken on October 6, 2011, would swear under oath that the signature on one page of a release of defined benefits package form was a forgery and not hers. That was the release on the defined benefits package on which Paul Chastant based his claim when he said she "had no rights to the money."

In questioning Laurie about Robert's defined benefit plan, Daniels asked, "Was it your understanding that he was cashing in his interest in the plan, he was cashing in on his benefits?"

"I had no understanding of that," Laurie replied.

Daniels persisted. "I have in front of me three pages, page 10, 11, and 12 of a Form 3."

Daniels was referring to a document form entitled "Consent of Spouse" that had been admitted into evidence (See Appendix F).

Page 10, "Marital Status and Personal Information," contained the printed name of "Laurie Chastant" on a line identifying her as the spouse of Robert Chastant, along with the signature of a notary public, Judith Vaughn (Appendix E).

"Do you recall signing these documents on page 10 and 12?" Daniels asked.

"I did not sign on page 10," Laurie asserted. "On page 10, that's Bobby writing my name right there and I don't see anything else. This is not my handwriting, none of this.

"And then on page 12, I signed this at home in the kitchen," she said, adding that she did not fill out any of the other information [a space for the printed Name of Spouse, location and the date of December 3]. "And I don't know who this notary is because it was—she wasn't in the kitchen with us that night."

"Is that your signature?" Daniels asked.

"Yes, that's my signature."

"And under your signature, where it says, 'Name of Spouse,' is that your writing in print of your---?"

"No."

"You did not fill that out?"

"No, I didn't."

"With regard to the notary, it looks like it's a Judith—"

"It looks like Vaughn in print," Laurie volunteered

The notary seal was stamped at the bottom of the page and identified the notary as Judith G. Vaughn.

"Do you know Judith Vaughn?" Daniels asked.

"No, I don't know her," Laurie replied with certainty.

"Do you know whether she was present when you signed your name?"

"No, she was not present." Laurie remained forceful in her denial.

Daniels pressed on. "Did you have any discussions with Dr. Chastant with regard to his cashing in his benefits under the defined benefit and profit-sharing plans?"

"He never told me he was going to cash it in. He told me he was unhappy with ARS [Administrative Retirement Services, a third-party administrator for business retirement plans] and that he was going to move his retirement to a different company such as Edward Jones, but he never said, 'I'm cashing it in.'"

"Did you read this document before you signed it?"

"No, I didn't."

Daniels asked Laurie if she and Robert Chastant had ever had any conversations about his cashing in his benefits with ARS to pay down his debt.

"No," she answered, "we never had any discussion about him cashing it in. He specifically told me he was going—he was unhappy with ARS, and that he was going to put his retirement with another company."

"Was it your understanding when you signed this document, page 12…that you were waiving any rights to Dr. Chastant's benefits under the defined benefit profit sharing plans?"

"No, I never read it. He just asked me to sign it, so I did."

"And you didn't know what you were signing, is that your testimony?"

"No, I didn't."

"But you remember where you signed it?"

"Yeah, he gave it to me in the kitchen and asked me to sign it."

"Did you go into ARS to ever discuss what you were signing with them?"

"No, I've never been to ARS."

"The first date above your signature, is that your handwriting?" Daniels asked.

"The only thing [that] is my signature is my handwriting," Laurie said, "but where it says, 'Date, December 3rd,' and printing my name, that's not my handwriting."

"So, you didn't fill out anything other than sign your signature?"

"Correct."

There were actually two sets of consent forms—one for Dr. Chastant and another for Laurie. Because as an employee of her husband's office, Laurie had her own individual plan and every participant was required to sign the consent forms in order for the plan to be closed out. So, in reality, there were two copies of page-10s and two page-12s. So, to simply say the signature on page 10 was not hers was misleading without knowing which page 10 she was referring to.

An examination of the prenuptial agreement signed between Robert and Laurie Futral, dated May 14, 2004, would seem to refute her claim. Her signature on page 3 of the prenup, other than the difference in the last name from Futral to Chastant, is strikingly similar to the signature on page 10 of her specific consent form. The signature of "Laurie" is identical in both documents and the "F" in her maiden name before her marriage and the middle initial "F" in her married signature also is the same. On her husband's form, she is merely listed as his "spouse" on page 10 and her name is not presented as her signature—just as he is listed as "spouse" on page 10 of her form. Her signature on his form is on page 12 and it appears to be authentic.

Despite her assertion that her signature had been forged on the document only ten days before the murder, suspicion of her complicity in her husband's death continued, particularly with Paul Chastant and the relationship would quickly become contentious. Even the guilty plea entered by Ismael Tovar, followed by his sentence of life imprisonment in the Louisiana State Penitentiary at Angola failed to quell the growing distrust between the Chastants and Laurie and her father.

Cessation of Communications

On March 30, 2011, just over three months following the murder of his brother, Paul Chastant sent an email to Assistant District Attorney Robert Chevalier of New Iberia. He opened his email by noting that he had tried unsuccessfully to call Chevalier the previous day before going into what he described as "a few items of concern" that he felt warranted revisiting by investigators.

He noted that Laurie had been "insistent" upon obtaining access to personal property, ostensibly located in the motor home that was parked at Dr. Chastant's clinic. "When moved to Bobby's office, William [apparently a reference to Laurie's father, William Futral] cleaned it, all of Laurie and Bobby's personal effects were removed and delivered to her. She remains insistent. We will be allowing access in the coming week. My concern is she may have something related to the case which would be evidence in the motor home." That concern was apparently motivated by his claim that Laurie's father, William Futral, had previously removed many personal effects from the motor home. "There were [sic] a substantial amount of graphic sexual DVDs we returned. Something electronic/video may remain which could relate to the case."

Paul Chastant also referenced a real estate agent named Sammy Kennedy, who he was told "may have seen something on the 13th." (No further mention of Kennedy was ever found in the reams of investigative files examined by the author.)

Paul said the tack room at the barn was also "a huge issue. "Laurie has made all kind [sic] of excuses for access. The court hearing requires us to give access. The Sheriff has looked at it several times. One additional hard look before she gets control may be merited," he wrote.

He added that he had also asked that James Daniels forward "any information obtained from ARS and Edward R. Jones for your files, adding that "historic information from all insurance carriers with regards to policy changes, in particular those which are beneficiary related," had also been requested and that the DA's office would be copied "with everything we receive."

"Again, we feel confident that the matters of my brother's death will continue to be high priority on the DA & Sheriff's agenda's [sic]. We remain at you [sic] service s [sic] is [sic] needed. Let's all work to make sure those involved are brought to justice."

The following day Chevalier replied, also via email, that he had forwarded Paul Chastant's email to Sheriff's Detective Adrienne Wells "who should be in contact with you shortly. I also spoke to your attorney Jimmy Daniels regarding the same."

Paul replied seventeen minutes later that Wells had called a few minutes earlier.

Thirty-three minutes after that email, Wells emailed Paul Chastant to ask, "Can you please send me something in writing granting permission for me and other Detectives [sic] that I may designate to assist in the search of the mobile RV which currently [is] being stored at 603 Rue De Lion. Also, when I speak to Liz at the office, I will get her to sign a voluntary consent to search form. I appreciate your assistance in the investigation."

By June 10, however, the bloom was off the rose insofar as Paul Chastant's faith in the Iberia Parish Sheriff's Office was concerned. Sheriff Louis Ackal, who once said he had "a million and one reasons" why Laurie Chastant might have wanted her husband dead, by now seemed to have lost all interest in pursuing her as a suspect.

On that date, Paul Chastant wrote in a blistering email to Ackal:

"I would appreciate the opportunity to speak with you and staff involved with the investigation of my brother Bobby's murder. In the recent past, I've called your office to discuss matters of the case and concerns of the family. As of yet, you have not extended the courtesy by either receiving a call or returning one. I did receive a followup [sic] call from a sargent [sic] of your staff. At which time I indicated that you were whom I wished to speak [to]. To my knowledge, you have made no effort to return my calls.

"I will be traveling to the area June 20, 2011, and would appreciate an appointment to meet with you in your office. I can make myself available at any time that date. Please respond by email, starting tomorrow morning. I will be traveling to Singapore and not return until June 18, 2011."

Asked if Ackal ever responded to that message, Paul Chastant said, "We met two times after the initial investigations. Once he stopped returning calls, he and I never talked again until a confrontation at an annual state sheriffs' conference." (Paul Chastant, who designs public and private prisons, would likely have been attending the conference as a vendor.)

"Our last meeting was in his office. My sister-in-law and I went together. We confronted him on our concerns that he was using the case to help his re-election effort. He assured us that the case was still active. Two deputies attended [that meeting]. Less than two months after being re-elected he [Ackal] dropped the case.

"At the meeting, he reaffirmed that he felt our sister-in-law [Laurie Chastant] was involved and [he] told us of her meetings with him. This was a first. We were concerned in that it was our understanding that their investigations were confidential."

Tom Aswell

A Few Things to Consider

It would be New Year's Eve 2011 before Paul Chastant would read Laurie Chastant's October 6 deposition and he was unhappy with her testimony. In a rambling January 1, 2012, email apparently hurriedly written and peppered with spelling, punctuation and grammatical errors to brother Bradley Chastant, Robert Chastant's daughter Megan, attorney James Daniels and three others, he wrote, "Read the whole damn thing last night. A few notes & things to consider.

"We need to verify Lauries [sic] medical timeline for the week prior to the 13th and her other treatment, care and medications. Bobby confided in me that Laurie was seeing a psychologist or other mental health service. Verified today that Dr. Ritter, who she saw Monday morning, was a physiologist specializing in physical recovery [Laurie Chastant, in fact, left Dr. Ritter's office before actually seeing Dr. Ritter]. She apparently had an appointment which had been canceled before the weekend and re-appointed by Bobby during the weekend. We need to know the particulars of the schedule changes. Also, we need to verify Lauries [sic] past schedules for appointments. Also, we need to know when she arrived at the office. She indicated that she was late & left around 9:15 What will the Dr. report [say], do they have a time sheet. [sic] Was it a routene [sic] visit, in and out. [sic]"

Paul also expressed his concern over Laurie's refusing to answer questions in her deposition about possible drug use. "It's interesting that she pleaded the 5th for this so rapidly. We need to know what she's hiding. Whats [sic] her concern and how does it relate to the murder. How can she plead the 5th if they arent [sic] related?"

Laurie, invoking her Fifth Amendment rights in that October 6 deposition, had refused to answer on three occasions when asked specific questions by attorney Daniels about any problems she may have had with drug abuse.

Paul Chastant continued in his email:

> Also, Kids [apparently addressing Robert Chastant's children], one of you told me of a friend of Lauries [sic] that your father didn't like hanging around. One of you mentioned that the lady supplies Lauries [sic] drugs, who is that person. [sic] Jamie [not explained] needs to depose her.
> Who is Melissa Rummel, any of you know. [sic]
> We need to contact and depose the two girl friends [sic] and get them to tell us of anything Bobby may have shared with them. Any issues with the marriage etc.
> Megan and Michele, which of you did Laurie call about Kristen. [sic] Had she called in the past to discuss marital issues. [sic] What and when!! [sic]
> Check histories. Laurie made a big deal out of the checks and that she put a notation for the use on each. We need to get the checks and find out. Also, at one time, Fran indicate [sic] that she had a discussion with Laurie recommending she not write checks for cash. Jamie, wouldn't hurt refreshing that issue with her. When and why was that addressed. If you don't already have it, we need the images of canceled checks from the stables account.
> Finally, I'm seeing conflict with the comments about Natalie and Ishmael. In particular, Laurie stated that both were gone by 7:40. Then she states that Natalie was in the residence before she left. Planned propoerly [sic] with Ishmael, moving the timeline which we can not [sic] verify forward, she could have easily completed all and made the appointment. We need the phone logs and histories. Jamie, now that we have the evidence, we need it all. Please request the telephone history.

There is no record that Paul Chastant's concerns and emotional outburst in his email were ever addressed to his satisfaction.

Letters from Tamara and David

While no documents have been found that would tie Laurie directly to any evidence of illegal drug use, there were two letters from a friend discovered by investigators, both from a woman named Tamara Chaplin, apparently living in New York, that do provide some insight into the character makeup of Laurie and her associates.

The first letter, dated August 9, 1994, a decade before Laurie and Robert Chastant were married, offered no indication of any drug use, though it did reveal her frustration with the man with whom she was living. It seemed from her letter that he was continuing to see other women. The second, undated letter, however, was a bit more revealing. She also wrote of her intentions to visit Laurie.

Her second letter also went into considerable detail about her affair with another man named Frank even as she continued living with the first man and she wrote openly of her drug dealing and drug use. "There are so many things that I want to tell you that I can't tell you on the phone," she wrote. Her letter continued:

> I slept with Frank again. We can't seem to stay away from each other. Only now he has taken off to Jefferson to hide because he owes this guy $1500 and now that he's gone, I've somehow taken over his business, if you know what I mean. I've been hooked up with his connection in Saratoga and I have to help get it for the guys at the [unintelligible]. That's one of the reasons why I am never home when you call. It's just like having another job, only I don't get paid with money. I just get high for free mostly.
>
> This is starting to become very hard. John has no idea what I'm doing and he's starting to wonder what's going on. I have to lie to him all the time about where I'm going and who

I'm talking to on the phone. And Shawn from the shop keeps calling and telling me to beep him and John wants to know why.

The guy that Frank got his stuff from in Saratoga is the one that I'm working with. His name is David. He's about 34 and just spent 10 years in jail for dealing and we know that he and the shop are being watched. I hope that I'm not in over my head. I never thought that I would get this involved and it's not something you can just walk away from. That can make a lot of people really pissed. Anyway, David and I have to spend a lot of time together and now I think that I want to sleep with him. When we first started this, he told me that he was crazy about me and wanted me really bad but he would not touch me because he says that he is a loser and way too old and that I don't need a drug-dealing convict to mess up my life. And I totally agreed.

I didn't even find him attractive—only now the more time we spend together, the harder it is. He treats me like a little angel. He won't let me pay for anything when we are on the road. He is always making sure my sugar level is alright [sic]. He always tells me how pretty and smart I am and that he wishes that I never got involved in the business. Compared to the girls he is used to, I am an angel and pure.

Now I have a feeling that he is falling in love with me. Last week we were making a buy. We were dealing with this black guy. One said to me, 'What's wrong with you? You look like a stuck-up little cunt.' David lost his mind, punched the guy and threw me in the van and took off. Because of that we had to wait in the van for four hours for another deal. He would of [sic] ignored the comment and got the stuff but he says that he can't allow anyone to disrespect his little angel.

The other night, we had to sit in a hotel for another two hours by ourselves and he never made a move on me. He says that he really wants to but he won't. All he did was touch my hair and stare into my eyes. I thought that he was going to kiss me but all he did was pull away and lock himself in the bathroom for almost 10 minutes.

The more he fights wanting me, the more I want him. I know that I can't and don't need to fall in love with him but I have a great, powerful need to have him. I've never wanted someone so bad in my life and if and when it does happen, it's going to be explosive. And guess what? His penis is pierced!!

Well, I have a lot more to tell, but I can't think of it right now. Oh, I know, when we talk on the phone, don't mention drugs at all. I worried that my phone may be tapped. If it's not now, it may be soon. Well, got to go. I'm at work I miss you and I love you.

Tamara

The correspondence with Tamara Chaplin is significant because of a sworn statement Tamara gave in Lafayette on March 26, 1995, which in retrospect, appears to have laid the groundwork for Laurie's divorce from her first husband, Navy petty officer David Moore, not to be confused with the David alluded to in Tamara's earlier letter:

Before me, the undersigned authority, personally came and appeared Tamara D. Chaplin, of Opelousas, St. Landry Parish, Louisiana, who being duly sworn did depose and state that:

She has known David and Laurie Moore for approximately 2-3 years from the time they lived in New York State;

That when PO2 David Moore received transfer orders to Virginia, she stayed with David and Laurie Moore looking at apartment books and college books for Virginia;

That she personally witnessed PO2 David Moore encouraging Laurie Moore as to the move and that on the night before David Moore and Laurie Moore left New York, PO2 David Moore was being very affectionate to Laurie Moore;

That David Moore informed her that the Moore's [sic] were going to spend a couple of weeks with family in Louisiana and that they would then move together to Virginia and pick up their household goods;

That a few days later, she (Tamara) received an [sic] hysterical phone call at approximately 1:00 o'clock in the morning, in which she was informed that PO2 Moore had informed her that he did not love her and was leaving her at her parent's [sic] house and would go to Virginia without her, informing her that he did not love her.

The sworn affidavit was dated and contained the signatures of Tamara D. Chaplin and a notary. But her statement, given under oath, did not square with an anguished letter Moore wrote to Laurie five months earlier.

That letter, written in longhand and dated October 25, 1994 read:

Laurie:

I know you're probably surprised that I'm writing you a letter, but there are some things I need to say to you and I think this is the best way to do it.

I found out about a week ago what you filed for in our divorce. I was shocked. Adultry [sic]? Do you really believe that I cheated on you? I never did, I swear. In many ways, I probably wasn't a very good husband but one thing I never did was cheat. If I would have, you would know about it because I would have told you.

You also filed for abandonment and say that I am somehow responsible for you being sick. If you remember, I tried to get back together with you before I left, so how is that abandonment? If you had wanted to come with me to Virginia, you could have. How can you possibly say I am responsible for your illness? I can't believe you said that! I did everything I possibly could to make you better. I went with you to visit the doctors and I was there every time I could be when you had to have some sort of test done. I paid for and am still paying for all your visits, tests and medicine without ever complaining one bit about it. If I remember correctly, you got sick after you left me for the first time. When you left, you were fine.

In the four or five months that we were apart is when you got really sick and I came to see you even though we were still apart because I was worried about you. You can say a lot of bad things about me, Laurie, and many of them are probably true, but I was always there for you when it came to your illness.

I didn't write this letter to bitch at you or to try to make you feel bad, so, if that's what it sounds like, I'm sorry. I know that I am probably responsible for many of the things that went wrong in our marriage, but so are you. I know I didn't spend enough time with you and go out with you and do things. I didn't express my feelings too often, neither. For all of this I am sorry....

David

Tom Aswell

Roszczynialski Explains Funds Distribution

Lori Roszczynialski, a pension consultant for Administrative Retirement Services (ARS), gave her deposition on March 15, 2012. She was able to shed critical light on the timing of Dr. Chastant's death and how that affected the disbursement of funds from his retirement and profit-sharing funds. She testified she began handling Robert Chastant's defined benefit and profit-sharing plans in 2006.

She testified that the plans included a death benefit for Laurie should Robert Chastant die while the plans were in force.

Daniels, in his questioning of Roszczynialski, inquired as to the status of the plans on December 13, the day of Chastant's death. "Both of the plans were in the process of being terminated," she explained. "The defined benefit plan, everyone [all the employees of Dr. Chastant's dental practice] had been paid out with the exception of Dr. Chastant, Laurie Chastant, and Megan Chastant [Dr. Chastant's daughter], and the profit-sharing plan had been terminated and we were in the process of doing distribution paperwork for those."

Daniels asked what she meant by the plans being terminated.

"When you have a retirement plan, it's active and ongoing until a point in time that you decide that you no longer want to continue your retirement plan, so you terminate the plan which ceases the accrual of benefits or anymore contributions going in. At that time, you do an accounting and you prepare distribution paperwork and the participants complete it based on their election, whether they want to roll it into an IRA or take a lump sum distribution."

"Is the fact that the plan being terminated, was that an election by someone?" Daniels asked.

"Dr. Chastant had decided to terminate the retirement plans."

Daniels handed Roszczynialski a copy of the Notice to Participant of Distribution Election which she described as a distribution of benefit packet. "The employee goes through and it gives them a special tax notice, explains to them what's going to happen as far as tax—the taxation of their distribution that they take," she explained, adding that participants have an option of whether to take a lump sum distribution, if they want to roll it into an IRA, or purchase an annuity. "They have all their options," she said. "They choose their option and then they have to continue to fill out paperwork if they're taking a lump sum, if they want state withholding taken out, if they're rolling into an IRA, they give us the information. So, this was the paperwork that he completed."

"Were these forms filled out by Dr. Chastant?" Daniels asked.

"Yes."

"And when were they filled out by Dr. Chastant?"

"He signed them in November, so I would assume they were completed in November."

"Would you tell us the year, please?"

"Yes, November 11, 2010."

Daniels then asked what Dr. Chastant's option had been with regard to the profit-sharing and the defined benefit plans.

"The defined benefit plan, he elected to roll that into an IRA with Edward Jones, Roszczynialski replied. "The profit-sharing plan, we, at the time of his death, paperwork had not been completed yet, so he did not sign anything on that."

"So, with regard to the election that Dr. Chastant made prior to his death, it had to do with the—terminating the defined benefit plan only?"

"Yes."

"And what is the purpose of page 10?" he asked, referring to paperwork for the defined benefit plan.

"Page 10, what happens in a defined benefit plan, if—because of the fact that it's a guaranteed benefit, if the participant were to elect to take a lump sum distribution, the spouse needs to sign off confirming that she is okay with that because she would be due…some form of an annuity, because that's the normal form of payment from a defined benefit plan."

"And did Laurie Chastant sign a Consent of Spouse form" (Appendix F)

"Yes."

Daniels then referred her to page 11, a Written Explanation of Qualified Joint and Survivor Annuity Form of Benefit. "Would you tell…what that document is?" he asked.

"It's a Consent of Spouse that she's waiving the survivor annuity benefits…In a defined benefit plan, you have an accrued benefit and the normal way—and the normal form of payout in a defined benefit plan is some form of an annuity, whether it's 100 percent joint and survivor, 50 percent joint and survivor. So, if he took his distribution and he's receiving an annuity and then he dies and his spouse continues to receive an annuity payment. He has the option of electing to take a lump sum distribution or to roll [it] over. The spouse has to sign off acknowledging that that's fine, but the benefit is not going to be paid in the form of an annuity."

"Can you tell me when ARS received the documents which are listed …as 'Exhibit No. 3'?

"I don't know the exact date, but it was maybe like December 5th or 6th, something around that time."

Daniels asked what else, if anything, needed to be done "in order to complete the termination of the defined benefit plan?"

"We were waiting on Megan Chastant's [Qualls] paperwork to come in because we had to pay her out before we could pay Dr. Chastant."

"What happens to the process of Dr. Chastant terminating his plan upon his death since he was killed before the plan was actually terminated?"

"Everything had to stop until a new trustee was appointed because …funds can't be dispersed out of the plan unless the trustee instructs these."

"So, is it your testimony that because he died before Megan was paid, that instead of rolling the funds over to the Edward Jones account, they would be paid to Laurie Chastant?" Daniels asked.

"Yes," Roszczynialski replied, "because that is his beneficiary."

"Even though she had earlier waived…signed a spousal consent form?"

"The only thing she waived was the annuity option. She didn't waive being the beneficiary, she waived the annuity option."

Legal delays notwithstanding, Laurie Chastant wanted what she thought was coming to her and she wanted it quickly—even as suspicion that she was complicit in her husband's murder gained currency with her in-laws.

A spate of lawsuits ensued, the first filed by Laurie in April 2011, less than four months after her husband's death. But the seeds of dissention and suspicion were sown even before a casket for Robert Chastant's burial could be selected at New Iberia's Pellerin Funeral Home.

Sparks Fly Over Funeral Arrangements

Paul Chastant, Robert's brother and executor of his estate, had barely arrived in New Iberia from his home in South Carolina when the bickering began—a not uncommon occurrence with families at funerals, especially when money is involved. "It occurred the night I got in on the 14th" when Laurie went to the funeral home to make arrangements, he testified in his deposition of January 13, 2012. "The first thing out of her mouth was, 'Don't you think we should cremate him? Bobby would have wanted to be cremated.'

"I told her that we are Catholic, that was not something that we typically consider." He said he and Robert were "very, very close...and I had never heard him refer to anything except a Catholic burial. And unless she had some kind of documentation to prove it, that we would not cremate him."

Asked by attorney James Daniels if Laurie ever told Paul that Robert desired to be cremated, Paul said, "No, I asked her and she said, 'No, I don't think so, but, you know, I just think he would have preferred it.'"

"Any other discussion about that?"

"No. I stopped it. It wasn't going to happen."

That dispute, though resolved to Paul's satisfaction, did not end the simmering ill feelings between Laurie and her in-laws who were already considering her a suspect in her husband's murder. Paul and another brother, Dr. Bradley Chastant, a Lafayette otolaryngologist (head and neck surgeon), were at Pellerin Funeral Home along with Laurie and her father, a retired state trooper and then a deputy with the St. Landry Parish Sheriff's Department. The rift spilled over to the choice of a coffin for Robert Chastant. "The selections that she made for coffins once she had a hint that she [and not her husband's estate] may be paying for the funeral were very, very low grade and very contrary to Bobby's personality," Paul insisted.

His memory of having to confront Laurie's father, William Futral, Jr., was also vastly different from Futral's recollection. Paul Chastant testified that when Futral "piped up," he had to ask him to leave or he would physically escort him from the funeral home.

Not so, Futral countered in his deposition of April 3, 2012. "I don't know if it was Bradley or Paul [who] decided he wanted to go pick out the casket, and I didn't get into that at all. That's between him and Laurie and I believe what actually happened after that was Laurie picked it out herself. So, no, we had no problem then."

"Did you have any problems at any point in time with either Bradley or Paul Chastant?" Daniels asked.

"Certainly not."

"Any argument with either one of them?"

"No."

"Anything else occur that you recall at the funeral home?"

"One thing I did find was a little unusual, I noticed that my daughter was crying, I was crying, but none of the Chastants were. I found that a little unusual."

Asked if Laurie told him that she paid for the funeral, Futral said, "I believe she did."

"Did you tell her you thought maybe the Chastants should have paid instead of her?" Daniels asked.

"We talked about it and I thought perhaps that the estate should have paid for it."

"And you told Laurie that?"

"Yes."

The payment of funeral expenses and the selection of a casket were not the only points of contention between the Chastants and the Futrals. Another sore subject concerned the disposition of a number of guns that were in Robert Chastant's home before his murder but which vanished shortly after his death.

"You were aware, were you not, that Dr. Chastant had several firearms in his home?" Daniels asked Laurie's father.

"Yes. He had shotguns and…well, basically shotguns."

Futral, during his deposition, at first agreed with Daniels's suggestion that he took the guns to protect his daughter but contradicted himself within minutes.

"Did you make any attempt the day of the murder or the next day to gather those weapons so that Laurie wouldn't hurt herself or anyone else?" asked Daniels.

"Yes, I did," Futral responded. "I took them and brought them and put them in a gun safe."

"At your house?"

"Yeah."

"Are they still there?"

"No."

"Where are they?"

"I had a threat of a flood last year, so I took them and I locked them up in an unused jail cell at [the] Palmetto Police Department."

"Are they still there?"

"I believe they are."

But when Daniels again asked why he removed the weapons (three shotguns and two .22 caliber rifles), Futral said, "I removed them because I wanted to keep them for safekeeping."

"And what do you mean by that, 'for safekeeping'?" Daniels asked.

"Well, just so that they would remain for whoever they wound up being for, because there was some other things in that house that didn't stay where they should have been."

"Who made the decision for you to take the firearms?" Daniels asked.

"I did."

"And did you do it with Laurie's blessing?"[2]

"I believe she saw me do it and didn't object."

The floor mat found in an outside storage compartment of Dr. Chastant's motor home raised other questions about the diligence, or lack of, in the investigation. It was the same motor home in which family friends stayed during the funeral.

Detective Adrienne Wells, in her December 8, 2011, deposition, described the mat as plural mats, as appearing to belong to a truck, though it was never determined for certain if there were one or two mats discovered by authorities.

"Did you participate in the search of the motor home?" she was asked by Daniels.

"Yes, I was there."

"What evidence was collected from the motor home?"

"The first time, nothing," she said. "I don't think anything was taken and then a while later, I was contacted by the family, Paul Chastant, to go back and look in the motor home because [he said] Laurie wanted to get into it, so I went back and got a consent to search."

Once the consent to search was signed, Wells said she went back to the motor home "and I found a floor mat, two floor mats, if I can recall correctly, in one of the compartments."

"One of the luggage compartments?"

"Yeah, on the outside."

"And I see ... it says 'Floor mat.' I assume that's what that is. It says, 'Hair and blood from claw.' What does that mean?"

"It should be the claw of the hammer," she said .

"What about the floor mats caught your attention when you searched the motor home," he asked.

"...After I found the floor mats, the next day I went [to] check the vehicles at the jail. The Avalanche [Laurie's vehicle] was the only vehicle without any floor mats and it [the discovered mat or mats] looked like truck floor mats."

Captain Gerald Savoy, deposed on the same day as Wells, said that almost exactly a year after submitting the floor mat (singular) to the Acadiana Crime Lab, results of the lab's analysis incredibly still had not been received by the sheriff's department even though he said Laurie remained a person of interest in the investigation. The crime lab's analysis of the floor mat, in fact, was never received nor, apparently, followed up on by the sheriff's department.

What was Laurie Chastant looking for in the motor home that prompted her to request permission to enter it while it was still considered as evidence? Paul Chastant, in an interview for this book, said his brother's blood was in Laurie's truck. "She said she wanted to go to the motor home to retrieve some personal belongings," he said. "Instead, she went directly to the compartment where the floormat was found and removed earlier by authorities. She then made only a cursory trip through the motor home's interior picking up a few assorted items."

Laurie denied that she ever checked the outside luggage compartment when she visited the motor home or that she was looking for any particular items.

In her deposition, Laurie said, "We had two mutual friends [Pam Harris and Donna Riley, both from Texas] that stayed one night in the motor home."

"When Pam and Donna were staying in the motor home that one night, that was the night before the funeral?"

"No," Laurie said. "It was the night of the funeral."

"…Since the day of Dr. Chastant's death, had you been inside the motor home?"

"Yes, I believe so."

"And what was the purpose for going in the motor home?"

"I took some of my clothes out of there."

"Did you have any reason from December 13th, other than the time you went to the office to look through the motor home, did you go into the luggage compartment of the motor home?"

"No, not that I recall."

"When you went to Dr. Chastant's office … to examine the motor home looking for personal belongings, was there anything that you were specifically looking for?"

"No, nothing in specific."

"Was there anything that you were looking for that you thought was there that was not there?"

"No, I don't think so."

Tom Aswell

Laurie Chastant v. Prudential Insurance

That feud, which had begun brewing at the funeral home, boiled over on January 4, 2011, less than a month after Dr. Chastant was murdered, when Laurie made a formal demand that insurance carriers and Paul Chastant turn over all insurance and retirement death benefits to her. When Prudential Insurance Co. of America which had issued a $600,000 policy on Robert Chastant's life, and Lincoln National Life Insurance Co., whose policy was for $700,000, did not comply, she filed suit against both companies on April 19, just four months and six days following the death of her husband.

Together, the two policies meant a world of difference to Laurie. She could receive more than two million dollars from her husband's death, including the $1.3 million from the two life insurance policies and the defined benefits and profit-sharing plans. Should she be implicated in the murder, however, she was looking instead at the possibility of prison – and no money.

In her lawsuit, she claimed that Paul Chastant breached his fiduciary duties to her by refusing to provide the proceeds of the plans in a proper and timely manner; attempting to discredit her by declaring her as unworthy to receive the proceeds and to remove her as beneficiary of the plans by claiming she was responsible for the murder of her husband, for using the proceeds of the plans to fund such attempts, and wrongfully directing that funds from the plans be used for legal services.

Ironically, more time and money would be spent on arriving at a determination of whether or not she was entitled to the benefits and whether Paul Chastant had a legal right to use money from the trust to defend the trust than on the question of whether she might have been involved in a murder plot.

The problem with her demand of payment of benefits and her subsequent lawsuit was (1) the death certificate had not yet been issued at the time of her demand letter and (2) she had yet to be eliminated as a suspect in the murder of her husband. In fact, a year after the murder she was still considered to be a "person of interest." Lincoln National Insurance, in its August 2011 answer to her lawsuit, said, "According to the Estate, [Laurie] Chastant remains a person of interest in connection with the death of the insured."

Louisiana has a so-called "Slayer Statute" on the books. The slayer statute prohibits someone involved in the death of an insured from receiving benefits, retirement, or inheritance of the decedent. It is important to note that conviction of murder requires proof beyond the shadow of a doubt. The Louisiana law that required only ten of twelve jurors to vote guilty to obtain a conviction in serious criminal cases was overturned in April 2020 and now necessitates a unanimous verdict. Louisiana was one of only two states that accepted only ten votes for a conviction at the time of Dr. Chastant's death. The slayer statute applies only to civil law, which needs only a preponderance of the evidence. That means that even a killer who is acquitted of murder in criminal court may still be legally denied any such benefits in a civil proceeding.

As trustee of his brother's estate and as trustee on behalf of Robert Chastant's retirement plans through his dental practice, Paul Chastant, was named along with Prudential and Lincoln National as a defendant in Laurie's lawsuits. As trustee, he said he felt he had a fiduciary responsibility to protect the assets of the estate and the insurance and retirement benefits from fraudulent claims. Accordingly, as long as she remained a suspect, or even a person of interest, he thought he had a legal duty—an obligation—not to pay out any of the benefits to Laurie until the investigation by the sheriff's department was completed.

Laurie countered by asserting that neither Prudential nor the Iberia Parish Sheriff's Office was empowered by Louisiana law to determine whether the state's slayer statute applied. "Prudential cannot substitute its own judgment for that of a court. Louisiana law requires that a court determine by final judgment whether a beneficiary under an insurance contract is disqualified," she said. Laurie, who was given no credit cards or checking account authority, other than the small account for the farm, was financially strapped and desperate. Guilty or innocent, she would not – could not – wait for the investigation to grind down. So, when her demand for payment was denied, with financial help from her father, she filed her first federal lawsuit in Louisiana's Western District Court in Lafayette on April 19, 2011.

Laurie Chastant attempted to invoke the federal ERISA (Employee Retirement Income Security Act) provisions in claiming the money from the defined benefit and the profit sharing plans, but attorney Nancy Picard of the Metairie law firm of Robein, Urann, Spencer, Picard & Cangemi, wrote that, "Cases clearly support [that] Louisiana's slayer statute is not preempted by ERISA; also the concept that an unworthy spouse should be excluded from ERISA plan benefits is supported by federal common law."

She also said, "The trustee [Paul Chastant] shall have the power to pay out of the trust assets all reasonable expenses of administration including, without limitation, fees paid to accountants, actuaries, appraisers and attorneys."

On April 19, 2012, almost a year after Laurie Chastant filed her initial lawsuit, Federal Judge Richard Haik signed a consent order placing the proceeds of the defined benefit and profit-sharing plans in the registry of the court and to formally recognize Paul Chastant as trust administrator (see Appendix D).

Tom Aswell

Dispute, Distrust Deepen

On September 17, 2012, Laurie filed a fourth amended complaint in which she said that after her husband's death, Paul Chastant "refused to distribute the proceeds of the plans" to her and that she "was forced to file suit against Paul in order to receive the proceeds of the plans.

"...Paul answered by alleging that Laurie had participated in murdering Dr. Chastant, and as such, was an unworthy beneficiary...and was barred from receiving the proceeds of the plans," the amended complaint said

Back on June 9, 2011, attorney James Daniels wrote Laurie Chastant's attorney, Steven "Buzz" Durio to confirm an agreement between the two sides that called for any funds received from Prudential to be deposited into the Registry of the Court

> ...with the proceeds thereafter only to be distributed following the final disposition of (Paul) Chastant's claims in the litigation regarding Laurie Ann Futral Chastant's worthiness as an heir and/or beneficiary to receive benefits from any life insurance policy and/or defined benefit and/or profit-sharing plan:

> The parties agree that all funds to be deposited into the Registry of the Court may only be distributed pursuant to settlement of all claims between the parties or a final judgment in the litigation.

> The parties further agree that should there be any sums owed by Lincoln National Insurance Company (Lincoln) for death benefits covering the life of Robert B. Chastant to any beneficiary or beneficiaries, Lincoln shall be directed by the parties that those funds are to be deposited in the court's registry.

The parties further agree that in the event criminal charges are brought by the District Attorney's Office in the 16th Judicial District Court, Iberia Parish, Louisiana, against Laurie Chastant alleging that she is criminally responsible for the death of Robert Brown Chastant, the parties shall stay any further proceedings in the litigation pending resolution of the criminal charges, with the parties reserving all rights, claims, causes of action and defenses in the litigation.

Both Daniels and Durio signed off on the letter.

Initial legal maneuvers quickly zeroed in on efforts to obtain critical information about the ongoing investigation from the sheriff's office and the sheriff's reluctance to release the information for fear of jeopardizing the investigation.

In a thirteen-page ruling, the court granted two motions to quash witness subpoenas.

Sheriff Louis Ackal filed the motions to quash which arose out of the issuance of two separate subpoenas to Captain Gerald Savoy, Commander of the sheriff's department's Bureau of Investigation and who had overall control of the murder investigation, to give his deposition.

Oddly, each side in the dispute wanted Savoy's testimony. One subpoena was issued by plaintiff Laurie Chastant and the other by defendant Paul Chastant.

In granting both motions to quash on September 8, 2011, Federal Magistrate Richard T. Haik wrote, "On June 14, 2011, Ismael Viera-Tovar pleaded guilty to the murder of Dr. Chastant in the 16th Judicial Court for the Parish of Iberia. The parties attempted to depose Viera after his plea, however, he refused to testify. Therefore, as he is 'unavailable,' the parties wish to depose Captain Savoy and review the investigative file materials to determine what Viera told the police. In particular, the defendant [Paul Chastant] contends he needs this information in order to oppose a motion for summary judgment filed by the plaintiff on August 26, 2011..."

Ackal, Haik said, based his motions to quash on a provision of Louisiana's Public Records Act "which exempts from 'public records' disclosure records or information pertaining to pending criminal litigation or any criminal litigation which can be reasonably anticipated, until such litigation has been finally adjudicated or otherwise settled."

Ackal argued that the public records provision "is inapplicable to the issues before the court. Laurie in turn said the court should conduct an *in-camera* inspection of the documents (only the presiding judge actually seeing the documents) before deciding the question before him. Haik at that time did, in fact, conduct an *in-camera* inspection of summaries of the interviews of Tovar.

"According to Savoy," Judge Haik wrote, "there is an ongoing criminal investigation into the murder of Dr. Chastant and the information contained in the summaries contains detailed information that would prejudice the investigation if disclosed. In addition, investigators are awaiting test results of DNA samples and carpet fiber evidence that are currently being analyzed at the Crime Lab which, once returned, may lead to interviews of additional witnesses."

The file materials, Judge Haik pointed out, contained other information as well, including the location of a witness which, if disclosed, "presents a security issue." He said the file also contained detective's notes, as well as notes of witness interviews, telephone call information and a listing of evidence accumulated to date.

"Other than in conjunction with the prosecution of Viera, the case has not been submitted to the Grand Jury, and until such time as the investigation is complete and the material is turned over to the District Attorney, Captain Savoy is not in a position to say whether the case ever will be submitted to the Grand Jury."

Judge Haik said that Savoy testified that the turnaround for results from the crime lab was difficult to determine given the volume of samples submitted. "However, the evidence was submitted approximately two months ago [some seven months *after* the murder] under a high-priority flag from his [Savoy's] office and 'assuming normal circumstances,' he would expect a turnaround time of two-three months from the date of the hearing."

As Savoy would eventually testify in his own deposition on December 8, 2011, three months after Haik's ruling to quash, the sheriff's office was still awaiting results from the crime lab—a full year after Robert Chastant's murder.

"The purpose of the Louisiana Public Records Act," Haik wrote in his decision, "is to keep the public reasonably informed, while at the same time, balancing the public's right of access against the public interest of protecting and preserving the public records from unreasonable dangers of loss or damage, or acts detrimental to the integrity of the public records. The act sets forth the means by which a person may obtain access to public records. It also recognizes exceptions which restrict access to some records."

One of the exceptions he cited was "records pertaining to pending criminal litigation or any criminal litigation which can be reasonably anticipated, until such litigation has been finally adjudicated or otherwise settled…"

Louisiana courts, he said, had defined "criminal litigation" to be an adversarial contest "begun by formal accusation and waged in judicial proceedings in the name of the state. Criminal litigation is 'pending' when the formal accusation is instituted either by the district attorney (bill of information) or by the grand jury (indictment).

"As there has been no indictment or bill of information filed against anyone other than the defendant Viera, even though that judgment may not yet be final, there is arguably no criminal litigation pending," Haik wrote. "Therefore, the issue is whether criminal litigation can be reasonably anticipated." He added that the exemption to disclosure under the Public Records Act "is applicable to bar the discovery sought at this stage of this litigation."

He said the investigation was ongoing and "continues to proceed to the point it can be submitted to the district attorney for determination of whether to bring the case to the Grand Jury" but had not reached that point because of delays in obtaining results from the Crime Lab.

Judge Haik somewhat cryptically noted that investigators "have not concluded that Viera, who pleaded guilty to the murder, acted alone" and that the plaintiff (Laurie Chastant) *"has not been eliminated as a suspect."* (emphasis author's).

Haik, following his retirement from the federal bench a few years later, would resurface to represent Ackal in criminal proceedings against his cousin, the sheriff.

Savoy would ultimately give his deposition, but not until December 8 and he would testify that the Acadiana Crime Lab still had not submitted results of its tests of evidence sent nearly a year before.

That was just one skirmish in what would become an ongoing, drawn-out legal battle between Laurie and her in-laws over the proceeds of Robert Chastant's life insurance and his defined benefit and profit-sharing plans.

Before that matter could be decided, Laurie would sue Paul Chastant as trustee of Robert's estate under provisions of the Employee Retirement Income Security Act (ERISA) for misuse of the plans' funds. Paul would counter with the claim that the expenditures were made in the interest of protecting the ERISA funds and his attorney would seek the legal opinion of an expert in succession law. Finally, Robert Chastant's children would file suit against Laurie for their father's wrongful death and Laurie, by now remarried (and with a brand-new prenuptial agreement of her own), would in turn sue the children. Meanwhile, the criminal investigation into whether or not Laurie was involved in the murder was pushed further and further into the background.

In the interim, her litigation against Prudential deliberately and methodically plodded its way through the courts.

Tom Aswell

Use of Benefit Funds Challenged

On November 9, 2011, almost eleven months following Robert Chastant's murder, Metairie attorney Nancy Picard who specializes in ERISA matters, addressed questions about Laurie's challenge to Paul Chastant's use of trust assets to pay his legal fees related to the ongoing dispute.

Noting that both the defined benefits and profit-sharing plans "establish the employer [Robert Chastant] as both administrator and the trustee" [while living] she wrote that each trust agreement gives the trustee broad general powers, including:

- To settle, compromise or submit to arbitration any claims, debts or damages due or owing to or from the trust, to commence or defend legal proceedings for or against the trust, and to represent the trust in all proceedings in any court of law or equity or before any other body or tribunal;

- To employ agents, including without limitation, investment advisors, appraisers, attorneys [including counsel for the employer] and accountants and to rely on advice given by them;

- To pay out of the trust assets all reasonable expenses of administration including, without limitation, fees paid to accountants, actuaries, appraisers and attorneys.

In summarizing her findings, Picard wrote, "…if the plan is sued and the trustee or administrator is sued independently i.e., for breach of fiduciary duty, in which case he could be reimbursed for his expenses if successful." These duties fell to Paul Chastant when he was named executor of his brother's estate.

On that same date, she reiterated her findings in an email to Daniels in which she said, "[The] trustee has the obligation to guard the assets of the trust from improper claims as well as the obligation to pay legitimate claims."

In an April 18, 2012 letter, attorney Daniels, representing Paul Chastant, addressed key issues put forward by Laurie's attorney, Steven Durio:

> "The Defined Benefit/Profit-Sharing plans are not rolled into any other account, but instead, they will remain with Edward Jones. As we discussed, it would be a conflict for Paul to roll those funds into an account in Laurie's name under any circumstances and then attempt to defend the lawsuit claiming that she is unqualified.

> "The recommendation by Buzz (Durio) that the Defined Benefit/Pension plan can be dismissed from the lawsuit would have the effective removal of the funds from the issues of the lawsuit and subject those funds only to Laurie's discretion."

As an alternative, Daniels suggested allowing Paul Chastant to voluntarily withdraw as trustee and an independent trustee be appointed in his stead.

Daniels also called for a complete waiver by Laurie of any claims against Paul Chastant as a result of any alleged conflict of interest "and in fact a waiver of any conflict of interest with Laurie Chastant and Paul Chastant reserving to themselves the claim for reimbursement for attorney's fees and costs, both past and future."

This was summarily rejected by Laurie Chastant.

Pre-nup and Insurance Benefits Challenged

Laurie would receive the money from the defined benefit and the profit-sharing plans but that would not bring the acrimonious litigation to an end. It continued in debates over insurance benefits, again argued before Judge Haik.

If the flurry of correspondence in the form of letters and emails were mere legal formalities, the testimony in the trial was anything but. The testimony of Paul Chastant, for example, was peppered with confrontational exchanges between him and Durio and even between Durio and Judge Richard Haik when Durio attempted to object to the answer to a question that he himself asked. At one point, Judge Haik had to send the jury out of the room while he chastised a woman in the courtroom who apparently was trying to send signals to the witness.

Paul Chastant's testimony began routinely enough with direct questioning from Daniels, who asked questions about his duties as executor of his brother's estate and the prenuptial agreement between Robert and Laurie. "Did you have any discussion with your brother and Laurie Chastant about a prenup?" he asked.

"Yes, I did," Paul answered. "At one of our family gatherings Laurie approached me. My wife and I had just gotten married a couple of years prior, and [Laurie] approached me and asked me how I felt about the prenups. At the time I told her I didn't agree with them personally, and didn't have one with my wife because I felt it was not a level of commitment that I understood. But in addition, I told her that I understood since Bobby had recently gone through a pretty hard divorce, that I understood why he would want to do so.

"At the time we discussed it at the family gathering, and Bobby was pretty well strapped for money as a result of his other divorce. And I suggested that he buy a policy—or get a policy of insurance and cover an amount that they came into agreement about."

"And did you have any discussions with Bobby Chastant and Laurie Chastant about amounts of—what type of life insurance they should be talking about?" Daniels asked.

Paul said he and his wife suggested a one-million-dollar policy, which he said was roughly equivalent to the settlement between Robert and his previous wife.

Paul said after learning Robert had been murdered, he immediately booked a flight to Louisiana, arriving around 6 p.m. on December 14, the day following his brother's death. "...The attorney, and he is also an accountant that handled the estate and defined benefits plan, called and told me I had to sign the will document and file the trust agreements.

Daniels asked, "Was your brother in the process of terminating those plans?"

"Yes."

"And were you presented with paperwork indicating his desire to terminate those plans?"

"Yes."

"Were you also provided with some paperwork where Laurie Chastant was terminating her interest in the plan?"

"Yes."

"Now, as we sit here today, has Laurie Chastant received all of her benefits under her portion of the defined benefit and profit-sharing plans?"

"Yes."

"And that was something you signed off on?"

"Most certainly."

"That was something you were told to do as the trustee, correct?"

"Yes."

Daniels then had a copy of the Consent of Spouse agreement projected onto a large screen. "Have you seen this document before?" he asked Paul Chastant.

"Yes, I have."

"And what does that document represent in connection with the defined benefit plan?"

"It's the consent of the spouse. And from what I understand—some of these things aren't really overly clear—but it the consent of the spouse where she released her rights to the defined benefit plan in the event of a termination."

"Mr. Chastant, what were the—what was the financial condition of your brother's financial affairs at the time of his death?"

After an objection by Laurie Chastant's attorney Steven Durio was overruled, Paul said, "He [Robert] was upside down. He had gone through a couple of hard years because of the economy [the 2008 financial crisis]. This dental practice—or his orthodontia practice—is very expensive. The estate was in debt almost $2.5 million. And his assets didn't equal the estate balance."

Referring back to the Consent of Spouse form exhibited on the screen, Daniels asked, "What date was that executed by Laurie Chastant?"

"December third."

"And…your brother was murdered on December thirteenth?"

"Yes, he was."

"Ten days prior to his murder?"

"Yes, it was."

"What were your brother's plans for the use of the funds that he was cashing in from his defined benefit plan?"

"He planned to use it to pay down his debt."

"Did a part of that debt have to do with the construction of a big barn?"

"Oh, yes."

"Could you describe it for the jury, the size and—"

"It was huge. Bobby approached me early on about—I'm an architect, and Bobby approached me early on to do it. Well, I refused to do it because of the size of the venture he was getting into. I told him he was going to get upside down and it was not going to be something he should do. It's huge. It is right off the highway and it's visually in your line of sight. You can't miss it. If you ever go to New Iberia and driving down the Loreauville Highway, it is evident."

Daniels asked if Paul was familiar with Robert's home.

"Yes, I am," he replied. "I built it." He added later in his testimony that he had designed the house for Robert and his previous wife and children.

"As you leave your brother's house and you head toward the town of New Iberia itself, do you pass the barn?"

"Most certainly. It's on the left."

"And can you see the barn and the front area of the barn easily from there?"

"You can't miss it. It's in your peripheral view."

Referring back to the defined benefit plan, Daniels asked if there were other documents indicating that Laurie was cashing in her benefits.

When Paul answered in the affirmative, Daniels then asked, "Do you know whether or not Laurie Chastant was aware of the amount of the death benefit in your brother's plan?"

"I would think she would have been."

"She knew she was entitled to the benefits, correct?"

"Yes."

"You had discussions with her after your brother's death concerning that?"

"Yes. First, at the funeral home when we went out to select the casket and make arrangements for the funeral.

"In fact, Laurie Chastant was an employee of your brother's orthodontia practice for a while; is that correct? And that's how she became a member of the plan herself?"

"That's correct."

Daniels then asked Paul to provide an approximation of the amount of money Robert had invested in the construction of the barn.

"He had over $850,000 tied up in the barn. At the time, it was about 70 percent complete. He had problems with the contractors. In fact, he had to run one of them off. At the time of his death, he was $460,000 in debt to the Teche Federal Bank and it was going to grow, I would say, another $250,000. The barn would have been about a million-dollar barn when he was finished."

"After Bobby's death, as executor of the estate, did you attempt to sell the barn?"

"Most certainly."

"And did you have any offers on it?"

"Not a one."

"Tell us a little bit about the size of the debt—at least at the time of your brother's death."

"Two-and-a-half-million. Loans to the banks for cars, vehicles, tractors, the barn, house, office, his program. He had a program that he championed. It was called *Kids ID*, where you go and identify kids. He did it over several parishes and he'd collect their DNA and it was a foundation essentially that he created."

"Is the estate still indebted to individuals?"

"Yes."

Shifting directions, Daniels asked Paul to describe his impression of Robert's and Laurie's marital relationship in the time leading up to Robert's death.

"It was greatly strained. Bobby was depressed, highly depressed. He knew where I stood in relationships and how I felt about them. He would come to me at the end of his prior two marriages, and we would work together to resolve them."

Paul testified that he had heard talk of Robert's affair with another woman but never had any conversation with Laurie on the subject.

He further testified that Robert had created the Sonriente Stables limited liability corporation name in accordance with his practice of "treating everything like business. He was going to do breeding of Peruvian Paso stallions and horses.

He said he was contacted by Detectives Gerald Savoy and Adrienne Wells and Sheriff Louis Ackal who asked for access to Robert's bank accounts. "I gave them free access to everything," he said. "I met with the sheriff the morning after we selected the coffins [sic] and I told them anything they wanted, that it was open territory. They didn't have to issue a subpoena."

Daniels then had the Sonriente Stables checking account statement from Community First Bank for December 2010 projected onto the screen. "When was the first time that you saw the copy of this bank statement?" he asked.

"When the sheriff's department presented it to me."

Daniels then had the second page of the statement brought up for viewing and asked if it showed checks written on the stables account.

"Yes, they are," Paul Chastant answered.

"And who are those checks signed by?"

"Laurie Chastant."

"And the first check, [number] 1539, what is the date on that check?"

"12-6."

"2010"

"2010. I'm sorry."

"And the amount on the check?'

"Six hundred dollars."

"Who is the check made payable to?"

"Cash."

"I'll ask you to look at the check following that check, check No. 1540. It's another check on the Sonriente Stables account?"

"That's correct."

"It was presented to you by the sheriff's department?"

"It was."

"Who is that check made payable to?"

"Cash."

"And for what amount?"

"Four hundred dollars."

Upon Daniels' questioning, Paul said that neither check noted the purpose of the checks on the memo lines.

"Has Laurie Chastant ever provided you with an explanation as to what these checks were for?" Daniels asked.

"No."

"Have these checks been tied to any expenses of Sonriente Stables?"

"Not that we know of. We can't identify it."

"You're aware, Mr. Chastant, are you not, that Ismael Viera [Tovar] confessed to the murder of your brother?"

"Yes, I am."

"You are aware, are you not, that Mr. Viera also said he was paid by Laurie Chastant?"

"Yes, I am."

"Do you know what amount Mr. Viera claimed to have been paid?"

"One thousand dollars."

"Mr. Chastant, did you have any conversations with Laurie Chastant in your preparation for the funeral of your brother, Dr. Chastant?"

"Yes, I did."

"Did you and she go together to the funeral home?"

"Yes, we did."

"In connection with the estate as executor, you understood that the estate was in a lot of debt?"

"From the conversation with Bobby, yes, and the executive [attorney/accountant], yes."

"What discussions, if any, did you and Laurie Chastant have in connection with payment for the funeral services?"

"I brought it to her attention the amounts in the two [insurance] policies that I was made aware of about an hour earlier at the accountant's office. I just knew he was having problems financially. And after we met and selected the coffin and made arrangements for the funeral, I—we were told the amount and my comment was, the only thing I know that the estate has are these two policies. One was a policy that funded the benefits plan, and I told her the amounts. And that I was told that we could assign that debt to the cost of the funeral, and there were a lot of objections relative to it. And the comment was, 'This is my money. You can't use my money. The estate should pay for this.'"

"Who said that?"

"Laurie said it. I was taken aback, obviously, and made a comment, you know, who doesn't want to pay for their husband's funeral?"

Daniels asked if the barn also included living quarters.

"It did," Paul replied.

"Do you know whether or not the plans were to sell your brother's home that you had designed and built and to actually—for Laurie Chastant and your brother to move into the barn?"

"Yes, it was."

"So, this was going to be Laurie Chastant's new home, and the business that they were going to run?"

"Yes."

With that, Daniels ended his direct examination and now it was Steven Durio's turn at cross examination. It was in his cross examination of Paul Chastant that Durio seemed to have demonstrated either faulty memory or a lack of preparation. He would engage in argumentative exchanges with Paul Chastant, would have apparent memory lapses of his own, object to the answer to a question that he himself asked and be called down by Judge Haik for arguing instead of asking questions.

Tom Aswell

Wrath Incurred on Cross Examination

Durio lost no time when it came his turn to question Paul Chastant.

"I think the first subject you discussed with Mr. Daniels was the question of Laurie's executing a consent as part of the process of terminating the plans. I think you gave us your understanding of those documents. Have you ever consulted with a lawyer about that, whether or not your understanding is correct?"

"Yes. James Daniels."

Referring back to the testimony of ARS pension consultant Lori Roszczynialski, Durio asked Paul Chastant if he recalled her saying that Laurie did not waive the death benefit, that she only waived the annuity that she would have received from the defined benefit plan.

"I heard her say that," Paul replied.

"You also heard her [Roszczynialski] say when asked about the IRA into which the defined benefit funds would be rolled as part of that process, that Laurie was the death beneficiary of that IRA into which those funds would go? Didn't you hear that?"

"I heard her have a question in her mind about it, but, yes."

"I think she said the beneficiary was Laurie because she spoke to Edward Jones about it, and she looked at the document?"

"Yes."

Apparently satisfied that he had made his point, Durio suddenly changed direction, asking if the barn was "really a lot more than a barn," something Paul Chastant had already testified to.

"It's a huge barn. It's a training barn and also a place for his motorhome and for him to do mechanical work and shop work. It was a huge facility."

"And there were living quarters on the upper story, am I correct?"

"They had not been completed, but yes."

"It was designed so that, as part of his plan to liquidate his debts, Bobby would be able to sell his home and take the money that he thought he could get in excess of the mortgage and apply it to move into the barn and finishing that upstairs so that he and Laurie could live there?"

"That was his intent, yes."

Durio then sparred with Paul in an attempt to show that a vehicle could have been driven into the building and not be seen from the road.

"Is it possible for someone to drive a vehicle into that building and it not be seen from the road?" Durio asked.

"It's possible. But at that time, it would have been hard because there were no doors on the building."

"Well, if you pulled into one gable but you weren't so far into the building that the vehicle could be seen through the other, wouldn't that be possible?"

"Yeah, but there were no roads to that at the time. The roads were all muddy around the barn and it was wet. The only road was in the front."

"Well, that front road, you could at least drive a vehicle into that?"

"It would have been difficult because you couldn't have turned around once you got in."

Durio then apparently committed the unpardonable sin of an attorney: asking a question to which he did not already know the answer.

"Eventually you were able to sell that barn, were you not?"

"I did not sell the barn."

"Did you dation [the legal act of conferring] it back to the bank?"

"I had no part of the negotiations. The bank—an individual approached the bank and made arrangements to take over the debt, assume the debt or the note. And as a part of it, he contacted us and we were released from the balance of the debt."

"So, you gave it back to the bank in exchange for a release of whatever excess debt…"

"I didn't give it back to the bank. We were trying to sell it at the time."

"You said it was an assumption, so this person assumed whatever excess debt there was to the bank, right?"

"I don't know what he did. All I did was sign the releases."

"It was Eddie Landry, wasn't it?"

"Ed Landry, yes."

"He's the attorney that represents the estate?"

"Yes, he is."

Durio then moved on to the prenuptial agreement in his cross examination.

"...Bobby suggested, am I correct, a pre-nup to Laurie? Am I correct about that?"

"To Laurie, yes, I would assume. I was approached after the fact."

"And as a result of this pre-nup, the debts that Bobby accumulated or the assets that he required [sic], remained his. Am I correct? And Laurie's assets, if she acquired any, remained hers?"

"Correct."

"Is it fair to say that Bobby was interested in horses when he was married the first time?"

"No, not the first marriage. He didn't have time. He was in dental school."

"When did he acquire his first horse?"

"When he got married to his second wife and his family started growing. He had one for each kid and his wife."

"Did he have any particular type of horses? Was it a specific breed?"

"We all evolved for different breeds. He started out with Tennessee Walkers. Then he got into the...we were in Paso Finos, my other, Bradley, and I, and it eventually evolved into Peruvian Pasos."

"How many horses did Bobby have at the time of his death?"

"I think it was around fourteen."

"Who got those horses?"

"After we went to court, we had them. And then we settled and gave them to Laurie in an agreement."

"Didn't Laurie claim ownership of some of those horses?"

"She claimed ownership of all the horses."

"And you claimed ownership of all the horses, as well?"

"Not me. Sonriente Stables."

"And you brought Laurie to court to defend her interest in the horses, right?"

"Yes, we did."

"And except for a horse that was registered in her name, the horses were given to you?"

"They were given to the estate."

"And how did Laurie get them back? What did you get in that settlement?"

"We gave them to her in a settlement. We got the right—we were trying to sell the house and she had the right of use of the house. And the only way we could sell it is by having it redone and cleaned up and prepared for sale. So, part of the agreement was to allow her to move into the barn—or into the motorhome shed and live in the trailer in there so that we could prepare the house for sale."

"What you're saying is that Laurie had a two-year right of habitation of the house, am I correct?"

"Correct."

"And, as part of your motion with the court to recover the horses, you also, in that motion, suggested that her right of habitation did not extend to the barn or the pasture where the horses were, or the adjacent lots, but all that extended to her—the actual house she was living in, right? And the court found you were wrong about that, that Laurie had access to all of those—or a two-year right of habitation to all those properties because they were used as a unit and she could not have taken care of those horses without all of those properties as a unit, right?"

"I don't think that's the way they defined it, but, yes, they did say she had right of use."

"And you got her to release all of those areas?"

"No. All I released was the house so we could prepare the house for sale."

"Didn't you sell the pasture before you even sold the house?"

"We had an agreement, if you remember, that stipulated that if we had an act of sale, we could sell it."

"And Laurie would have to move out within sixty days?"

"Correct."

"And that's what happened?"

"Exactly."

"Before you sold the house, you sold the pasture and you said, 'Laurie, move out of the house, and go into the motorhome shed,' right?"

"I didn't tell her to go into the motorhome shed. That's something y'all came up with in the deal, and I agreed to it."

"That was the only piece of the property you would allow her to remain on, right?"

"Not really. I couldn't restrict her from anything except the house."

"Well, you could keep her from getting the horses, couldn't you?"

"Excuse me?" Paul replied. "I don't understand the question."

"Didn't you tell her the only way she would get her horses back if she released her two-year right of habitation on all that other property, including the house and the pasture, and the only thing she could stay on—and she would have to get out of that in sixty days if you sold it—was the motorhome shed?"

"I think you are elaborating [sic]. The situation was…"

"All I need is a yes or no."

"I'm not going to say yes or no because it's not a yes-or-no statement."

"Well, you have to answer my question and if you want to explain…"

"Simplify it and make a little bit more direct and I'll answer it."

At that point, Judge Haik interrupted the exchange to instruct Chastant to answer the question "and then you can explain it." He then directed Durio to repeat his question.

"Isn't it true that the only way Laurie could get her horses back, the ones that she had cared for for years, was to give up her right to inhabit everything else, including even the pasture and the motorhome shed, on six-days' [sic] notice if you sold it?"

"We offered that prior to going to court, yes."

"Isn't that what was finally agreed?"

"Yes. Can I elaborate now?"

Told by Haik that he could explain his response, Chastant said, "At the time we were trying to liquidate the assets of the estate. The estate was in incredible debt. We had to sell the house. It was incumbered at $590,000. And that was the intent. If it sat there for two years, we would not have been able to do so, and that was the intent."

Durio and Paul Chastant became embroiled in another dispute when Durio shifted to the issue of the vehicle Laurie Chastant was driving at the time of her husband's death.

"At the time of Dr. Chastant's death, was Laurie driving a vehicle?"

"Yes, she was. A Chevrolet Avalanche."

"And you asked her to give that vehicle back to you, did you not?"

"I didn't speak to her. I went through the courts because of the property of the estate."

"Well, no, at first you did speak to her. You offered..."

"I did not speak to her until after we picked it up."

"Excuse me. Didn't you offer to sell that vehicle to her before you sequestered it?"

"No, sir, I didn't. That happened after, when you got involved."

"When did you sequester that vehicle?"

"I can't tell you the exact date, but you can check the records of the day you got involved with the case. Because I spoke to you that day as well, sir, and I told you that they were picking it up. We were getting a writ to pick it up. I had not spoken to Laurie."

Durio appeared to stumble at this point. "I'm going to have to...I don't want to debate this whole thing with you. That's not my purpose, but let's start at the beginning."

That prompted another interruption by Judge Haik, who admonished Durio, saying, "If you'd ask one question at a time, maybe he can answer."

Attempting to regroup, Durio continued. "At the time of Bobby's death and the funeral, did Laurie have a lawyer?"

"A gentleman named Buzz. I don't know his name."

"His name was Buzz, too?" (Durio's nickname also was Buzz.)

"Correct."

"But it wasn't me?"

"No, it was not. A friend of yours, apparently."

"Didn't you tell that gentleman, 'I will sell the truck, which is in the name of Sonriente Stables, that Laurie does not own, to her for X amount'?"

"No, I did not."

"Didn't you tell him 'You only have three days to tell me whether you want it or not'?"

"I think you are fabricating that. I did not."

"Didn't you hire Mr. [James] Daniels and send him to court *ex parte*, that is, without notice to anybody on the other side, like Laurie or Buzz—the other Buzz—and get an order for the sheriff's department from the court telling the sheriff's department to go out and take that truck away from her?"

"Yes, I did. But I did it because the sheriff's department requested that I do so because they thought they had evidence in it."

Ignoring Paul Chastant's mention of possible evidence in the truck, Durio continued: "How long after Bobby's death did you sequester the truck Laurie was driving?"

"It was probably a week-and-a-half to two weeks."

"It was December 28th, wasn't it?"

"Okay. A week-and-a-half or two."

"And all of that happened before I became her lawyer?"

"I talked to you that day, sir. When we were at the courthouse, I called you myself and told you that we were going to pick up the truck, please notify your client, because the other Buzz was the one that told me that you are now part of the case. And I personally called you to give you that courtesy so there would be no disruption when we got to the house."

"That's not the way I remember it," said Durio, now appearing to be on the defensive.

"Then you have a bad memory, sir," Chastant shot back.

"No, that's not correct," said Durio, prompting yet another interjection by Judge Haik.

"Is that a question?" Haik asked.

"I don't want to argue with him," Durio answered.

"Well, either it's a question or it's not," Haik said. "You ask questions."

Trying to recover from his apparent fumble, Durio continued: "Did you call Laurie and tell her you were picking up her truck?"

"No, sir. I did call you," Chastant reiterated.

"Did you call Buzz, the previous Buzz, and tell him you were picking up her truck?"

"Before I called you, I called him because I thought he was involved with the case. He told me that you were now involved and gave me your number. I called you to make your client aware so it wouldn't be a shock and there would not be something happening at the house. So, I made them aware. And that's exactly the first conversation I ever had with you, and I remember it distinctly."

"And you think that was before the truck was sequestered?"

"It was about an hour before we picked it up."

"An hour before you picked it up?"

"At most. I went from there, from the courthouse, with the writ that James [Daniels] got for me, to the sheriff's department, waited for a gentleman to ride with me, and we went to the house."

"So, you didn't call Laurie?"

"No, I did not."

"Or Buzz?"

"I did call Buzz before talking to you."

"Excuse me. I understand that. But you didn't call any of us until you already had Jimmy [Daniels] at the courthouse with a draft of the motion and an order, and you were picking up the order to pick up the truck?"

"I did not because I was asked to pick up the truck by the sheriff's department and they didn't want it to be told in advance. They told me that after. They asked me that morning and I made the arrangements."

Having made no dent in Paul Chastant's version of events surrounding the Avalanche, Durio abruptly changed course to questions about Robert Chastant's funeral, the sale of Robert's practice and Paul's concerns about Laurie's possible involvement in the murder of his older brother.

"Do you recall Laurie saying, 'Why isn't the estate paying for the funeral?', a claim Paul had already made during direct questioning by Daniels.

"Yeah."

"And what did you tell her?"

"I told her exactly what I said earlier, that the only thing I knew about it, I had not talked to anybody about the accounts at that time except these two policies, the defined benefit plan and the insurance policy, and I knew nothing about the accounts of the estate."

"So, when she asked you, what did you tell her?"

"That's all I told her," Chastant said.

"My question is very simply, when she asked you why isn't the estate paying for the funeral, what did you tell her?"

"I told her that I knew nothing of the accounts of the estate. I didn't know if the estate had any money, that Bobby had expressed to me that the estate was in bad shape and I didn't know if we would be able to pay for it. I had not been able to see any of the accounts or the books at that time."

"So, she assigned the Prudential policy to the funeral home to pay for the funeral?"

"That's correct."

"Did you tell her at that time that the estate was broke?"

"I didn't tell her at that time. I had no idea."

"When did you first tell her [that] the estate was broke?"

"I never told her the estate was broke. I told them it was upside down."

"How is upside down different from broke?"

"We still had opportunities—we had a practice that we were trying to sell. We didn't know the value of the practice at the time. And we actually sold it for under its value because we wanted to try to get somebody in there to maintain the patients and the staff."

"You described a conversation in which you told the sheriff's department they could have access to anything because you were greatly concerned about what was going on."

"Yes, I was."

"What did you mean when you said you were greatly concerned about what was going on? You had a conversation with the sheriff's department sometime between December 13th and December 28th when you seized the truck."

"I had several conversations with the sheriff's department."

"And in one of those conversations, you said you told them they could have access to anything because you were greatly concerned about what was going on."

"I'll tell you how my concern started," Paul Chastant began.

"I don't want to know what the sheriff told you," Durio said. "I want to know what you meant."

"I meant I thought Laurie was involved with my brother's murder."

"So, the business about seizing the truck was not so much the sheriff's department; it was you wanting to give them the truck?"

Chastant's answer caused Durio to make an amateur's error.

"No," Paul Chastant said. The sheriff's department approached me, as I said earlier. They approached me and asked me…"

"Objection."

Judge Haik: "Wait, wait, wait. You asked him that question." Then to Chastant, the judge said, "You can answer that question."

"They approached me and asked me to get them the vehicle, and I did."

"Did you tell Laurie the sheriff's department would like to have your vehicle to search or to test or anything?" Durio continued. "Did you ask her that?"

"No, I did not. But the sheriff's department…"

"Wait, wait, wait," Judge Haik said. "That answer is no. That was a simple question."

"Do you know," Durio continued, "if the sheriff's department ever asked Laurie if they could look at her vehicle or inspect it or search it?"

"I couldn't tell you that."

Durio then turned his line of questioning to the two checks for cash that Laurie had written only days before her husband was killed.

"These are checks that you found or are they checks that the sheriff's department found?"

"As I said earlier, the sheriff's department did," Chastant said.

"And they brought them to you, is that what you're saying?"

"That's correct. They brought me the statement and asked for the checks."

"Did you ever ask Laurie what these checks were for?"

"Not me personally. The estate did."

So, you have never heard Laurie explain these checks?"

"Not from her."

"These two checks were never discussed in Laurie's deposition, were they?" Durio asked, zeroing in on Daniels' mistakenly referring to the checks as being for $1000 each instead of for $600 and $400.

"I don't know," Chastant said. "I know two checks were discussed. I have no way of knowing if those particular ones were addressed, 1539 and 1540."

"Isn't it true that in her deposition, Laurie was asked about two one thousand-dollar checks, one thousand dollars each, which she supposedly wrote out, and supposedly to cash, and supposedly with the memo blank? Isn't that true?"

"I don't know."

"You didn't read the deposition well enough to know if it was those two other checks or these two checks that were actually discussed there?"

"No. I don't know if anybody could," Chastant said.

Durio continued to stumble into unexpected answers during his cross examination of Paul Chastant when he broached the subject of Robert Chastant's indebtedness.

"I think you told the jury that Bobby had discussed his personal debt with you before his death. Am I correct?"

"Correct. Not the specifics, but he told me he was in debt, incredible debt."

"And he also told you, according to your testimony earlier, that he intended to cash in some of his retirement benefits and pay?"

"He didn't tell me that," Paul said.

"He did not?"

"He did not."

"How did you find out?"

"I talked to the gentleman at Edward R. Jones about a week after [Robert's death], and he verified it. But I was also told that by Lori Roszczynialski when I went there the day after his death and the attorneys came in and we talked to the attorney and Lori."

Durio then posed a curious question that seemed to contradict the one he had just asked when he asked, "Isn't it true that you didn't know Bobby was moving assets to pay off his debts until after he died?"

"That's correct," he said before adding, "I knew he had his house for sale. I knew that."

Turning to the earlier testimony of Laurie's father, William Futral, Durio then asked, "You heard Bill Futral's testimony, did you not?"

"Yes, I did."

"And Bill said he doesn't remember any disagreement or problem with you at the funeral home?"

"Yes."

"And you think otherwise?"

"I think Bill was confused yesterday. There were a lot of things he said which were confusing."

"When you realized the estate didn't have the money to pay for the funeral, when was that? That was before or after you spoke with Laurie?"

"I never said that I didn't know the estate couldn't pay for the funeral. They could have after the fact, after I was there, after I realized what the books said."

"Well, I think you said you reflected at the time, 'what kind of woman won't pay for her husband's funeral?'"

"I sure did."

"Did you reflect on what kind of estate won't pay for the burial of the man who died?"

"I never referred to that, or inferred it. The money that was in the trust was the estate's money at the time and the money that was in the insurance policy. Bobby had paid for those."

"Have you ever tried to pay Laurie back?"

"No, I have not."

"You said you have a duty to protect the money in the estate and in the accounts. Am I correct about that?"

"I don't remember saying it, but, yes, I do."

"That would include the money that is in the defined benefit [and] profit-sharing plan that, if the jury decides she didn't participate in the killing, would be Laurie's? Would you agree, based on Ms. Roszczynialski's deposition, that all the money left in the defined benefit [and] profit-sharing plan, is money designated for Laurie?"

"She was named the beneficiary, yes," Paul agreed.

"And you say you have a duty to protect that money?"

"It's my obligation."

"For who [sic] are you protecting it?"

"It's my job. It's my responsibility under the law from my understanding."

"As the trustee of the defined benefit and profit-sharing plan, are you protecting it for Laurie's interest?"

"If she is entitled to it, she will get it."

"Will she get all of it? Every penny?"

"I would hope so."

"None of it has been spent in the meantime?"

"Money has been spent to fund legal fees, which was set up in the original agreement that Bobby and I had between he and I [sic] and the estate. I am not a rich man. I'm an architect, and believe it or not, we don't make much money. When Bobby and I set up this agreement, we agreed that I would have the right to use the funds to protect the interest of the estate by using the funds within the defined benefit plan and the trust."

"As I understand it, then, you've been paying Mr. Daniels's fees, to press this claim against Laurie to deprive her of this money, with the money that, if she is correct, she is supposed to get?"

"Yes."

"And about a month-and-a-half ago, you consented to an order of this court to stop you from doing that?"

"Yes, sir. But you knew we were using it about three months before that and [you] did nothing about it."

"When Laurie was allowed to remain living in the motorhome shed on the premises, did she have a trailer?"

"I heard so. I never saw it."

"Did the estate pay for that trailer?"

"No, sir."

"So, Laurie had to pay for a trailer to live in in the motorhome shed for the last sixty days before you sold it?"

"I know nothing about her arrangements."

"Do you remember when you announced to Laurie that…you would offer her an opportunity to buy the riding lawn mower to cut the grass? Do you remember that?"

"You approached us. We were selling the assets of the estate and you asked for the riding lawn mower. You approached us, sir."

"You don't remember Laurie cutting the grass, personally getting on the riding lawn mower and cutting the grass, before it ever became for sale?"

"I never went by the house. I live in South Carolina. I'm sure she did."

"How was Laurie feeding these horses?" Durio asked, setting up an incident that would halt proceedings and incur the ire of Judge Haik when a spectator apparently tried to signal answers to the witness.

"We were paying for the feed."

"Who was paying for the feed?"

"We were."

"The estate was paying for feed?"

"I'm sure she wrote checks and we reimbursed. We paid for a lot of things while she was still there. We paid utilities. And eventually, I had to pay for feed. And we still have a bill right now. That's one of the outstanding things of the estate was paying – the feed bill.

"Was she feeding the horses hay?"

"I would think."

"And what was she using to feed the horses hay?"

"Originally a tractor."

"What happened to the tractor?"

"The tractor was sold. It was—actually, it was dationed. Kubota came back and picked it up because we couldn't pay for it anymore."

"Did you call Laurie or me?"

"You were communicated through our attorney. Mr. Daniels"

"You contend Mr. Daniels notified me?"

"I don't remember what happened, sir. I don't remember what transpired."

"So, you're not saying that Mr. Daniels notified me?"

"I don't know who notified you."

"Are you saying that anybody notified me?"

"I have no idea."

Durio continued that same line of questioning in an attempt to show that Paul had failed to notify Laurie that the tractor would be picked up even though Paul had repeatedly said all communication with Laurie was done through the attorneys. Durio seemed to get hung up on seemingly insignificant disputes, pushing the issue of whether or not Laurie was implicated in the murder into the background.

"Do you recall discussing with Mr. Daniels," Durio asked, "the fact that I had called him to let him know that Ms. Chastant was going to make a criminal complaint because the tractor had disappeared?"

"I don't know about that level of particulars, but I know you and he [Daniels] were in contact."

"And it turned out that you had consented to have the tractor picked up?"

"Yes."

"But you had not told Laurie or me?"

"At that time, I was not communicating with Laurie."

"Or me?"

"I was communicating to you through Mr. Daniels."

"Are you aware of a criminal complaint made against Laurie and investigated by the Iberia Parish Sheriff's Office based upon the allegation that she was not feeding the animals?"

"We had gotten contacted by some neighbors that said she wasn't taking care of the animals."

"Wasn't that Suzy?"

"I have no idea," Chastant said.

"I don't know who Suzy is, but wasn't that the second wife?"

"I think you are making an inference, sir. It was one of the neighbors is what I was told."

"Who?"

"I have no idea. I was contacted by my niece, Megan and in turn, I talked to Mr. Daniels and he conveyed that to you."

"I'm asking about the criminal complaint, not information conveyed to me.," Durio said.

"You asked if Suzy is involved and I don't think she was. I don't know."

"Wasn't Suzy the person that made the criminal complaint?"

"I have no way of knowing."

Suddenly, Judge Haik cut in. "We're going to remove the jury."

"Excuse me?" Durio responded.

"Let's remove the jury for one moment. Don't talk about the case. We'll be right back in. Don't get too comfortable."

Once the jury had been removed from the courtroom, Haik began dressing down an unidentified spectator seated in the courtroom who apparently was attempting to flash signals to Paul Chastant.

"Suzy, don't raise your hand, don't shake your head, don't do anything. If you cannot do that, I'm going to ask you to leave."

"Okay," the unidentified audience member—apparently Suzy—replied.

"Now this is a trial with a jury," Haik continued. "Paul is on the stand. He is going to answer the questions. If you are going to be a witness, you are going to be sent outside and called back in. Do you understand?"

"Yes."

"I am not going to have that kind of thing going on in my courtroom. You are not a witness and you are not to make any expressions whatsoever during this trial. Do you understand me?"

"Yes, sir."

"All right," said Haik. Anybody else misunderstand that? If you cannot refrain from doing anything in this trial, please leave. And I know it is emotional. And Mr. Durio has a right to ask questions just like your attorney—just like Mr. Daniels has a right to ask questions. I will not have anybody in the audience making any gestures or signing anything or waving hands or doing anything else. Do we understand one another?"

"Yes, sir."

"All right. This is a trial. Okay? [sic] This is not something that people can just raise their hand or shake their head or do something to say or do anything in response to Mr. Durio's question to Mr. Paul Chastant. Everybody understand that? And that goes for every other witness that comes up here, all right. Now, if you won't do that, please leave. If you can do that, you may stay. But the next time it happens, you're gone. Do you understand me?"

"Yes, sir."

Early Win for Laurie

After a short recess following the furor over someone named Suzy, who had interrupted the proceedings by signaling the witness, Durio moved on to the wrongful death lawsuit against Laurie Chastant by Robert Chastant's children.

"When we had opening arguments, your attorney, I believe, argued that you had not filed a suit against Laurie Chastant, that you were brought into this suit?"

"Correct."

"But you are aware that there is a lawsuit against Laurie Chastant for wrongful death, are you not?"

"The children have filed suit, yes."

"Did you have anything to do with that lawsuit?"

"Yes."

"What did you personally have to do with that lawsuit?"

"Personally, nothing. All I did was talk to the kids about it. I told them it was an opportunity. At that time everybody in the family was concerned that Laurie had a responsibility in the murder. In addition, we were told by Mr. Duhé…"

"Excuse me, Your Honor."

"Wait, wait, wait," Haik said. "When you asked the question, you opened the door."

"I told them that Mr. Duhé…" Chastant began again.

"Excuse me," Durio said. "While you were…"

"You asked the question," Haik said again. "I'm going to allow the question. You asked the question."

"I told them," Chastant began once more, "because of the terms of prescription, that Mr. Duhé advised that we pursue wrongful death."

"Mr. Bo Duhé?"

"Mr. Bo [M. Bofill] Duhé, the DA in Iberia Parish."

"So, Mr. Duhé said that if you think you have a claim against Laurie, you need to file it within the prescriptive period, the one-year that you have to file such a claim?"

"Yes. He told all the family in a meeting after the sentencing of Mr. Viera."

That was the last of Durio's cross-examination but Chastant's attorney, James Daniels, jumped right back into the wrongful death lawsuit discussion during re-direct examination.

"Mr. Chastant, I do want to know what Bo Duhé told you," he said.

"Mr. Duhé told us that we should consider filing a claim for wrongful death."

"And when was that told to you and the family?"

"The day of the sentencing of Mr. Viera."

"I want to talk to you a little bit about the home residence. Did your brother, Dr. Chastant, have a mortgage on that residence?"

"Yes, he did."

"Who was the mortgage with?"

"Iberia Bank."

"What were the approximate monthly payments?"

"I think they were $5,600 to $6000."

"Per month?"

"Per month."

"And after several months after your brother's death, was the estate able to continue to make payments to Iberia Bank?"

"No."

"What happened to that loan?"

"They were going to foreclose."

"And as a result, were you attempting to sell the residence? Did you list the house?"

"Yes."

"In fact, you listed all of the property? Everything? The property, the big barn, the little barn?"

"Everything."

"The orthodontic practice?"

"Yes."

"The motorhome?"

"Everything. Tractors, cars, everything."

"In connection with showing the house, were there any problems with showing the property?"

"Every time, the game changed. We had to give Laurie two-days' notice and when we'd go to show the house, she wouldn't allow it."

"Would it have been advantageous to the estate and creditors if the bank foreclosed on the home?"

"No. We would have no opportunity to recapitalize any of the profits, the potential profits."

Paul Chastant explained the estate was trying to sell the home in order to put money back into the estate so that the estate's debts could be resolved.

"Who was paying the taxes on the property," Daniels asked.

"We were."

"Who was paying the insurance on the property?"

"We were."

"Now, Mr. Durio made the statement that Laurie assigned the Prudential insurance policy, the proceeds of the policy, to Pellerin Funeral Home. Did you hear that statement?"

"Yeah."

"Did she assign the entire policy to the Prudential [sic] Funeral Home?"

"A very small part."

"To pay for the funeral?"

"Exactly.

"And to your knowledge, have you paid out of the defined benefit plan anything other than the trustee's expenses and the trustee's attorneys' fees?"

"No, I have not."

Did the estate pay for any of the expenses at the home?"

"Yes."

"What other expenses?"

"A lot. One of which was a $5,560 liquor bill."

"Let's go beyond that. Let's talk about, like grass cutting?"

"Yes."

"Pool service?"

"Yeah. We rebuilt the pool."

"And finally, the Kubota tractor. Was that heavily mortgaged?"

"It was totally mortgaged."

"Did the estate have money to pay the note on the tractor?"

"It was a very high note. No, we did not."

"So, you gave the vendor, the Kubota people, the permission to pick it up if they forgave the rest of the debt?"

"They called me up and asked me, and they actually suggested that. Yes."

Despite Paul Chastant's testimony in defense of protecting the assets of the defined benefit and profit-sharing plans, as well as benefits of the life insurance policies, and despite the fact that the question of Laurie's possible involvement in her husband's murder was left unresolved, the trial jury inexplicably ruled in Laurie's favor.

Phone Records Clash with Testimony

As part of the testimony in the insurance dispute, Robert Chastant's phone records (See Appendix I) showed that he received a 37-second call from Ismael at 7:37 a.m. on December 13.

Then, beginning at 9:15, 9:20, 9:28 and 9:29, there were four consecutive calls from Laurie to Dr. Chastant's phone interrupted by one from an unidentified caller at 9:36, then another from Laurie at 9:38 followed by another unknown caller at 9:44.

Then, at 10:02, a call was placed from Robert Chastant's phone to Laurie followed by three more calls within the next two minutes from Laurie to her husband's phone. The duration of each of those calls between the two cellphones ranged from three to thirteen seconds.

Then, there is a call from Laurie to Robert Chastant's phone at 10:15 followed immediately by three calls from Robert Chastant's cellphone to Laurie and then four more calls from Laurie to Robert's number between 10:18 and 11:35.

Only one of those, the 10:18 call from Laurie to Robert's cellphone, lasted more than 21 seconds, that one for a minute and eight seconds.

It's important to note that some, if not most, of those exchanges were text messages, according to Laurie Chastant's own testimony.

It's also critical to note that Ada Credcur and her co-worker claimed that Laurie Chastant was in Dr. Ritter's office before 7:30 a.m. Ada Credeur, in fact, testified in her sworn deposition that Laurie was already at the clinic when she arrived at approximately 7:30 a.m. Laurie, however, said in her deposition that she arrived at Dr. Ritter's office somewhere around 8:10 a.m.

Laurie also testified under oath, and told investigators as well, that Dr. Chastant was outside on his cellphone when she came downstairs that morning. The only call Dr. Chastant made or received early that morning was from Viera at 7:37 a.m., phone records show (see Appendix I, Item 191 on the printout of his phone records). Viera testified that Laurie Chastant was standing outside the residence when he and Dr. Chastant left for the barn that morning.

It would appear, therefore, that Ms. Credeur and her co-worker were simply mistaken about the time that Laurie Chastant arrived at the doctor's office, "especially considering that Laurie Chastant claims to have seen her husband on the phone when she came downstairs that morning," attorney James Daniels wrote to Assistant District Attorney Bo Duhé on April 12, 2012.

"Even if Laurie Chastant left immediately [following the departure of] her husband and Viera, [she testified she left 10-15 minutes later], it would take her somewhere in the neighborhood of 15 minutes to get to Dr. Ritter's office," Daniels wrote.

"In the past, you have told me that the D.A.'s office had a problem with the time line because of Ms. Credeur and her co-worker's statements to the police. It is clear to me that the phone records of Dr. Chastant and Mr. Viera prove that Ms. Credeur and co-worker are simply wrong as attested to by Laurie Chastant, Viera and the phone records, because there is no way that Laurie Chastant could have been at Dr. Ritter's office at 7:30 or even 7:45."

The phone records printout (Appendix I) is a record of calls to and from Dr. Robert Chastant's cellphone (337-519-0343) on the day he was murdered. Laurie's is 337-519-7998 and Ismael Viera Tovar's number is 337-201-6408. The second column gives the date of the call, the third the duration of the call and the fourth, the number making the call.

If the investigation undertaken by the Iberia Parish Sheriff's Office and the district attorney's office could be described in a single word, that word would have to be *fiasco*. In fact, if one were to write a manual for botching an investigation, the Robert Chastant murder case would serve as a textbook illustration.

From the failure to properly preserve evidence from the crime scene to foot-dragging by the Acadiana Crime Lab to Keystone Kops-like investigation that included overlooking a key bit of evidence right under detectives' noses, the investigation of the murder of Dr. Robert Chastant was a disaster from start to finish.

The Acadiana Criminalistics Lab serves the parishes of Acadia, Evangeline, Iberia, Lafayette, St. Landry, St. Martin, St. Mary and Vermilion. The sheriff of each parish is automatically a member of the crime lab commission. Louis Ackal, as sheriff of Iberia Parish, was a member of the commission at the time of the murder investigation as was the sheriff of St. Landry Parish where Laurie's father, William Futral, was employed as a deputy.

A motion-activated camera like those used by deer hunters was installed at the barn so that Dr. Chastant might be able to learn who was taking tools that were disappearing from the barn. But the camera, which might have provided valuable information about the murder, was missing as well. It would turn up more than a year after all proceedings were over—in the bed of Dr. Chastant's pickup truck that had been in the possession of the sheriff's department all that time. Because the truck had been kept outdoors, the camera was lying submerged in standing water, inoperable and of no use.

In another example of ineptitude, there were records of a fourth telephone number, 337-560-5841, which was the landline number for the Chastant residence. The records for calls to and from that number during the crucial days leading up to and including the day of the murder are incomplete. There is a gap between an incoming call at 1:48 p.m. on December 9 and an incoming call at 8:23 a.m. on December 14 (See Appendix H). There were either no incoming or outgoing calls for four days and twenty hours, which seems improbable, at best, or the records for the date of Dr. Chastant's murder are missing.

Tom Aswell

Inexperience, Indifference Hamper Investigation

Almost lost in the legal maneuvering over disbursement of insurance benefits and proceeds from the defined benefit and profit-sharing plans was the issue of actual guilt or innocence of Laurie Chastant.

The fact that the criminal investigation was somehow relegated to a secondary role is largely attributable to the inability—or unwillingness—of the Iberia Parish Sheriff's Office to conduct a thorough and professional murder investigation.

No fewer than fourteen officials from the department participated in the search for Dr. Robert Chastant's body and in the investigation of his violent death. Yet, not one of the reports written by those deputies alluded to any questioning of Laurie Chastant or of any efforts put forth to reconcile time discrepancies in the account of her arrival at her doctor's office the morning of the murder.

Nor were the written reports by the inexperienced and seemingly unmotivated deputies completed in a timely manner, some being written a full month after the fact, when memories of important details might tend to fade as evidenced by the numerous lapses of memory exhibited during their depositions taken even later.

As further illustration of the ineffectiveness of the Iberia Parish Sheriff's Office, Detective Adrienne Wells possessed a sum total of six years in law enforcement—three years in communications, two years on patrol and less than six months' experience as a detective. Yet, she was the lead detective on the case throughout the duration of the investigation.

And Detective Rusty Vallot, also with six years' law enforcement experience, less than two years as detective, missed the time that Dr. Chastant's body was found by a full twelve hours, listing the time (in military parlance) as 0900 hours instead of 2100 hours. Copies of other reports follow Vallot's example.

Detective Wells filed a fifteen-page report and a three-page supplemental report, some of the key points of which appeared earlier in this book. Incredibly, neither was dated. She explained in her deposition of December 8, 2011, almost a year after the murder, that the reports were not dated because she had written her report "over several days throughout the investigation leading up to the end before I turned it in." She estimated that she turned in her fifteen-page report on January 27, 2011, more than six weeks after Robert Chastant's murder, reflecting an inexcusable lack of urgency in pursuing the case.

Like the reports filed by the other detectives, it was filled with grammatical, punctuation and spelling errors, redundancies, and seemingly useless information. She also noted that Dr. Chastant's truck was taken in by authorities "for processing." Forensics investigators, however, somehow managed to overlook the video camera which had been removed from the barn and which might have rendered valuable information had it not been submerged in water in the bed of the truck for more than a year following the murder.

After locating the missing doctor's vehicle in the Walmart parking lot, she observed surveillance film of the parking lot which revealed that "a Hispanic male subject later identified as Ismael Viera" drove Dr. Chastant's 2009 white Chevrolet Silverado Super Duty truck to the store's parking lot and emerged "a few minutes later" to enter the right real passenger door of an Eddie Bauer model Ford Expedition driven by Jam Romero.

Soon after locating Dr. Chastant's truck sheriff's deputy Wayne Norris "arrived on the scene to process the vehicle," Detective Wells wrote, adding that she then instructed that the truck was to be stored "for further processing." Somehow, all that processing managed to overlook for an entire year the motion-activated camera that had gone missing from the barn.

At approximately 9:30 p.m., Wells was advised that a body, possibly that of Dr. Chastant, had been discovered at the barn. The body, she wrote, "appeared to be in a fetal position, upper body was sitting on its knees." She wrote in her report that Dr. Carl Ditch "advised that the body appeared to still be warm."

For Dr. Chastant to have been attacked thirteen hours earlier on a cold December day and his body remain warm that long would seem to indicate he didn't die from his injuries for up to twelve hours later.

Wells observed tire tracks that appeared to belong to a small utility truck that ran from the trash pile to the rear of the barn. During a search of the property, detectives located blood spatter on the ground in front of the barn, a cigarette and broken lenses from a pair of sunglasses near the blood spatter.

In walking investigators through a reenactment of the crime, Ismael described how Dr. Chastant allegedly slapped him twice in a dispute over Ismael's misplacing Dr. Chastant's tools. When Dr. Chastant turned to walk away, Ismael said he struck him twice in the back of the head with a claw hammer and then, after Dr. Chastant fell face forward to the ground, he hit him two more times while he was on the ground and then turned the body over and struck him twice more in the neck area with the flat part of the hammer.

He told detectives that he placed a garbage bag over the mortally-injured doctor and physically carried him to the back of the property where he covered the body with scrap wood. He said Dr. Chastant was so heavy that he had to take two rest breaks during the process.

Wells wrote in her report that Ismael said he then drove his vehicle back to the pool house and had Nayeli drive him back to the point where the barn's driveway meets the highway. He then walked to the barn and drove Dr. Chastant's truck to the Walmart parking lot. That story would take a dramatic twist when Ismael later implicated Laurie in the killing and concealment of Dr. Chastant's body.

Before Dr. Chastant's body was discovered and he was still considered missing, Ismael told of an unidentified, black-haired woman driving up and leaving with Dr. Chastant who instructed Ismael to drive the doctor's truck to Walmart and leave it. After Ismael had admitted killing his employer and after implicating his wife in the crime, he was asked who came up with the story of the mystery woman. "Ismael advised Laurie came up with the story," Wells wrote in her report. "Ismael said they [he and Laurie] discussed the story the same day she paid him to kill D. Chastant."

During questioning of Ismael, State trooper Frank Garcia asked him why he wrapped the body in the trash bags. Laurie instructed him to do so, he replied. She appeared at the barn right after Ismael killed Dr. Chastant and did not want to see her husband covered with blood. She then left the barn in her black Avalanche and returned in the smaller utility truck and helped Ismael load Dr. Chastant's body into the truck. While Ismael transported the body to the rear of the barn, Laurie stayed behind and covered up the blood with dirt, he told investigators.

Detective Wells conducted an interview with Terry Romero who said he met Ismael at the horse race located at Evangeline Downs racetrack. He met Ismael about a year before the murder. He said Ismael worked for Romero during the summer of that year. He worked for maybe a month. Terry said they already knew Natalie because her father worked for him and his wife Jan. He paid Ismael about $300.00 a week – in cash – and Natalie earned approximately $150 a week but she did not work long for the Romeros. Terry said he met Dr. Chastant at his barn located on Sugar Oaks Road, adding that Ismael was looking for a job and did not have anywhere to stay. Romero allowed Ismael to live in the pool house behind his residence. Ismael and Nayeli were soon working for Dr. Chastant who Romero said was proud of having Ismael work for him.

Then, near the end of her lengthy report, Detective Wells had an interesting entry that would normally raise red flags and set off whistles with an experienced investigator. She wrote in her report that on the morning of December 21, 2010, she received a phone call from Laurie Chastant who advised she had a couple of questions.

She then asked if Wells had any additional information in the ongoing investigation. When Detective Wells advised that the case is still under investigation, Laurie then asked if her husband's wallet had been located. Told it may have been found, she then asked if she could have his driver's license. When Wells told her that was not possible because it was considered part of the evidence in the case, Laurie then asked if the computers were pertinent to the case. Wells said that after computers are processed, they would be returned. Laurie then asked if we knew when Ismael would go in front of the grand jury. Detective Wells was unable to answer the question," the detective wrote.

Was Laurie fishing for information about whether or not she was a suspect? Or were her questions legitimate inquiries into the status of the case against her husband's murderer? It may never be known because neither the sheriff's office nor the district attorney's office ever followed up on her cryptic questions.

Missed Signs, but Finally a Coherent Report

Viera stood five-feet-six and weighed only one hundred sixty pounds compared to Dr. Chastant, who was six-feet, five-inches tall, nearly a full foot taller than his killer, and outweighed Viera by thirty-five pounds. It would have been difficult, if not impossible for Viera to lift the one hundred eighty-five-pound dead man and carry him through the barn to the trash pile.

Despite the verbiage in her report, Detective Wells overlooked several key points:

Underscoring the sloppiness of her report was the paragraph in which she said she prepared a search warrant for AT&T call data records of *her own* cell phone when she obviously meant the records of Nayeli or Viera. Unexplained was why detectives waited a full week before it occurred to them to upload data from Jan Romero's cell phone. And for a report containing so much mundane detail, it failed to provide a last name for one of the investigators with the first name Adrena.

There was nothing in her effusive, unintelligible tome to indicate whether or not Viera was ever examined for evidence, such as red marks, bruising, abrasions or a swollen face, of having been slapped. Nor was there any indication that Laurie Chastant was ever brought in by detectives for questioning about her possible part in the murder scheme.

Most important, Detective Wells never mentioned the disappearance of a motion-activated camera that was in the barn which may have held key evidence to the killing. The camera would reappear more than a year later in the back of Dr. Chastant's truck, submerged in water and by then, non-functional and useless. The truck had been in the possession of the sheriff's office all that time and was supposedly taken by the department for "processing."

Detective Wells did provide an undated, three-page "Supplement" report that did little to shed additional light on the events of December 13, 2010 although two glaring missteps did jump off the page:

It took more than three months, from December 13, 2010, to March 31, 2011, for investigators to get around to conducting a search of Dr. Chastant's motor home. In any professional department, that would have been a routine step in the normal course of a homicide investigation.

And it took nearly five full months, from December 13, 2010, to May 9, 2011, for investigators to finally decide to check the sign-in sheet at the office of Dr. Kenneth Ritter. Why would the sheriff's department omit what seems like basic steps in the investigation?

Amateurism is the only plausible explanation.

The only report completed promptly and thoroughly was that of Louisiana State Trooper Frank Garcia. Assigned as an interpreter on December 13, the day of the murder, he filed a typewritten, five-page report four days later, on December 17, 2010. Interestingly, his was also the cleanest and most concise, from the standpoint of grammar and spelling, of all the reports submitted.

He said that after being called in to question the suspect, Viera initially denied any knowledge of Dr. Chastant's whereabouts. But during Trooper Garcia's questioning, Sheriff Louis Ackal entered the interrogation room to inform Garcia that Chastant's body had been found at the horse barn the Chastants owned. "Initially, Viera denied having any involvement in Dr. Chastant's murder," Garcia wrote in his report. "A few minutes later, Viera lowered his head and stated that he was the one who killed Dr. Chastant."

Viera related to Garcia the details of Dr. Chastant's slapping him and then turning to walk back in the direction of his parked truck. This occurred at approximately 8:30 a.m., he said, adding that he grabbed the hammer and struck Dr. Chastant once in the back of the head. That was in variance with what he would later say: that he struck the doctor several times. He told Garcia that after he moved Dr. Chastant's body to the trash pile he returned to his own vehicle and drove it to the pool house where he and Nayeli lived and had her drive him to the barn where he then drove Dr. Chastant's truck to Walmart and called Nayeli to have Jan Romero pick him up. That part of his account also would later change when he implicated Laurie Chastant.

Garcia wrote that Viera, after confessing to the murder, agreed to reenact the crime for investigators. Garcia said two areas of pooled blood and blood spatter were located but had been partially covered with dirt. Viera said that after he placed Dr. Chastant's body in the wood pile, he attempted to cover the blood with a post hole digger. That also would be counter to his later story in which he said Laurie covered the blood while he moved the body.

"Viera requested to speak with his wife," Garcia wrote in his report. "While Viera was talking with his wife, I video monitored the conversation in a separate room. Viera pleaded and tried to coerce his wife to admit guilt by saying that she drove him back to the barn in the gray Suzuki utility cart. Viera's wife became irate with Viera. She continually told Viera that she did not know what was happening and that she was not going to lie by saying she drove him back to the barn."

Returned to the interrogation room, Viera admitted to Garcia that Nayeli did not assist him in any manner but, again contradicting what he would later allege, said that it was he who retrieved the utility truck to use in disposing of Dr. Chastant's body. He said he then drove the utility cart back to Dr. Chastant's residence and walked back to the barn (a walk of about five minutes) to retrieve Dr. Chastant's truck and drove it to Walmart at which time he called Nayeli to pick him up.

"After speaking with Viera, I explained that he was being charged with 2nd Degree Murder, and then I explained the booking procedure," Garcia wrote. "Viera stated that he understood.

"Having no further information, the interview was concluded."

But then came the bombshell.

On December 15, at approximately 6:30 p.m., Garcia was informed that Viera wanted to talk to him about the homicide. Upon his arrival, investigating deputies told him that Viera was claiming to have been paid by Laurie Chastant to kill Dr. Chastant. "Prior to speaking with him, I read Viera his rights per Miranda," Garcia wrote. "Viera stated that he understood his rights and signed the LA State Police Miranda Rights Form (Spanish version)."

Garcia, in his report, wrote:

According to Viera, on or about December 7, 2010, he returned to his residence to each [sic] lunch. As Viera was exiting his residence, he was approached by Laurie Chastant. Laurie Chastant and Viera conversed about marital problems Dr. Chastant and she were having and during the conversation, Laurie Chastant asked Viera if he would be willing to kill Dr. Chastant. Initially, Viera refused to accept the offer. Laurie Chastant asked if Viera would be willing to kill Dr. Chastant for money, but Viera again refused. Laurie Chastant offered Viera $800 to kill Dr. Chastant, but Viera again refused. Finally, Laurie Chastant offered Viera $1,000 to kill Dr. Chastant, and Viera accepted the offer. Laurie Chastant removed the cash (in $100 bill denominations) from her front pants pocket and gave it to Viera. Viera put the money in his pants pocket and returned to work. After Laurie Chastant gave Viera the money, they did not converse any more between December 7, 2010, and December 13, 2010 [the day of the murder].

On December 13, 2010, after Viera killed Dr. Chastant, Laurie Chastant arrived at the barn. Viera stated that Laurie Chastant's arrival was not planned. Viera explained that Laurie Chastant had a doctor's appointment in New Iberia and she must have seen their vehicles at the barn as she was passing by. When Laurie Chastant arrived, she saw Dr. Chastant on the ground but she did not react to the sight of the murder. Viera said Dr. Chastant was already dead when his wife arrived but the only thing Laurie Chastant did was to start to cry a little. Laurie Chastant departed the scene, returned to her residence, retrieved the Suzuki utility cart and returned to the barn. Laurie Chastant instructed Viera to get a trash bag and wrap Dr. Chastant in the bag. Viera removed two trash bags from the barn and wrapped Dr. Chastant's upper body in the trash bags. Viera grabbed Dr. Chastant's upper body and Laurie Chastant grabbed the doctor's feet. Both subjects placed Dr. Chastant in the rear of the Suzuki utility cart.

Once Laurie Chastant and Viera placed Dr. Chastant in the rear of the utility cart, Viera drove the cart to the trash pile that was located behind the barn. Viera stated that Laurie Chastant remained at the location of the murder and covered the blood pools with dirt. Viera placed Dr. Chastant's body in the trash pile and covered it with several items that were already in the trash pile. When Viera returned to the location of the murder, Laurie Chastant had finished covering the blood with dirt. Laurie Chastant instructed Viera to take Dr. Chastant's vehicle to Walmart and leave it in the parking lot. Laurie Chastant took control of the Suzuki utility cart and drove it back [to] the residence. Viera drove Dr. Chastant's vehicle to Walmart and called his wife to pick him up.

With regards to the manner in which the murder was committed, Viera's statement about what he did *was consistent with previous statements* (emphasis author's) However, Viera added that after he struck Dr. Chastant in the back of the neck, as he was lying on the ground, he turned Dr. Chastant onto his back and struck him in the throat with the side of the hammer.

I questioned Viera about missing money and credit cards that were in Dr. Chastant's possession. Viera stated that when he rolled Dr. Chastant's body over, he saw several credit cards lying on the ground. Viera assumed that the credit cards had fallen out of Dr. Chastant's pants pocket. Viera retrieved the credit cards and later placed them in a shoe. Viera placed the shoe in the second-floor loft of his residence. Viera was adamant that he did not take any money from Dr. Chastant. Viera said the money his wife sent to Mexico was the payment money he received from Laurie Chastant to kill Dr. Chastant. Viera stated that Dr. Chastant always paid him in cash so Viera's wife did not question where the money came from.

Viera stated that Laurie Chastant wanted to pay him (and not another worker) because Viera happened to be exiting his residence at the same time as Laurie Chastant. Viera was adamant that he was never involved in any type of relationship with Laurie Chastant. Viera added that he was scared to tell the truth about being paid to kill Dr. Chastant due to the fact that he felt threatened by Dr. Chastant's sons. Viera had seen one of Dr. Chastant's sons target practicing with a weapon, and Viera was scared that the son would harm him if he told the truth.

With regards to the text messages that were received and sent on Dr. Chastant's cellular telephone, Viera stated that Laurie Chastant and he were conversing. I went over each of the texts, and Viera stated that all the outgoing texts after 0830 hours were from him. All the incoming texts during that same time were from Laurie Chastant.

Other than the detailed report of Trooper Frank Garcia, the only consistency in the entire series of events was that of Ismael Viera Tovar, who remained steadfast in his insistence that he was paid a thousand dollars by Laurie Chastant to kill her husband—even when informed by his attorney of the difference between second degree murder and a life sentence and premeditated murder i.e., a contracted murder, and a possible death penalty

Ismael was formally indicted on a charge of second-degree murder by a grand jury of the Sixteenth Judicial District Court on March 16, 2011. The indictment consisted of a single paragraph in the form presented below:

IN HERE, the Grand Jurors of the Sixteenth Judicial District, State of Louisiana, on the 16th day of March 2011, having been duly empaneled and sworn to inquire, in and for the body of the parish of IBERIA, to the name and by the authority of the said State, upon their Oath, charges that in the Parish of IBERIA, and within the jurisdiction of the Sixteenth Judicial District Court of Louisiana, committed the offense(s) of: ON OR ABOUT DECEMBER 13, 2010, IN THE PARISH OF IBERIA, ISMAEL VIERA-TOVAR DID KNOWINGLY OR INTENTIONALLY COMMIT R.S. 14:30.1 SECOND DEGREE

MURDER, by killing Robert Chastant in the second degree contrary to the law of the State of Louisiana and against the peace and dignity of the same.

Three months later, on June 11, he entered a plea of guilty:

On or about the date alleged in the Bill of Indictment, in the parish of Iberia, the defendant, Ismael Viera-Tovar, produced a hammer and struck the victim multiple times in the back of his head and neck area, causing fatal injuries. The attack occurred shortly after a verbal argument between the two, as the victim was walking away from the defendant.

Tom Aswell

Problems with Wells' Deposition

If Detective Adrienne Wells's written report was convoluted and uninformative, there was little improvement in her oral deposition of December 8, 2011, taken almost a year to the day after Dr. Chastant was murdered.

She was questioned in the matter of Laurie Chastant's suit against her husband's estate by Laurie's attorney Steven Durio, and James Daniel, representing Paul Chastant as executor for the succession of his slain brother. Attorney Steven Elledge, representing the Iberia Parish Sheriff's Office, was also in attendance but asked no questions of Detective Wells, though he did provide certain information on investigative procedures from time to time.

In the interest of reducing redundancies, some of her deposition transcript has been condensed. Durio opened the questioning:

> Durio: How long have you been an employee of the sheriff's department?
>
> Wells: With the sheriff's office, a total of six years. However, it's three years communications, two years on patrol, and at the time of this case, I had started working in detectives [sic] in July.
>
> Durio: Prior to coming to the sheriff's department, you had never had a law enforcement role before?
>
> Wells: No.
>
> Durio: So, he [Deputy John McBride] indicated that Laurie was the first person to report Dr. Chastant being missing?
>
> Wells: Yes.

Durio: What time did that occur? Do you know?

Wells: He responded to the doctor's office at 10:02 hours.

Durio: Did you participate in the discussion about how to charge him and how he should be charged, whether he should have been charged with first degree, second degree, anything like that?

Wells: No.

Durio: And ultimately, he pled guilty?

Wells: Yes.

Durio: And he's been sentenced to life in prison?

Wells: Yes.

Durio: Is there anybody besides you, Ms. Wells, in this department that would know better than you what's in that book that you have on these materials?

Wells: I would be the only one because I put it together and organized it.

Daniels then took over the questioning:

Daniels: Detective Wells, were you the lead investigator in connection with Dr. Chastant's murder investigation?

Wells: Yes.

Daniels: You put together this book?

Wells: Yes.

Daniels: What is this book called?

Wells: It's a case file.

Daniels: Do you have typewritten reports in the case file?

Wells: Yes.

Daniels: How many reports are in there that you prepared?

Wells: Oh, one, my original investigative report.

Daniels: And when was that prepared?

Wells: It was prepared over several days.

Daniels: Is it dated?

Wells: I did it over several days throughout the investigation leading up to the end before I turned it in.

Daniels: And when did you turn that in?

Wells: Let's see, January 27th.

Daniels: 2010, obviously, correct?

Wells: 2011.

Daniels: Detective Wells, you were the lead homicide investigator in connection with Dr. Chastant's murder?

Wells: I was the lead detective throughout the whole thing, from the missing report up until we found out it was a homicide.

Daniels: The file still open?

Wells: With the D.A.'s office.

Daniels: What about the sheriff's department?

Wells: It's going to remain open.

Daniels: Can you tell me whether or not from the sheriff's department standpoint, if Laurie Chastant is still considered to be a person of interest?

Wells: We're waiting for further reports to come in.

Daniels: In other words, there's evidence at the Acadiana Crime Lab, is that correct?

Wells: Some of it.

Daniels: Did you collect evidence in connection with the homicide investigation?

Wells: Some. I can't recall what.

Daniels: And has the evidence collected here in your homicide investigation been processed?

Wells: Yes, to my knowledge. We're just waiting on reports from the lab.

Daniels: So, you haven't gotten returns of the evidence?

Wells: We're waiting on the Acadiana Crime Lab report.

Daniels: What will that report tell you?

Wells: I'm not sure.

Daniels: The evidence was forwarded to the Acadiana Crime Lab for what purpose?

Wells: To be processed.

Daniels: Okay, what were you looking for in particular? Can you tell me?

Wells: No.

Daniels: You don't know?

Wells: No. We just…we just send it off.

Daniels: What type of evidence are we talking about?

Wells: We're just waiting on the report, you know, from the lab.

Daniels: What type of evidence was sent to the Acadiana Crime Lab?

Wells: We got swabs, we got carpet padding, we have a hammer, shoes, the list…

Daniels: Are you waiting for the report back from the Acadiana Crime Lab in order to determine whether or not anyone else will be charged in Dr. Chastant's homicide?

Wells: Yes, basically.

Daniels: Is there anyone…other than Laurie Chastant considered to be a person of interest in connection with Dr. Chastant's murder at this time?

Wells: Possibly.

Daniels: And who is this individual?

Wells: Ismael's girlfriend.

Daniels: Does your file reflect a location of Ms. Natalie?

Wells: No.

Daniels: When was the last time that you've spoken to her?

Wells: The last time was a few days---I think the night of the murder and then we---Detective Buddy Fleming brought her back in because supposedly she was packing up to go somewhere.

Daniels: We were asking you earlier if you had an address, if somewhere in the file it indicated an address?

Wells: No.

Daniels: Or a phone number for Ms. Zuniga?

Wells: No, I don't have any contact information.

Daniels: And it is your testimony that she is still considered possibly to be a person of interest in connection with this homicide?

Wells: Possibly.

Daniels: And why is that?

Wells: Everybody is a person of interest.

Daniels: Well, I'm not.

Wells: Yeah, in the whole situation.

Daniels: Well, I'm trying to find out what is it about your investigation that points you that possibly she's a person of interest?

Wells: I'm not really sure what it is, but...I mean, there's some things that I'm not---that happened, that I'm not really sure if it's true.

Daniels: Tell us...what Mr. Viera told the sheriff's department during your homicide investigation about why he killed Dr. Chastant.

Wells: Because basically, you know, there was an argument and he was mad.

Daniels: Is that all he told the sheriff's department?

Wells: No...a few days later, he came back and retold the story.

Daniels: And what did he tell the sheriff's department at that time?

Wells: He implemented Laurie helped...that he was paid to kill the doctor.

Daniels: Did Mr. Viera voluntarily testify or give a statement to the sheriff's department about Laurie's involvement?

Wells: Yes.

Daniels: He wasn't coerced to do so?

Wells: Huh-uh.

Daniels: You'll have to say "no."

Wells: No, not to my knowledge, not with me.

Daniels: And he wasn't offered anything in exchange for his statements concerning Laurie Chastant?

Wells: No.

Daniels: What else did Mr. Viera tell the sheriff's department with regard to Laurie Chastant's involvement?

Wells: He said---you want detail?

Daniels: Yes, please.

Wells: Okay. He said that he was approached by her, if I can recall right, it was on a Tuesday and the conversation took place of her wanting the doctor killed and she offered him some money. He said, "That's not enough," and she came back and offered him more. And then he said yes.

Daniels: Did he tell you anything else concerning Laurie's involvement?

Wells: He said she got out the truck, went helped him, and she instructed him to put trash bags over him and helped him and he went put him in the back.

Daniels: Did he say why she instructed him to do that [place the trash bags over Chastant]?

Wells. I can't recall.

Daniels: Do you know whether or not those trash bags were processed for evidence?

Wells: I'm not sure. I think they went with the body, I'm not sure.

Daniels: Because my question was, do you know whether or not it [sic] was dusted for prints?

Wells: I'm not sure.

Daniels: To your knowledge, did Mr. Viera ever change his story concerning Laurie Chastant's involvement in the murder?

Wells: I'm not sure.

Daniels: Would your investigation reveal that if he changed his mind after that point? In other words, did he ever retract that statement?

Wells: I didn't talk to him after that because he was assigned to an attorney.

Daniels: Did you ever have any conversations with Mr. Viera's attorney?

Wells: No.

Daniels: How many search warrants were issued? Do you recall?

Wells: I don't recall.

Daniels: Was a search warrant issued in connection with the Chastant residence?

Wells: Yes.

Daniels: Did you participate in that search?

Wells: It depends what residence, the pool house or the big residence?

Daniels: Let's talk about the main residence first. Did you participate in that search?

Wells: No.

Daniels: Let's talk about the pool house, then. Did you participate in that search?

Wells: Yes.

Daniels: And what were you looking for, specifically?

Wells: I was looking for the doctor's wallet, his credit cards, money and, you know, any items that would constitute [sic] with the murder, you know, any evidence that we can look for.

Daniels: What did you find at the pool house?

Wells: We found a wallet with the doctor's credit cards…He [Viera] told us that he had some money in a blue container, and it was all the way at the bottom. I found it. It was a white cylinder and it had like $223. He said that was the money left over from the $1,000.

Daniels: Do you know whether or not that $223 was ever processed?

Wells: I'm not sure if it was processed. It is in evidence.

Daniels: Did you participate in the search of the motor home?

Wells: Yes, I was there.

Daniels: What evidence was collected from the motor home?

Wells: The first time, nothing. I don't think anything was taken and then, a while later, I was contacted by the family, Paul Chastant, to go back and look in the motor home because Laurie wanted to get into it, so I went back and got a consent to search with Elizabeth Breaux and she signed it and we was [sic] sent look and I found a floor mat, two floor mats, if I can recall correctly, in one of the compartments.

Daniels: One of the luggage compartments?

Wells: Yeah, on the outside.

Daniels: And has that floor mat been processed?

Wells: Yes, it should be at the Acadiana Crime Lab.

Daniels: And I see it on Page 1 at the bottom. It says, "Floor mat." I assume that's what that is. It says, "Hair and blood from claw." What does that mean?

Wells: It should be the claw of the hammer. I didn't prepare this list, so it was prepared by my evidence custodian.

Daniels: What about the floor mats caught your attention when you searched the motor home?

Wells: The floor mats in the---were---after I found the floor mats, the next day I went to check the vehicles at the jail. The Avalanche was the only vehicle without any floor mats and it looked like truck floor mats.

Daniels: Was it the same style or color of the other floor mats of the Avalanche?

Wells: The Avalanche doesn't have any floor mats.

Daniels: So, there are no floor mats in it?

Wells: No.

Daniels: Did the floor mats match the Avalanche?

Wells: I didn't put it in the Avalanche to try.

Daniels: It's my understanding that fiber samples are being analyzed from the floor mats to determine whether or not they came from the Avalanche?

Wells: Yes.

Daniels: Was there blood evidence on the floor mats?

Wells: I'm not sure. I didn't process it.

Daniels: Was there anything on the floor—any other matter on the floor mats that looked like it may have some evidentiary value that's being processed?

Wells: I'm not sure. Whenever we collected the floor mats, I sent them to my lab and my crime scene technician went through them and submitted them to ACL.

Daniels: Was there any skull or brain matter on the floor mats?

Wells: No.

Daniels: Do you know that for a fact?

Wells: I would have seen it.

Daniels: And you know that even though ACL has not sent back a report on the floor mats?

Wells: Uh-Huh. Yes.

Daniels: So, you've been told by somebody at Acadiana Crime Lab that there was no blood evidence on the floor mats?

Wells: I talked to the district attorney and asked him, I said, "Did they find anything on the floor mats?" and they told me no.

Daniels: So, as we sit here today, Detective Wells, you're still waiting to find out whether or not the floor mats belong to the Avalanche?

Wells: Yes, sir. I haven't gotten any word.

Daniels: Now, I just see one floor mat. Was there more than one, or do you recall?

Wells: That would be it.

Daniels: Just one?

Wells: I can't recall what---there was only one.

Daniels: Is this your report, Detective Wells?

Wells: Yes.

Daniels: And this would have been typed by you?

Wells: Yes.

Daniels: It says, "During the search, Detective Wells located a black floor mat which appeared to belong to a pickup truck that was located in the second compartment on the exterior of the RV upside down. Detective Wells looked at the mat closer and located two hairs on the mat." Do we know whose hairs those were?

Wells: No.

Daniels: Still waiting on the results from the crime lab?

Wells: Yes.

Daniels: When do you expect the return on the evidence from the Acadiana Crime Lab?

Wells: I don't know.

Daniels: Have you spoken to anyone over there recently?

Wells: No.

Daniels: Do you know whether or not the evidence that has been submitted to the crime lab is there on any type of priority or rush basis or just regular?

Wells: No, I'm not sure.

Daniels: You don't know if it's handled rush or ASAP-type request?

Wells: We've been waiting a while.

Daniels: What did the DA's office told [sic] you about their investigation?

Wells: They're just waiting on the report from the crime lab.

Daniels: Is their investigation still ongoing?

Wells: Yes.

Daniels: Do you recall that Ms. Chastant had claimed that when she got up that morning, Dr. Chastant was outside on his phone?

Wells: Yes.

Daniels: He came in, his truck was running, he came in, gave her a kiss goodbye and then left? That's what she told Detective Papion, correct?

Wells: Yes.

Daniels: I took Ms. Chastant's deposition a few months ago, and she testified that morning that she got up at---she got up and made him coffee...and he had coffee at the house before he left. So, that statement would be contrary to what she told Detective Papion, correct? That's not what your report, your investigative report, reflects what Ms. Chastant told the detectives in this case, is it?

Wells: I'm not sure.

Daniels: The fact that Dr. Chastant's blood was found in the Isuzu vehicle, that evidence is consistent with Mr. Viera's last statement about Dr. Chastant being placed in that vehicle and driven to the wood pile?

Wells: yes.

Daniels: And what did Mr. Viera tell you in your investigation with regard to how the Isuzu arrived at the big barn that day or if it was already there? Do you recall?

Wells: I can't remember.

Daniels: Do you recall whether or not he told the detectives that Laurie Chastant drove it to the property?

Wells: I don't remember.

Daniels: So, you received on December 15th, you received a telephone call from Laurie Chastant?

Wells: Yes, she called me on the office phone and she was saying that Natalie lied to her, that Natalie told her Terry Romero picked up Ismael from the pool house.

Daniels: And Ms. Chastant was saying that was a lie?

Wells: Yeah, to her, from speaking with them.

Daniels: You make a comment there was a male subject in the background guiding her. What did you mean by that?

Wells: It sounded like---like---I don't know if you know Trevor Qualls. That's who it sounded like.

Daniels: Trever who?

Wells: Qualls. He was talking, telling her what to say, kind of.

Daniels: Who is Trevor Qualls?

Wells: The son-in-law. He's married to Megan.

Daniels: Did she say that who it was?

Wells: No, I didn't ask. I was in the middle of doing other stuff.

Daniels: What did Mr. Viera tell you and the other detectives concerning Laurie Chastant's involvement that day?

Wells: He said as soon as he finished killing the doctor, Laurie showed up at the barn all of a sudden. He advised she saw the doctor's truck and the car in front of the barn. She pulled in to see, at which point he already killed the doctor. Laurie instructed him to get the bags to cover him up. Then her reaction was after she observed the doctor being dead, her reaction was appeared to like she wanted to cry. She had tears in her eyes, but never cried. She told him to get the bags to cover the upper body, and then Laurie grabbed---Ismael grabbed the upper body, Laurie grabbed the lower part of the ankle. They placed him in the rear of the grey Suzuki truck. Then he said she covered up the blood in the front of the barn.

Daniels: Did you all question him concerning the origination of the story he had told earlier about the lady picking Dr. Chastant up in the pickup truck?

Wells: Yes. He said Laurie came up with the story and they discussed the story the same day she paid him to kill the doctor.

Daniels: Where was this Isuzu [Suzuki] truck found after Dr. Chastant's murder?

Wells: If I can recall right, it was at the house.

Daniels: Back at the Chastant house?

Wells: Yes.

Daniels: Did Mr. Viera tell you and the other detective how the truck got from the barn to the other house?

Wells: He may have. He tried to say in the interview with Carmen Garcia that Natalie [Nayeli] drove the truck and then we confronted Natalie with it and she broke down, so I don't think she drove it.

Daniels: Is it safe to say that your investigation of Dr. Chastant's homicide remains open?

Wells: Yes.

Daniels: Is the reason it remains open is that you want to see if that evidence, once processed, either points to or perhaps implicates someone else's involvement with the murder?

Wells: Yes.

Daniels: Did you obtain the OnStar information with regard to the OnStar for the Avalanche, Laurie Chastant's vehicle?

Wells: I think I did. I'm not sure if they sent me anything. I submitted a search warrant for her vehicle. However, they could only give me a limited amount of information. It wasn't anything pertinent. They didn't give me a route, only whenever she pressed her button inside her vehicle, they gave me the GPS coordinates, which I tracked…on Google Map and it tracked in front of the barn. It could be off. We're really not sure.

Daniels: You're talking about on the day of the murder?

Wells: Yes, at the time she notified OnStar that her husband was missing. She pressed the button in her truck…and then she told them that her husband was missing and they told her she needs to file a police report. I guess she pressed it around the time she was looking for the doctor, and she went to the doctor's office, and that's whenever they called.

Daniels: And the general location of her OnStar at that time, you said, in front of the barn?

Wells: Yes.

Daniels: What's the plus or minus accuracy of that point?

Wells: I'm not sure. Records for the black Chevy Avalanche, the time OnStar activated the case, is at 11:05. However, I'm not sure if it's Eastern or Central time.

Daniels: And we don't know if it's Daylight Savings Time or not.

Wells: I'm not sure. I'm assuming it's Eastern.

Daniels: Other than waiting on the evidence to come back from the Acadiana Crime Lab, are you awaiting anything else, to speak to anyone else at the present time, concerning the investigation?

Wells: Not at this time.

Tom Aswell

Detectives' Collective Memory Lapses

Wells indicated that Jason Ramsey, the contractor doing remodeling work on the rent house on Caroline Street, said that Dr. Chastant was supposed to pay him $2,880 on the day he was killed. Only two thousand dollars was recovered from Dr. Chastant's jacket pocket. Natalie, she said, sent eight hundred dollars to her mother in Mexico via a Western Union transaction at the New Iberia Winn Dixie. She was charged a fifty-dollar processing fee, plus $9.99 tax. She paid $880 and received $20.01 in change. She said the transaction was executed at 9:34 a.m. central time. Wells said Viera claimed the money recovered in the pool house was left over from the thousand dollars Laurie Chastant paid him.

During their depositions, Detective Wells, her supervisor, Captain Gerald Savoy, and Sergeant Carmen Garcia answered "I don't recall," "I don't know," "I can't remember," or some other variation of memory lapse of crucial details no fewer than ninety-four times.

Only Detectives Dusty Vallot, Emayla Papion and Richard Fleming seemed to display any signs of fact retention, making similar claims only seven times between them.

Savoy, the most veteran of the lot with eighteen years' experience in law enforcement. fourteen of those in nearby St. Martin Parish, at the time of his deposition on December 8, 2011, was described as the "top of the pyramid" in the Iberia Parish Sheriff's Office. Six years following his deposition, he was sentenced to eighty-seven months in federal prison in an unrelated matter over the mistreatment of prisoners in the Iberia Parish Jail.

Savoy successfully quashed an earlier attempt to obtain his deposition in September after both attorneys, Daniels and Durio, had insisted it would be premature and potentially damaging to the investigation for Savoy or Wells, who was deposed the same day as Savoy, to give their depositions while the district attorney's investigation was ongoing.

In a November 21 letter to Steven Elledge, special counsel for the sheriff's department, Daniels reinforced his interpretation of Louisiana Disciplinary Rule 3.8, the Special Responsibilities of a Prosecutor, as his reason for concern:

The prosecutor in a criminal case shall:

- (f) Except for statements that are necessary to inform the public of the nature and extent of the prosecutor's action and that serve a legitimate law enforcement purpose, refrain from making extra-judicial comments that have a substantially [sic] likelihood of heightening public condemnation of the accused and exercise reasonable care to prevent investigators, law enforcement personnel, employees or other persons assisting or associated with the prosecutor in a criminal case from making an extra-judicial statement that the prosecutor would be prohibited from making under Rule 3.6 or this Rule.

"Inasmuch as the Iberia Parish Sheriff's Department is the investigative arm of the District Attorney's office," the letter read, "we believe that this Disciplinary Rule prohibits the Sheriff's Department from allowing its employees to make such extrajudicial comments and/or statements during an ongoing investigation.

"When I informed the Chastant family that these depositions were going to go forward in the light of the ongoing investigation by the District Attorney's office and that the District Attorney's office objected to same, they were very upset, to say the least. Both the District Attorney's office and the Chastant family feel that releasing this information to potential murder suspects in this case will only aid them in any future defense and it would be irresponsible considering all of the above. Should the District Attorney's office decide to bring this matter to the Iberia Parish

Grand Jury, it may well jeopardize any advantage it has by disclosing the evidence obtained through the investigation at this time.

"Accordingly, we ask that the Iberia Parish Sheriff's Department coordinate with the Iberia Parish District Attorney's office regarding the Iberia Parish District Attorney's office ongoing investigation and reconsider its position with regard to opening up its entire investigative file in the civil proceedings until such time as the Iberia Parish District Attorney's office has been able to complete its investigation and make a decision regarding bringing this matter to an Iberia Parish Grand Jury.

"In that the depositions of Captain Savoy and Inspector Wells have been scheduled for the near future, the family would appreciate written responses confirming or denying your final determination to cooperate with the Iberia Parish District Attorney."

Tom Aswell

Savoy Vague, Evasive in Deposition

Despite Daniels's letter, the depositions of Savoy and Wells went forward as rescheduled on December 8. Still, by the time his sworn testimony was taken on that date, Savoy would prove to be vague, evasive and generally non-responsive to questions about the investigation.

He did not know, for example, how the sheriff's department first received information that Robert Chastant was missing, even though he was in charge of the overall investigation. He did, however, recall that Viera told detectives that Laurie Chastant had paid him to kill her husband.

James Daniels: Captain Savoy, is the sheriff's investigation still ongoing?

Savoy: Yes.

Daniels: Is Laurie Chastant, Dr. Chastant's wife, is she still considered to be a person of interest with regard to the sheriff's investigation?

Savoy: Person of interest.

Daniels: It's my understanding that there is still evidence at the Acadiana Crime Lab which has not been processed.

Savoy: Yes, there is.

Daniels: Did you know whether or not any other evidence was collected from the motor home, other than the floor mat, was collected, when the motor home was searched?

Savoy: No.

Daniels: When do you expect a return on the evidence?

Savoy: I don't know. To give a specific date, approximate, I don't know. We just a couple of weeks ago received something from 2004.

Daniels: So, when you testified in court in Lafayette, you were being optimistic that you thought you might have it within six to eight weeks?

Savoy: Yes, being very optimistic. And they knew the importance of this case.

Daniels: Have you been informed by anyone from the district attorney's office that they were waiting on the results from the Acadiana Crime Lab before making a decision whether to present this matter to the grand jury?

Savoy: No.

Daniels: What did Mr. Viera have to say about why the garbage bag was placed over---on Dr. Chastant?

Savoy: He claimed that...he covered it at the request of Laurie because she couldn't stand seeing him like that.

Daniels: Did Mr. Viera give any testimony during his interrogation whether or not Laurie participated in the murder?

Savoy: He said that she helped him load Dr. Chastant's body into the small work truck that was used to transport the body from the actual scene where the beating took place to the rear of the property.

Captain Savoy testified in his deposition that Viera said he was approached on two separate occasions by Laurie Chastant about killing her husband but said he did not recall the time lapse between the two solicitations.

When Daniels asked if Laurie Chastant's truck was seized by the sheriff's office, Savoy said it was "taken as evidence."

"Was evidence found in the truck?" Daniels asked.

"Possible evidence," Savoy responded. "We're still waiting on the Acadiana Crime Lab.

Daniels asked what type evidence was submitted to the crime lab from Laurie's Avalanche. Savoy answered "DNA swabs" and "possible" blood evidence. Daniels then asked about the motion-activated video camera that was missing from the barn only to be discovered by Daniels more than a year later submerged in water in the bed of Dr. Chastant's truck.

Daniels: People were looking for a video camera. I call it a game camera, like a deer camera, that we were told that Dr. Chastant had placed on the property. Do you know whether or not that camera was ever located?

Savoy: It was never located.

Daniels: Do you know anything about the marital problems between Laurie Chastant and Dr. Chastant?

Savoy: She did claim that he was having an affair. She claimed that he was supposed to fly out to maybe Dallas to speak---to see her. He cancelled it because she [Laurie] wanted to go or something to that effect, but from what I remember, it was still ongoing.

Daniels: Did it come up during the course of the investigation whether or not Laurie Chastant was seeing anyone else or having an affair during the marriage?

Savoy: No.

Daniels: Do you know whether or not that was asked of her?

Savoy. I'm not sure.

Daniels ended Savoy's deposition by discussing the difference between second-degree and first-degree murder: "Mr. Viera was charged initially with second-degree murder," he said. "Who made that decision about his charge?"

Savoy explained that Detective Adrienne Wells "spoke with the district attorney's office and they...came to the conclusion of second degree."

Daniels: With assuming Mr. Viera was paid to kill Dr. Chastant, does that change the level or degree of the homicide?

Savoy: Yeah, right.

Daniels: And that would be a first-degree murder charge?

Savoy: Yes.

Daniels: So, by confessing that he was paid to do so, he was actually putting himself in a worse position?

Savoy: Yeah.

That was the end of Savoy's testimony.

Det. Fleming's Timeline Contradicts Laurie's

Other members of the Iberia Parish Sheriff's Office investigative team who gave sworn depositions included Detective Dusty Vallot who had only six years' experience in law enforcement and all of six months as a detective at the time of Dr. Chastant's murder; Detective Emalaya Papion, who had two years' law enforcement experience on December 13, 2010, including a year as a probation and parole officer for the State of Louisiana and who had been a detective just over three months, and Sergeant Carmen Garcia, who, on seventeen occasions, claimed to have a faulty memory of events pertaining to the Chastant murder investigation.

Besides Captain Gerald Savoy and State Trooper Frank Garcia, the only law enforcement officer involved in the investigation with any real experience was Detective Richard Fleming who, while employed by the sheriff's department for less than two years at the time of the murder, was employed as a Louisiana State Trooper from August 1981 until his retirement in July 2009. He was initially assigned to Troop I and remained there until January 1985 except for three-plus years he spent as a detective in Region II.

His time in Troop I would have overlapped with times Laurie's father, William Futral, spent there after his original Troop K became part of Troop I in 1988. It was possible, even probable, that Ackal, Fleming and Futral knew each other—or at least knew *of* each other—earlier in their careers while employed as Louisiana State Troopers.

Fleming filed a three-page report in which he noted that Laurie Chastant "stated that Dr. Chastant was having an affair but was unsure if it was sexual. Mrs. Chastant also stated that Dr. Chastant has hit her in the past." Fleming went on to say that Laurie told him that she and her husband had argued over his plans to fly to Texas to spend the weekend with Kristen McClean.

Ismael's girlfriend Nayeli Zuniga (alternately referred to as Gutierrez) more or less confirmed the budding affair to Fleming when she told him that Laurie, in a conversation with Nayeli, said she had confronted Dr. Chastant about the affair around December 8 or 9. Nayeli further asserted that Laurie said she was going to leave because she did not want her husband "to give her gonorrhea." She told Nayeli that the other woman was from the Dallas area, approximately twenty-five years of age "and very pretty." According to Nayeli, she said her husband was spending a lot of money on the woman, buying her expensive dresses. Laurie then said to Nayeli, "Look at me. I don't have anything expensive. I don't have anything pretty." Nayeli said Laurie left town with friends in a motor home the day following their exchange.

"While Agent [Tim] Hanks was speaking to Mrs. Chastant, Mrs. Chastant also stated that Dr. Chastant's ex-wife's name is Susan Hall," Fleming wrote in his report. "Mrs. Chastant stated that Ms. Hall and Dr. Chastant had a horrible relationship and they had not spoken to one another in years.

"At approximately 2215 hours, Captain Savoy notified me that the body of Dr. Robert Chastant had been found [and] not to notify Mrs. Chastant until further notice." Fifteen minutes later, Savoy instructed Fleming to have Lieutenant Gary Louviere accompany him in notifying Laurie of the discovery of Dr. Chastant's body.

It was Fleming who was assigned to retrieve Dr. Chastant's DNA from the Lafayette Parish coroner's office and forward it to the Acadiana Crime Lab.

Fleming's deposition should have raised red flags for both the sheriff's and district attorney's offices because the time sequence he described was at odds with the time line provided by Laurie Chastant and Dr. Kenneth Ritter's office manager Ada Credeur .

Laurie testified in her deposition that she left for Dr. Ritter's office between 7:40 a.m. and 7:50 a.m. and Ada Credeur testified that when she arrived for work at the doctor's office at 7:30 a.m., Laurie was already there. Laurie, she said, received word around 9:00 a.m. that her husband had not shown up at his office.

But Fleming said in his deposition that Nayeli told him that she met with Laurie that morning at 8:00 "and the doctor's wife was upset" saying that her husband was missing.

Attorney Daniels asked Fleming to read a paragraph from his typed report:

Fleming: Upon returning home, Nayeli met with the doctor's wife to receive instructions on what she was to do the next day. An unsolicited response, Nayeli stated that the doctor's wife was crying when she met with her at this time. Nayeli asked the doctor's wife what was wrong to which she responded her husband had not shown up for work. The doctor's wife also stated that Ismael and the doctor were in the barn, and that she [doctor's wife] left at 8:00 a.m. for an appointment. The doctor's wife stated that the doctor never made it to work...

Nayeli apologized to the doctor's wife, stating, "I'm so sorry you're going through that." The doctor's wife replied that she was going to a doctor's appointment. Nayeli stated that this occurred at 8:00 a.m. on this day.

If Nayeli's timeline was correct, that would mean Laurie was crying about her husband's being missing an hour before she was notified of the fact.

Tom Aswell

Sgt. Garcia Corroborates Fleming Testimony

The deposition of Sergeant Carmen Garcia read much the same as that of Detective Fleming. Given on January 18, 2012, the same day as Fleming's, Garcia testified that Nayeli said she arrived at the Chastant residence "at approximately 8:30" the morning of December 13 and Laurie was crying.

> Sgt. Garcia: She [Laurie] could not reach or make contact with Dr. Chastant. Nayeli said Ms. Laurie said that Dr. Chastant was missing and that she could not find him. Nayeli said Laurie walked out and said she had to leave because she had a nine o'clock appointment with her doctor.

> Daniels: Now, Sergeant Garcia, what I'm going to ask you, according to these notes, what Ms. Gutierrez [Nayeli] told you was that before Ms. Chastant left for her doctor's appointment, she was at home crying because she could not locate her husband? What did Ms. Gutierrez tell you with regard to Ms. Chastant---what Ms. Chastant told her that morning?

> Sgt. Garcia: Exactly what I just read to you.

> Daniels: Did Ms. Gutierrez tell you that Ms. Chastant told her that her husband was missing before or after her doctor's appointment?

> Sgt. Garcia: She [Laurie] told her that---she advised me [Nayeli] of that before she went to her doctor's appointment.

> Attorney Durio took over the questioning of Sergeant Garcia at that point:

> Durio: What was the time of your interview with Ms. Gutierrez?

Sgt. Garcia: I'm not sure, sir. I didn't put it on my report. (This was another in a long line of oversights and omissions in the investigation.)

Durio: What day was it [that Dr. Chastant's murder] occurred?

Sgt. Garcia: After my interview, what you see right here [in her report], after this interview, I have nothing further to mention about anything because I don't know what went on.

Durio: Why not?

Sgt. Garcia: Because I had nothing to do with the interview of Mr. Viera or Nayeli after they found out that Dr. Chastant was pronounced---or found, his body was found out at the barn.

Durio: Can you explain to me why, after the body was found, you had no further contact with anybody?

Sgt. Garcia: Because I had already spent hours with this Spanish-speaking male, finding out what I did find out, and…they brought in a fresh guy to continue with the interview.

Durio: On the 13th?

Sgt. Garcia: On the 13th.

Durio: When we started on this series of questions, I was talking about an interview on the 14th that had---Mr. Fleming wrote about in the ARRMS [Automated Reports Management Mapping System] report…

Sgt. Garcia: Right, and I advised you that I don't know anything about Mr. Fleming writing something in the report on the 14th because I didn't have anything to do with it.

Durio: Have you ever spoken to Lieutenant---Detective Wells about this information you just read us indicating that Ms. Gutierrez said that Mrs. Chastant was at the home around 8:30 in the morning when she got there? Did you ever tell that to Detective Wells?

Sgt. Garcia: No, sir.

Durio: Do you know if the file or the investigation reflects that Mrs. Chastant was somewhere else at that time?

Sgt. Garcia: I'm not aware of any of that.

Durio: You haven't been told or heard that Mrs. Chastant was at the doctor's office at that time?

Sgt. Garcia: No, sir.

Tom Aswell

Papion First to Interview Laurie Chastant

Detective Emayla Papion also gave her deposition on January 18, 2012, the same date as Garcia and Fleming. Papion was the detective who took the initial statement from Laurie Chastant when Dr. Chastant was still missing.

Daniels: I want to ask you a little bit about your interview with Laurie Chastant. Do you remember when that was?

Papion: The morning of December 13th.

Daniels: Do you recall what time?

Papion: Approximately 10:00, 10:30 a.m.

Daniels: Did she tell you anything concerning their relationship?

Papion: She told me that they had been arguing the past few days over Kristen McClain, who was someone she found out he may or may not have had a physical relationship with.

Daniels: What, if anything, did she tell you about the morning that Dr. Chastant went missing, starting with the early morning, the last time she saw him?

Papion: She advised she had woke [sic] that morning, the morning of December 13, 2010, and she went downstairs. Dr. Chastant was outside, either emailing or texting someone on his phone and smoking a cigarette. She said when he finished, he came back inside, kissed her goodbye and left for the day to go to work.

Daniels: So, when she saw him initially that day, he was already outside?

Papion: Yes.

Daniels: Did Ms. Chastant indicate to you whether or not she saw Dr. Chastant after he left that morning?

Papion: She said she didn't.

Daniels: And that interview with Laurie Chastant was conducted on what date?

Papion: December 13, 2010.

Daniels: Was it completed by you on that date?

Papion: Yes, sir.

Daniels: And when was it typed by you, typed up?

Papion: It would have been probably the beginning of January.

Daniels: I noticed in your report you said that Laurie told you that she left the house after Dr. Chastant. Do you recall about when that was?

Papion: She didn't give me an exact time that she left. She just told me she had a doctor's appointment that morning.

Daniels: She told you she went to the doctor?

Papion: Yes, sir.

Daniels: Did you make any attempt to confirm that?

Papion: Another detective went out to the doctor's office and confirmed that she was there.

Daniels: Who was that other detective?

Papion: Jason Comeaux.

Daniels: And do you know when, you know, at what time she was at the office, what time during the morning she was at the doctor's office? Did she sign in when she left, [that] sort of thing?

Papion: According to my interview, she didn't tell me what time she got there, but she got a phone call at approximately 9:20 in the morning and Dr.---I'm sorry, Jason---Agent Jason Comeaux was able to confirm that was approximately the time she left.

An illustration of the compartmentalization of the Iberia Parish Sheriff's Office and the lack of communication and coordination between investigators manifested itself during the January 18, 2012, deposition of Detective Dusty Vallot. Attorney Steven Durio said, "In your report, the portion that Mr. Daniels asked you about, you mentioned that the $2200 cash was found in a jacket pocket. Do you know what kind of jacket pocket?"

"I don't," Vallot said.

"Was the jacket itself taken into evidence?"

"I'm not sure. I wasn't inside when the evidence was being taken."

"Do you have any way of knowing whether or not that was a jacket that belonged to Mr. Viera?" Durio asked.

"No, sir, I don't."

"Or to Dr. Chastant?"

"I don't."

"In your report, you say that you were present when someone, some detective, discovered a hammer with what appeared to be blood on it in a trash bag located inside the barn."

"Yes, sir," Vallot replied.

"So, he admitted to using the hammer as the hammer to kill Dr. Chastant? Are you aware that there was a hammer also found in his [Viera's] vehicle?

"No, sir."

"You're not aware of any indication in any of these reports of investigation that there was also a hammer found there in the Toyota vehicle?

"No, sir, I didn't read any other reports except mine."

Daniels Grills Laurie

Laurie Chastant's deposition in her consolidated lawsuit against Prudential and Lincoln National was taken on October 6, 2011, ten months after the murder of her husband.

Following a few preliminary questions about how she met Dr. Chastant, their moving in together following his divorce from his second wife and their marriage on May 24, 2004, attorney James Daniels broached the subject of Ismael Viera's employment and his operation of the Chastants' vehicles.

Daniels: Which vehicle did he have access to?

Laurie Chastant: He drove the mini truck and he also, at some point, drove Bobby's white truck and possibly backed up or drove my truck. He was not allowed to go driving any of these down the road…It was from the house to the little barn or from the house to the new barn and back, but not all over town.

Daniels: You told us earlier that Natalie [Nayeli] and Mr. Viera were paid $300 each per week?

Laurie: Yes.

Daniels: Did they pay for their own groceries?

Laurie: Yes.

Daniels: And I assume that you and Dr. Chastant paid for the utilities on the pool house where they were living?

Laurie: Yes. Those utilities were included in the same bill as our house.

Daniels: And how were Natalie and Mr. Viera paid? Were they paid by check or cash?

Laurie: Cash.

Daniels: And were there any withholdings taken from their weekly paychecks?

Laurie: You mean taxes?

Daniels: Taxes or any other withholdings?

Laurie: No.

Daniels: Were either Natalie or Mr. Viera, were they legally within the United States?

Laurie: It is my understanding that they were not here legally.

Daniels: How would you describe your relationship, marital relationship, with Dr. Chastant? Were you happily married?

Laurie: Yes.

Daniels: You all were faithful to one another?

Laurie: I was faithful to him. He had had some sort of---not necessarily an affair, but he had something with a girl. There were two girls. One was in 2009 and the other was in 2010.

Daniels: What about the 2010? What is the name of that individual?

Laurie: Kristen McClain.

Daniels: Had you ever spoken to Ms. McClain?

Laurie: I did speak to her. It was sometime in October or November.

Daniels: What did Ms. McClain tell you?

Laurie: She told me that it was my fault that my husband looked elsewhere.

Daniels then attempted to get Laurie to admit she had written two checks totaling a thousand dollars which was the money allegedly paid Ismael to kill Dr. Chastant. Instead of suggesting the two checks combined for a thousand dollars, however, he inadvertently asked if she had written two checks for a thousand dollars each, thus providing Laurie an opportunity to provide a denial without committing perjury.

Daniels: I'm sure you know there were two checks that were made out to cash on the Sonriente Stables account in the month of December prior to Dr. Chastant's death. Are you aware of that, for $1,000 each?

Laurie: No, I'm not.

Daniels: Do you recall cashing any checks for cash on the Sonriente Stables account for $1,000 in either the month of November or December 2010?

Laurie: No, I don't recall.

Daniels: Isn't it true that you confided in Natalie concerning your relationship with Dr. Chastant?

Laurie: I confided in her one time. I told her that he had a girlfriend.

Laurie Chastant then gave a conflicting account of when she left her house for her doctor's appointment the morning of the murder. She had told detectives that Dr. Chastant was already outside on his phone when she came down from the upstairs bedroom and that after he got off the phone, he came in, kissed her goodbye and left. She said in her interviews that both her husband and Viera left and that she left for her appointment after their departures. The office manager for the doctor's office said Laurie was already in the office when she arrived for work at 7:30 a.m. Laurie's deposition was a significant departure from that timeline.

Daniels: What was the work schedule for both Natalie and Mr. Viera for Monday morning?

Laurie: She was supposed to come and work at the house and he was supposed to go to the rent house.

Daniels: On Monday, December 13th, did in fact Natalie stay at the home to do work?

Laurie: Yes.

Daniels: And Viera was to be going to the Caroline Street property?

Laurie: Yes.

Daniels: How was he to get there?

Laurie: He had a car.

Daniel: And did he leave that morning to go to the Caroline Street property?

Laurie: I don't know because I left before they would have left. (This was in direct contradiction to statements she gave sheriffs' deputies, including Detective Emayla Papion.)

Daniels: What time did you leave the home?

Laurie: About 7:40, 7:50, somewhere like that.

Daniels: What time was the appointment?

Laurie: Eight o'clock.

Daniels: And what time did you arrive at his [the doctor's] office for your appointment?

Laurie: I got there a little bit after 8:00.

Daniels: That morning, you made breakfast for Dr. Chastant?

Laurie: I made him coffee. He didn't eat breakfast. (This was yet another inconsistency.)

Daniels: When you left the home, was Natalie already inside?

Laurie: Yes. She had just walked in when I was leaving.

Daniels: So, you leave the house, you get to your appointment with Dr. Ritter's office, and you left somewhere between 9:15 and 9:30?

Laurie: Yes. I went driving down the road looking for Bobby.

Daniels: What did you tell the police officer?

Laurie: I told him that Bobby was missing, which he knew, and I also showed him my cell phone because I had started getting text messages from Bobby's phone and I showed him the text messages that I was getting.

Daniels: What kind of text messaging were you getting from Bobby's phone?

Laurie: "I okay. Go Home. Go home now."

Daniels: Did you text back?

Laurie: I did.

Daniels: When did you get these text messages?

Laurie: As I was driving from the house to the barn, I mean, to the office (an inadvertent slip?) I got the text messages.

Daniels: What did you text back before you arrived at the office?

Laurie: "No, call me. You have patients. We are looking for you. The police…" something like that, you know. "Me and the police are looking for you." I mean, I wanted him to call me. I didn't want to get these text messages saying, "no, go home."

Daniels: Now, you had been married to Dr. Chastant for quite a while, hadn't you?

Laurie: Yes, we had been married since 2004.

Daniels: Was he a physically violent person?

Laurie: He had struck me a couple of times, but it hadn't happened in years and I would not consider him physically violent towards other men.

Daniels: Isn't it true that the sheriff's department informed you that Viera told them that you had paid him to kill…

Laurie: They never told me that.

Daniels: When was the first time you learned that Viera had told the sheriff's department that?

Laurie: I was sitting in this office and you told me.

Daniels: Other than the December 13, 2010, when you were looking for Dr. Chastant's truck and you drove onto the barn property, have you been out there since then?

Laurie: I don't think so.

Daniels: What about any of your family members?

Laurie: No, I don't think they would have any reason to go there.

Daniels then appeared to catch Laurie off guard with questions about possible drug abuse on her part. Following his first question, a break was called in the proceedings before she invoked her Fifth Amendment rights, refusing to answer specific questions about drug use.

Daniels: I understand you were hospitalized for a few days, a month or two before Dr. Chastant's death?

Laurie: Yes, for Crohn's Disease.

Daniels: Ms. Chastant, during the five or six years, have you had any problems with drug problems, narcotic problems?

Laurie: I really don't see how that's relevant.

At this point, a break in the proceedings was taken before Daniels restated his question.

Daniels: Your response to the last question that I asked concerning drug use?

Laurie: On the advice of counsel, I refuse to answer that question, relying upon my constitutional rights included in the Fifth Amendment to the U.S. Constitution and based upon Article I, Section 13 of the Louisiana Constitution.

Daniels: During your marriage with Dr. Chastant, did you have any problems with drug use?

Laurie: On the advice of counsel, I refuse to answer that question, relying upon my constitutional rights included in the Fifth Amendment to the U.S. Constitution and based upon Article I, Section 13 of the Louisiana Constitution.

Daniels: In connection with your relationship with Dr. Chastant, did you and Dr. Chastant have any relationship problems as a result of any alleged use of narcotics on your part?

Laurie: On the advice of counsel, I refuse to answer that question, relying upon my constitutional rights included in the Fifth Amendment to the U.S. Constitution and based upon Article I, Section 13 of the Louisiana Constitution.

Daniels: With regard to your hospitalization that you told us about for Crohn's Disease, was that hospitalization also due in part as a result of any drug use?

Laurie: No.

Daniels: With regard to the motor home…did you, other than the time you examined the motor home at Dr. Chastant's office, you remember, we set it up, you wanted to go look through it in connection with the lawsuit?

Laurie: Yes, I do remember that time.

Daniels: And what was the purpose for going in the motor home?

Laurie: I took some of my clothes out of there.

Daniels: Did you have any reason from December 13th, other than the time you went to the office to look through the motor home, did you go into the luggage compartment of the motor home?

Laurie: No, not that I recall.

Daniels: Is it your testimony, Ms. Chastant, that you have---to your recollection, that you have not placed anything in the motor home since the death of your husband?

Laurie: Nothing to my recollection.

Daniels: Isn't it true, Ms. Chastant, that the reason that in order to entice you to sign the matrimony agreement, you insisted on Dr. Chastant purchasing some life insurance on himself naming you as beneficiary?

Laurie: No, there was no enticement for me to sign the agreement.

Daniels: And what is your understanding now of the amount of life insurance with Lincoln?

Laurie: I think it was $600,000.

Daniels: And how about Prudential?

Laurie: I think it's $700,000.

Daniels: And what about the Defined Benefit Plan?

Laurie: I was told that it is about $700,000, also.

Daniels: How was it, Ms. Chastant, that you discovered that Dr. Chastant was seeing this woman in Dallas?

Laurie: He had asked me to put some packets together, some different paperwork, and some of that paperwork I was going to need to get off of his computer and print it out, and when I hit enter on the computer, there was an email that he had left up that he was sending to Kristen McClain.

Daniels: What did the email say?

Laurie: It was of a personal nature and I don't remember the exact words to it, that she was pretty and sexy and that they would have fun together.

Daniels: And when was this, approximately, that you discovered this email?

Laurie: It was sometime in October or November.

Daniels: Were there any other emails that you found in the computer between Dr. Chastant and Ms. McClain?

Laurie: They had a few emails back and forth.

Daniels: And have you ever printed those emails up?

Laurie: I printed one of them, yes.

Daniels: Did you ever contact Ms. McClain by email?

Laurie: Yes, possibly twice, maybe just once.

Daniels: What did you tell her in your emails to her?

Laurie: I was angry and I told her to leave my husband alone and I called her some names, home wrecker, whore, those kinds of things.

Daniels: Let's talk a little bit about the Defined Benefits and Profit-Sharing plans of Dr. Chastant. You were an employee of the orthodontic clinic at some point in time, correct?

Laurie: Yes.

Daniels: And so, you were a beneficiary or at least you were a participant, I should say, in the Defined Benefit, Profit-Sharing plans?

Laurie: Yes.

Daniels: And as I appreciate it, you've cashed in and received your benefit from the plan?

Laurie: Yes.

Daniels: Was it at some point in time prior to Dr. Chastant's death, that he asked you to sign any documentation relinquishing any rights that you had as spouse to his interest in the plan?

Laurie: You asked me about that. He's never asked me to relinquish anything.

Daniels: Do you recall signing any documentation regarding the Defined Benefits and Profit-Sharing plans?

Laurie: In regards to my own, he told me to go to Edward Jones and sign some paperwork over there.

Daniels: And what about his interest in the plan, was it your understanding that he was cashing his interest in the plan, he was cashing in on his benefits?

Laurie: I had no understanding of that.

Daniels: Ms. Chastant, I have in front of me three pages, Page 10, 11, and 12 of Form 3. Look on Page 10. It's part of a document. It's Notice to Participant of Distribution Election, pages 10 and 12. There are two spaces of Page 10—one on page 10 and one on page 12, that appears to be your signature. I'm going to ask you if you can identify that as being your signature. Do you recall signing these documents on page 10 and 12?

Laurie: I did not sign on page 10. On page 10, that's Bobby writing my name right there and I don't see anything else. This is not my handwriting, none of this. And then on page 12, I signed this at home in the kitchen, but I did not fill any of this out right here, and I don't know who this notary is because it was---she wasn't in the kitchen with us that night.

Daniels: You said that you signed this document in your kitchen one night. Do you remember when that was?

Laurie: No, I don't recall the night, the date.

Daniels: Do you recall whether it was December 3rd?

Laurie: I don't recall the date.

Daniels: Is that your signature?

Laurie: Yes, that's my signature.

Daniels: And under your signature, where it says, "Name of spouse," is that your writing in print of your...

Laurie: No.

Daniels: You did not fill that out?

Laurie: No, I didn't.

Daniels: With regard to the notary, it looks like it's a Judith...

Laurie: It looks like Vaughn in print.

Daniels: Yeah, okay, Judith Vaughn. Do you know Judith Vaughn?

Laurie: No, I don't know her.

Daniels: Do you know whether she was present when you signed your name?

Laurie: No, she was not present.

Daniels: Did you have any discussions with Dr. Chastant with regard to his cashing in his benefits under the Defined Benefit and Profit-Sharing plans?

Laurie: He never told me he was going to cash it in. He told me he was unhappy with ARS and that he was going to move his retirement to a different company such as Edward Jones, but he never said, "I'm cashing it in."

Daniels: So, you didn't fill out anything other than sign your signature?

Laurie: Correct.

Daniels: And you didn't read it before your signed it?

Laurie: No, I didn't.

Daniels: And you don't know Judith Vaughn?

Laurie: No, I don't know her.

Daniels: Ms. Chastant, …do you recall speaking with Megan Chastant in the month before Dr. Chastant's death and you informed her that Dr. Chastant had informed you that he would be spending time with his new girlfriend in Texas and was specifically not planning to participate in Christmas with the Christmas activities of the family?

Laurie: That did not occur.

Daniels: Was it your understanding that you and Dr. Chastant were separate in property?

Laurie: Yes.

Daniels: And that pursuant to the matrimonial agreement, that if an item was purchased in one of your names, it was going to be that individual's possession?

Laurie: Yes.

Daniels: Have you ever hired a private investigator prior to Mr. Chastant's death?

Laurie: No.

Daniels: Has anyone ever provided you with pictures of Dr. Chastant with another woman?

Laurie: No.

Daniels: It was my understanding that there was a game, I'll call it a game camera. Do you know what that is?

Laurie. Yes.

Daniels: Did you and Dr. Chastant ever place or have placed a game camera or cameras out at the big barn property prior to his death?

Laurie: He placed one out there at some point when Keith Shorrette and Ed Perry were working out there.

Daniels: Whatever happened to that camera?

Laurie: I'm not sure what happened to it.

Daniels: Did you inform the sheriff's department about that camera following Dr. Chastant's death?

Laurie: Yes.

Daniels: And did you show them where the camera had been placed?

Laurie: I was not sure where he had placed it since he had removed it from the barn but I did tell them where it had been at one time.

Daniels: Do you know whether or not anyone has found that camera?

Laurie: No, I don't.

Daniels: To your knowledge, other than yourself and Dr. Chastant, who else knew that the camera was put in place?

Laurie: I don't think anybody else knew.

Daniels: Did Mr. Viera know?

Laurie: I don't know.

Daniels: Do you know whether or not Dr. Chastant had any conversations with Mr. Viera concerning the camera?

Laurie: I don't know.

Daniels: Did you have any conversations with Mr. Viera concerning the camera?

Laurie: No.

Daniels: Did you have any conversations with Natalie [Nayeli] concerning the camera?

Laurie: No.

Daniels: It's my understanding…Mr. Chastant's body was found December 13th, that night?

Laurie: That's what the police told me, yes.

Daniels: Did you go out to the property that night?

Laurie: No.

Were you told whether or not Dr. Chastant's body was wrapped in anything when they found him?

Laurie: No.

Daniels: Were you shown pictures of any bag? Plastic bag or otherwise that he may have been wrapped in?

Laurie: No.

Daniels: So, you don't know of anything, the condition the body was in when they found him?

Laurie: No, I don't.

Daniels: Have you been told by the sheriff's department or anyone else that Dr. Chastant's murder occurred at the barn or on the barn property?

Laurie: They told me that Ismael killed him at the barn.

Daniels: And as we sit here today, that's your understanding that this crime took place at the barn?

Laurie: That's my understanding.

Daniels: You don't have any information to indicate that it may have occurred somewhere else?

Laurie: No, I've always understood that it happened there.

Daniels: Have you ever been told by anyone that Mr. Viera has testified that you paid him to kill Dr. Chastant, other than Mr. Durio?

Laurie: No.

Daniels: Have you ever been told by anyone that Mr. Viera has testified that you, in fact, helped him move the body?

Laurie: No, I haven't

Daniels: You haven't been told that by anyone?

Laurie: No, I have not.

Daniels: And where are the locations of the other firearms, including the long guns, and by long guns, I mean shotguns and rifles that belonged to Dr. Chastant at the time of his death?

Laurie: I have no idea.

Daniels: Have you asked any of your relatives that were staying with you following Dr. Chastant's death whether they removed any of the firearms from the home?

Laurie: No, I haven't asked anyone.

Daniels: You are aware that I made claim that they---that the firearms were missing and that they be returned. You were made aware of that, weren't you?

Laurie: Yes, and I don't see what that has to do with me asking my family if they took them.

Daniels: Well, you were living in the home following Dr. Chastant's death, correct?

Laurie: Yes.

Daniels: And you don't know where those firearms are?

Laurie: No, I don't.

Daniels: So, you didn't bother to ask anybody from your family if they removed any?

Laurie: I wouldn't think that my family would have taken anything because my family wouldn't have just taken something out of the house. In addition, there are many things that disappeared from my bedroom, my closet, and upstairs on the day that the kids demanded to go through everything and remove whatever they felt like removing, when they came up with trash bags, big black trash bags, and took whatever they wanted while I was laying [sic] in bed sick.

Connections between
Laurie's Dad, Sheriff Ackal

William Futral is Laurie Chastant's father. He is a deputy sheriff in St. Landry Parish. Prior to that, he served for more than thirty years as a Louisiana State Trooper, having retired in July 2005. Both positions would have placed the two in close association, both in proximity and professionally, with Iberia Parish Sheriff Louis Ackal, also a retired State trooper.

Ackal was hired in 1966 as a trooper and assigned to Troop C where he worked as a road trooper. In 1970, he was transferred to State Police headquarters in Baton Rouge and worked narcotics cases. He spent a short time in executive security before being promoted to lieutenant in 1972 and reassigned to investigations at Region II in Lafayette.

He remained in Region II investigations until he was transferred to work as a shift supervisor at Troop I in Lafayette in 1976. By mid-1977, he was named the Troop Executive Officer where he remained until his promotion to Troop Commander by Colonel Bo Garrison in August 1980. Garrison transferred Ackal to Region II where he was the Region Executive Officer and supervised narcotics and detective operations.

Prior to 1983, the command of investigative operations was regionalized. There were three region majors and the majors oversaw patrol and investigative operations in their respective areas. A captain in each region would oversee both narcotics and detective sections. A reorganization in 1983 removed investigative operations from the three region majors and all investigations were centralized out of one headquarters command and the component was renamed Criminal Investigations Bureau (CIB). One captain would oversee statewide detective operations and one captain would oversee statewide narcotics operations. Ackal was named the captain over statewide narcotics operations.

He remained in that position until Wiley McCormick was named State Police Superintendent in 1984. He retired in July 1984 and in

January 1996, when Gov. Mike Foster took office, he was brought back as Executive Officer, an appointive, unclassified position. In June 1996, he was named as a confidential assistant, an unclassified political patronage position. He remained at that post until his second retirement in September 1998.

Futral, meanwhile, began his career with the State Police in Troop K in Opelousas in July 1974. He retired in 2005 at the rank of sergeant.

His supervisor wrote in his performance evaluation in 1995, "Sgt. Futral is dependable, cooperative and loyal. He uses his knowledge and experience to plan and organize shift responsibilities effectively. He has excellent decision-making skills."

Troop K was disbanded in 1988 and became part of Troop I but would have been in Region II during the time Ackal was Region Executive Officer from 1980 to 1983.

Ackal was elected Sheriff of Iberia Parish in 2007 and took office in 2008. William Futral began work as a deputy with the St. Landry Parish Sheriff's Office in July 2008, the same year that yet another retired State trooper, Bobby Guidroz, took office as sheriff of that parish.

With their State Police and their respective sheriffs' departments careers coinciding as they did, it's highly unlikely Ackal and Futral did not have at least a passing acquaintance during that time.

Futral was deposed on April 3, 2012. Attorney James Daniels began the questioning:

Daniels: Tell me a little bit, if you would please, what you thought of the marriage between your daughter and Dr. Chastant.

Futral: Well, at first, when they first got married, I thought that he was a little too old for her, but we became good friends and I got to where I really liked and admired him. And then I approved of it.

Daniels: Would you spend a lot of time at Dr. Chastant and Laurie's house after they got married?

Futral: Quite a bit, yes. We'd barbecue and have a swimming party and one thing or another or just cook whatever.

Daniels: Did Laurie ever discuss with you the fact that Dr. Chastant had had an affair with someone in 2009?

Futral: No.

Daniels: Did she discuss with you the fact that he was---she thought he was having an affair in December or November, December of 2010?

Futral: No.

Daniels: When did you find out about that?

Futral: Much later, after December 13th.

Daniels: Mr. Futral, if you could tell me the best that you can, Laurie's exact words to you when she called you the first time that morning to tell you that her husband was missing.

Futral: She called me. She said her husband, Bobby, was missing. He didn't go to the office and she didn't know where he was at.

Daniels: She was at home when she called you?

Futral: I believe so, yes.

Daniels: Was Laurie crying when she told you this on the first telephone call?

Futral: No, I don't think so, but she was just---it sounded like she was very concerned.

Daniels: So, what did you do after the initial telephone call?

Futral: I just waited until later on that afternoon and found out that they had not located him. And then I went over to meet her.

Daniels: Did you have a conversation with Sheriff Ackal that day?

Futral: We met with Sheriff Ackal. He met us in the---not in his office, but in the bottom of the sheriff's office, and I told him hello and shook hands with him. And at that time, Bobby's body hadn't been found. When I just said, "how you doing?" he recognized me. I'd seen him before, working before. He was a Troop Commander at Troop I. I didn't work for him, but I knew who he was.

Daniels: What did you do after it was announced that they had found Bobby's body? Did you stay at the sheriff's department? Did you go back home?

Futral: We stayed there for some time, then we went back home.

Daniels: Were the sheriff's deputies questioning Laurie?

Futral: They did question her, yes.

Daniels: Do you know an ex-trooper by the name of Fleming? Bob Fleming, I think his name is, Robert Fleming. (The individual's name was actually Richard Fleming, a detective with the Iberia Parish Sheriff's Department.)

Futral: Yes.

Daniels: Do you know whether or not he works for the Iberia Parish Sheriff's Department?

Futral: I believe he does.

Daniels: You were aware, were you not, that Dr. Chastant had several firearms in his home?

Futral: Yes.

Daniels: Did you make any attempt the day of the murder or the next day to gather those weapons so that Laurie wouldn't hurt herself or anyone else?

Futral: Yes, I did. I took them and brought them and put them in a gun safe.

Daniels: At your house?

Futral: Yeah.

Daniels: Are they still there?

Futral: No.

Daniels: Where are they?

Futral: I had a threat of a flood last year, so I took them and I locked them up in an unused jail cell at Palmetto Police Department.

Daniels: Mr. Futral, we have taken the position that the firearms are property of the estate, and we have been asking trying to find out where they were or what happened to them. And I would ask that you bring those firearms back and give them back to Mr. Durio so he can give them to---pass them on to the trustee for disposition. Will you agree to do that?

Futral: I'll discuss it with Mr. Durio.

Daniels: Did Mr. Durio know that you had these firearms locked in this jail cell?

Futral: No.

Daniels: Had you ever discussed that with him?

Futral: No.

Daniels: Is there some reason you will not return those firearms?

Futral: I don't know who they belong to.

Daniels: They don't belong to you, do they?

Futral: No.

Daniels: Does Laurie---does your daughter maintain that they belong to her?

Futral: I don't know. I'll ask her.

Daniels: Did you ever discus with her the fact that you had those firearms?

Futral: Quite some time ago. About a year, I think.

Daniels: Why did you remove the three shotguns and the two .22s?

Futral: I removed them because I wanted to keep them for safekeeping.

Daniels: And what do you mean by that, for safekeeping?

Futral: Well, just so that they would remain for whoever they wound up being for because there was some other things in that house that didn't stay where they should have been.

Daniels: Who made the decision for you to take the firearms?

Futral: I did.

Daniels: And did you do it with Laurie's blessing?

Futral: I believe she saw me do it and didn't object.

Daniels: Did you tell her that you were going to take them for safekeeping?

Futral: Yes.

Daniels: Did you assist your daughter, Laurie, in making the funeral arrangements?

Futral: No, I didn't assist her with that, but I was there with her when they were being made.

Daniels: Did you have any problems at any point in time with either Bradley or Paul Chastant? Any argument with either one of them?

Futral: Certainly not.

Daniels: Well, tell us what---anything else occur[red] that you recall at the funeral home.

Futral: You know, one thing I did find was a little unusual, I noticed that my daughter was crying. I was crying, but none of the Chastants were. I found that a little unusual.

Daniels: So, at the funeral itself, you're saying you thought it was odd that Laurie was crying and you were crying, but the Chastant family was not.

Futral: Yes, I thought that was unusual.

Daniels: You are aware that at some point in time, Ismael Viera confessed to the sheriff's department that he killed Dr. Chastant?

Futral: Yes.

Daniels: Were you made aware at some point in time that he told the sheriff's department that Laurie had paid him to kill Dr. Chastant?

Futral: Yes, my daughter told me that that was one of the stories that he had, yeah.

Daniels: When did she tell you that?

Futral: On more than one occasion after it happened. She told me that it was strange because every time he gave a statement, it was different.

Daniels: Do you recall when Laurie told you this?

Futral: No. No date and time. I can't give you that.

Daniels: Did you ever ask Laurie whether or not that was true?

Futral: No, I didn't need to ask her that. I know it's not.

Daniels: Did she tell you it was not true?

Futral: I didn't ask her. But she, in a way, she told me by her bereavement. Her crying, missing her husband, and I think she may have said, "They must be crazy to believe that."

Daniels: But do you recall her ever saying to you, "I did not pay Ismael to kill Bobby"? Did she ever make an affirmative statement, "I didn't do it"?

Futral: She said that he said that. And I didn't ask her whether that was true or not because, like I said, I know darn good and well it's not.

Daniels: Okay, so you never asked her?

Futral: I didn't question her about that. But I was told about it.

Daniels: Did Laurie tell you that she paid for the funeral?

Futral: I believe she did.

Daniels: Tell me why you believe that.

Futral: Because I believe she told me that she had paid for it.

Daniels: Can you recall that conversation you had with her, whether you---did you tell her you thought maybe the Chastants should have paid instead of her?

Futral: We talked about it, and I thought perhaps that the estate should have paid for it.

Daniels: And you told Laurie that?

Futral: Yes.

Daniels: Over the past year-and-a-half or so since December 13th, have you loaned Laurie any money?

Futral: Yes, approximately $36,000.

Daniels: Do you know what that was for?

Futral: Yes, living expenses; medical expenses, whatever normally expenses people would incur over a year's time.

Daniels: Have you ever had any conversations with Laurie about her using---ingesting drugs or narcotics?

Futral: No.

Tom Aswell

Paul Chastant's Acrimonious Deposition

If the depositions of Laurie and her father appeared to get somewhat testy at times, the hostility that had simmered below the surface between the Futrals and the Chastants burst like a festering boil when Paul Chastant was deposed a third time on December 29, 2014. His first and second depositions, back on January 13, 2012, and May 22, 2012, were given in connection with Laurie's lawsuit against Prudential Insurance.

Two-and-one-half years later, he would give another but this time in another lawsuit: Robert Chastant, Michele Chastant Stark and Megan Duval-Chastant Qualls—Dr. Chastant's children—v. Laurie Futral Chastant. A second son, William, was not a plaintiff in the suit.

In that first deposition, Paul Chastant's attorney, did most of the questioning but in the third and most contentious – Daniel Phillips, Durio's partner in the law firm representing Laurie, opened the questioning and Paul Chastant never attempted to conceal his contempt for Durio, Durio's associate, or his former sister-in-law, by now remarried to a music teacher at the University of Louisiana Lafayette.

Daniels opened the deposition with a few perfunctory questions to set the stage for what quickly became an acrimonious exchange between Paul Chastant and Laurie's attorney.

"In connection with the wrongful death suit filed by Robert Jr., Megan, and Michele, did you at any time inform them that you would represent them in connection with those claims?" Daniels asked.

"No, actually quite the contrary. They asked my advice on who to seek for attorneys. I referred them to you in this very office in your conference room. I told them I could not participate because I was precluded to do so. I did not have a right to do so."

Phillips immediately objected, saying that called for a legal opinion which Paul Chastant was not qualified to give. "It wasn't an opinion," Chastant shot back. "It was advice given to me."

Daniels then asked if the wrongful death lawsuit ever made any claim on assets of Dr. Chastant's estate, defined benefit or profit-sharing plans or any other matters over which Laurie had sued Paul Chastant as executor of Dr. Robert Chastant's estate.

"None whatsoever," Paul replied, adding that the children had no claim to the defined benefit plan.

Phillips's questioning began innocently enough as he lobbed routine questions at Paul Chastant about specifics of his brother's will and the Prudential and Lincoln National insurance policies. Even so, his questions were peppered with frequent objections by Daniels who either said relevant documents spoke for themselves or that Phillips's questions called for legal opinions.

Phillips: Would you agree that Lincoln National Life Insurance lawsuit named you as a defendant in this claim?

Chastant: I still don't see the relevance of this, but go ahead. We're talking about a wrongful death suit. This has already been closed. It's almost like harassment.

Phillips: Would you turn to Page 7? There's a paragraph labeled "B." It says, "As a result of the death of the insured," which is alleged to be Dr. Chastant, your brother, "and following the incontestability review period, certain death benefits became due and payable to Chastant," which I believe is how they refer to Laurie Ann Futral Chastant, as indicated in Paragraph 2 on Page 6 of this pleading. Back to Paragraph 8, "As the sole and primary beneficiary on the policy, in the event that Chastant is determined to be disqualified as a beneficiary within the meaning of Louisiana Revised Statute 22:901 to the estate of the insured." Would you agree that that's what it says?

Daniels: I'm going to object. First of all, this is a pleading filed by the insurance company and it's a statement that the insurance company made and what you're asking him to call for is a legal conclusion, and not only that, but based upon what somebody else has alleged.

Phillips: Do you recognize this document?

Chastant: Not fresh in my mind.

Phillips: If I told you that this was a copy of the answer which you filed to the counterclaim which was filed by Lincoln National that we just reviewed, would you have any reason to disbelieve it?

Chastant: I have no reason to disbelieve it.

Phillips: Lincoln National, and you agreed with me, they allege that if my client, Ms. Chastant at the time, would have been disqualified as the beneficiary of that policy, then the funds would pass to the estate, correct?

Chastant: Best of my understanding.

Phillips: You're admitting the allegations that the contents of the policy, the Lincoln policy, would have passed to the estate if Ms. Chastant would have been disqualified.

Chastant: I'll say I'm admitting to the fact that I understand that this document was produced in response to those questions, and I had legal counsel help me do so. So, I used his advice to make sure I was compliant with the law, so that's my admission.

Phillips: Now, was it your contention that Ms. Chastant or---Ms. Chastant at the time, my client...

Chastant: Futral, the name on the suit was Futral and we should use Futral. What is it now, Ingram?

Daniels: Yeah.

Phillips: Well, in the wrongful death suit, she's named as Laurie Futral Chastant.

Chastant: Whatever.

Phillips: Can we just call her Laurie?

Chastant: There you go, good for you.

Phillips: As trustee, did you have any understanding of where those proceeds would go if she were disqualified?

Chastant: Best of my knowledge, it would probably go to the other---the heirs. I think the kids were secondary beneficiaries.

Phillips: You never talked about it, you never discussed, you never thought about…

Chastant: With whom?

Phillips: With anybody at any time.

Chastant: I talked about a lot of things with my attorneys, and that was about it.

Phillips: I won't ask you about what you talked about with your attorney.

Chastant: If you're trying to allude that I had conversations with the kids, they were never engaged at this level. The kids never got involved with the handling of the trust or with the benefits at all. It was too sensitive a matter and I didn't bring it to any of my family, ever.

Phillips: In the federal suit in which you appeared as executor and as trustee of the plans, your contention was that Laurie should be disqualified as the beneficiary of these policies and the plans, correct?

Chastant: I didn't file a lawsuit. She filed a suit against us. I don't think I ever stated that she should be disqualified.

Phillips: I object to the response as non-responsive.

Daniels: He has a right to explain his answer.

Chastant: I was told by the sheriff's department on several occasions and asked to give them evidence so she could be pursued as the prime suspect. I'm sorry, I don't remember your question now.

Phillips: I asked you if you were contending that Laurie should be disqualified as a beneficiary of the policies and plans.

Chastant: I don't know if I contended that or not.

Phillips: But you did litigate the issue of whether she participated in causing the death of Dr. Chastant, correct?

Chastant: No, that was not part of the litigation. The litigation was solely financial. We were precluded from bringing any evidence which could have proved her being a part of the case. We were told that it could only be financial questions dealing with that case, and there was issues like---I guess I better not say some of her improprieties, but there was some improprieties that we had evidence on which we could not even bring that your partner prevented us from bringing by getting---petitioning the judge, that we could have shown her true nature that we found out through the sheriff's department. So, I mean the bottom line is I don't know how to answer that. All I know is we could only bring in financial issues.

Phillips: Do you recall in the federal suit whether you submitted claims that Laurie should be disqualified as a beneficiary of the plan?

Chastant: I don't remember what we claimed. That's three-and-a-half years ago. He died four years ago.

Phillips: Well, if I told you that you made those claims, would you disagree?

Chastant: It would depend on the substance. I'd have to know exactly what I said and to what question I responded.

Phillips: So, you're saying you don't understand the question?

Chastant: No, I'm not saying I don't understand the question. What I'm saying is the question could be leading and I want to make sure that the answer that I give is specific to the question I'm being asked in total, the individual question, and your question is very voluminous. I want to know a very specific question.

Phillips: At trial, in the prior federal matter, did you claim that Laurie participated in causing Dr. Chastant's death?

Chastant: If I said anything, I said that I was told that she participated in the death by the sheriff, that he felt that she did, and he told me on several occasions with his chief deputy and the lady in charge of the case.

Phillips: I'm not asking you to tell me what you testified to at trial, I'm asking you to tell me what claims you were making at the trial, what claims you were litigating, either as a…

Chastant: I wasn't litigating, they were litigating me. I was the defendant and I was answering the questions that were posed to me at the time.

Phillips: But as the defense, didn't you claim that she participated in causing Dr. Chastant's death?

Chastant: I don't remember what I exactly claimed. I really don't. I mean, it's been a lot of things that I've dealt with in the last four years closing out this estate.

Phillips: So, you have no recollection at all?

Chastant: I have some recollection, but the answer to the question is ask me a specific question I can say "yes" or "no" to. I'm not going to elaborate.

Phillips: Well, if I told you that you did make that claim, would you disagree with me?

Chastant: I wouldn't disagree with it, no. If you told me, it would probably be based on fact. I could have only claimed that it was the best of my knowledge or it was my assumption based on information as provided to me by the sheriff. I could never claim, and I still can't claim that I know beyond a shadow of a doubt that she participated. All I do know is that the man that did kill my brother, and testified to killing my brother, also told us---told the sheriff and testified that she participated in the murder. And that's what I know. Do I know it's factual or not? No, I do not. I don't think anybody does but the good Lord. She'll have to deal with that in the future.

Phillips: Do you believe that she participated in causing Dr. Chastant's death?

Daniels: Objection.

Chastant: Objection, you're asking opinion.

Phillips: I don't think you can object.

Daniels: Well, I'm objecting. I think I can object.

Chastant: My answer is, I'm not going to reply. That's leading.

Daniels: No, it calls for an opinion.

Chastant: I've already stated my opinion. I've already stated the fact that I believe that she was brought into this trial by testimony of the murderer, the guy that confessed to the murder, and he said that she was part of the murder, and I was subsequently told that she was a prime suspect and asked to participate and help by the sheriff's department, which I did.

Daniels: Okay, that's good enough.

Phillips: Do you recall what the outcome was of the prior federal matter?

Chastant: It was settled on her behalf. We paid her. From what I understand, it was released to her. To the best of my knowledge, she's got the money. I have no idea what happened. It was released to her. The judge made a ruling in her behalf.

Phillips: Has a court ruled that the estate is insolvent?

Daniels: Let me object. I don't know that a court ever rules that an estate is insolvent.

Chastant: My answer is the last I heard was it was in abeyance because of a claim made by Mr.---his partner, and that's all I know at this stage. But I do know there's been an abeyance, put in abeyance, because of the claim made by your partner, or your boss, Buzz Durio.

Phillips: Did you file an accounting...of the assets of the estate...and liabilities, as well?

Chastant: Yes, we did.

Phillips: Are you claiming that the estate is insolvent based on the results of that accounting?

Chastant: The estate is insolvent on its own right. The accounting just verifies it, or documents it.

Phillips: Why do you believe the estate is insolvent?

Chastant: Because it has no money to pay the outstanding debtors, creditors, whatever.

Phillips: So, you contend that the estate's liability is greater than its assets?

Chastant: There you go. That's a good term for it. Yeah.

Phillips: So, I guess to summarize, you're contending that the wrongful death and survivor claims are for Dr. Chastant's children to assert, not for the estate?

Chastant: No, sir.

Daniels: And it's by law, counsel. You know that.

Phillips: Now, since this prior federal matter concluded, are you aware of any other evidence that's been discovered that might suggest that Laurie had anything to do with causing Dr. Chastant's death?

Chastant: I'm not going to answer that. I'm not going to answer that---that's not even a fair question. I'm not going to answer that.

Phillips: Well, I don't think you have the right to tell me what you're not going to answer.

Chastant: I'm not going to answer.

Phillips: I need an answer unless your counsel...

Chastant: I don't know, I don't know. That's the perfect answer.

Phillips: Has there been any evidence that you know of that makes you think or believe that Laurie caused her husband's death that has come up since the end of…

Chastant: I don't know.

Phillips: That's a "yes" or "no" question.

Chastant: No, no. Hey, let me tell you something. You're not going to intimidate me to answer the question and I'm not going to answer the question. I answered it legally. I do not know.

Phillips: I object to the response.…

Chastant: Good

Phillips: …as not responsive.

Daniels: All right.

Phillips: Let me ask it again.

Daniels: You're not going to ask it again. You have your objection. He's answered the question.

Phillips: "I don't know" is not an acceptable answer to that question. It's either "yes" or "no." Either there is evidence that makes you think that or there's not.

Chastant: There are a lot of questions that y'all asked are unacceptable. And a lot of questions that your partner asked are unacceptable. Y'all try to infer that I had a vendetta against Laurie since day one. I never did until I was told by the fricking sheriff and the testimony of the damn guy that killed my brother, the murderer of my brother that bludgeoned him to death, did I feel any objection to the woman, and I've tried to be as reasonable as possible. You guys are the ones that bring up the crap. My answer is I don't know. I'll answer it as many times you want, keep this poor lady here as long as you want. The answer is going to be the same, because if you know one thing about me, I will not back down. Bottom line is the answer is I don't know

Daniels: You're not going to ask the same question again because that's going to be his answer. If you don't like his answer, then bring him in front of the judge and let the judge say he's got to answer it different, but his answer is he doesn't know. That's a fair answer.

Chastant: I don't know what the sheriff's department are doing, I don't know what the DA is doing. I don't know. Are you going to ask me if the case is still open? I know that. I'll answer you, yes.

Phillips: Which case?

Chastant: The lawsuit or the case against who murdered my brother. Take that to your bank.

Phillips: What's the basis of your knowledge for that?

Chastant: I don't know. I just told you what I told you.

Phillips: But you told me that it was open and I asked you why you think that and you said you don't know.

Chastant: I might have given you an opinion. Ask a specific question.

Phillips: If you're going to tell me something, I think I'm entitled to know why you think that.

Chastant: I don't have to expound upon anything.

Phillips: I think you do.

Chastant: Think what you want.

Phillips: We'll have to file a motion to compel and get you to come down here from Dallas to appear before the judge. It's a simple question, isn't it?

Daniels: What is the question?

Phillips: If you could just answer, we would probably all be out of here by now, but the question was---I'm not even sure I remember it.

Daniels: Yeah, that's the problem. You're asking him to answer a question you don't even know what it is.

Phillips: Mr. Chastant, you testified that the case was still open and ongoing. I asked what case that was and I believe you said it was the case involving your brother's death, correct?

Chastant: Correct.

Phillips: Would that be the criminal case?

Chastant: I don't know what it is. I don't know the civil case, criminal case. I don't know which one would be---where it would be filed. I don't know all that stuff. I'm an architect. I was told the case remains open by the DA

Phillips: When did he tell you that?

Chastant: A long time ago.

Phillips: Was it before or after the federal suit was finished?

Chastant: Sometime after.

Phillips: In the federal suit, you presented a lot of evidence that was an attempt to try to show that Laurie participated in causing Dr. Chastant's death, correct?

Chastant: The evidence I sent defended myself, presented defending myself because I was the defendant. I was not pursuing Laurie in that case. I was defending the estate.

Phillips: What was your defense in that suit?

Chastant: You got a copy of it, read it.

Phillips: This is not about what I know, it's what you know.

Chastant: I don't know how to respond. It's not a question. You want me to sit here and elaborate? Ask me a question and I'll answer it.

Phillips: I did ask you.

Chastant: No, you asked me what was I defending. I was defending the estate.

Phillips: And then I asked you what was the basis of your defense.

Chastant: That I was sued by Laurie and we were defending the estate I was obligated. I was legally obligated as trustee and executor of the estate to file the claim to support the estate because there was thought given to me by the sheriff's department and the DA that she could be a part of the murder, so legally and responsibly and that's, I think, the decision of Judge Haik that I had to represent the interest of the estate, period. Does that answer your question?

Phillips: Not exactly.

Chastant: Well, you're not going to get what you want because you always ask questions without an end.

Phillips: I'm going to object to that as argumentative.

Chastant: I'm sure you can.

Phillips: The question was a simple question. What was the basis of your defense? You said you were defending the trust.

Chastant: I answered the question.

Phillips: How did you do that?

Daniels: He just answered it. Asked and answered.

Phillips: I don't think he did. I reserve the right to file a motion to compel on that question.

Daniels: All right, you can reserve any right you want. Next question. Half-hour ago was one more, so let's go.

Phillips: Well, let me finish my objection or at least my statement that I'm going to reserve the rights to file a motion to compel an answer to this question.

Chastant: Y'all are the most vindictive people I've ever met. You're going to carry this case on forever and ever and ever. Even if we offer---try to make an adjustment with you guys to settle everything and close it out, not this one, because I'm not involved with one that we're being---you're leading into other cases which really aren't germane, but the reality is, y'all are going to pursue it as long as you can.

Phillips: Mr. Chastant, I didn't solicit that statement.

Chastant: I know you didn't solicit that statement. I've got a right to say what I want. It's a fact. I sure hope the judge reads it. It ain't us that's holding that shit up. I'd love to go on with my life.

Phillips: I'm not going to sit here and argue with you here.

Chastant: You didn't lose your brother, either. You didn't have your brother bludgeoned either, did you? You didn't have a brother that you loved killed, okay? You ain't got a clue how that feels.

Phillips: Mr. Chastant, I'm not trying to harass you. I'm not trying to bring up any type of emotions. I'm just here to ask some questions.

Chastant: Okay, ask your questions. Ask specific questions and I'll respond to them.

Phillips: Mr. Chastant, if you'd let me finish the questions...

Chastant: That wasn't a question. That was a statement.

Phillips: I think that's all I have.

That was the end of a contentious exchange.

Tom Aswell

Viera: "I Feel Like You're Interrogating Me"

Ismael Viera Tovar gave two depositions thirteen days apart, on March 29 and April 11, 2012. Both sessions were video depositions, with attorneys in a New Iberia office and Ismael sitting somewhere in the Louisiana State Penitentiary at Angola. He had initially refused to give a deposition because of the presence of Laurie Chastant. For whatever reason, he obviously felt intimidated by her immediacy. Because Ismael refused to testify if Laurie Chastant was present, attorneys were under a court order not to disclose to him her attendance off-camera in the room in New Iberia at the subsequent sessions.

By this time, he had dismissed his public defender, Nancy Dunning and had no legal counsel present at the deposition.

His testimony revealed how he felt threatened by Laurie Chastant when he discussed what he perceived as an implied threat to his family.

The presence of an interpreter notwithstanding, the language barrier and the logistics of participants being in two separate locations, made both depositions cumbersome. In the interest of brevity, repeated failures in understanding and the repetition of questions have been deleted in transcribing his testimony.

Attorney Daniels began the questioning by asking Ismael when Laurie Chastant offered him money to kill her husband.

Ismael: It was on a Monday. It was Monday of the week.

Daniels: Do you remember what month?

Ismael: In November.

Daniels: How much money did she offer you?

Ismael: She gave me $800 and then $200.

Daniels: And did you tell Ms. Chastant that you agreed to kill Dr. Chastant?

Ismael: No, I told her I did not want to do it.

Daniels: Did you keep the money?

Ismael: Yes.

Daniels: Did you have any other conversations with Ms. Chastant?

Ismael: She said if I didn't do it, she would hurt me, my girlfriend and the child.

Daniels: Did you tell Ms. Chastant that you would kill her husband?

Ismael: No.

Daniels: Did Ms. Chastant ask for the money back?

Ismael: No.

Daniels: Tell us, please, what happened on December 13th.

Ismael: There was an argument between the doctor and I [sic]. He hit me twice and that's when I hit him. Then the wife came and then she told me to put him in the bags.

Daniels: What bags are you talking about, Mr. Viera?

Ismael: Black plastic bags.

Daniels: Where did the bags come from?

Ismael: From the barn. They were used to put trash in.

Daniels: Was Ms. Chastant supposed to come to the barn that day?

Ismael: No.

Daniels: What did you do with the bags?

Ismael: I put the body of the man in the bag.

Daniels: Did Laurie Chastant assist you?

Ismael: Yes.

Durio: I have to voice an objection to this question because it's leading.

Daniels: Tell me, Mr. Viera, what Laurie Chastant did at the barn that day.

Ismael: She helped me to put his body in the small vehicle. She told me to take the pickup truck to Walmart.

Daniels: Why were you to bring the pickup truck to Walmart?

Ismael: I do not know.

Daniels: Mr. Viera, when Laurie Chastant arrived at the barn, had you already killed Dr. Chastant?

Ismael: Yes.

Daniels: What did Laurie Chastant do at the barn after she arrived?

Ismael: I took the car to the house and she brought me back so that I would get the pickup.

Daniels: Did Laurie Chastant do anything else while she was on the property?

Ismael: She covered blood with soil.

Daniels: Did Laurie Chastant ask you why you killed Dr. Chastant?

Ismael: No.

Daniels: Who did you call on the phone?

Ismael: The doctor.

Daniels: What did you tell him?

Ismael: That I was bringing the things he told me to put in the barn.

Daniels: Did you ask Dr. Chastant to come to the barn?

Ismael: Yes.

Daniels: Mr. Viera, did you drive yourself to the barn or did someone go with you?

Ismael: I went by myself.

Daniels: How did Dr. Chastant get to the barn?

Ismael: He was ahead of me.

Daniels: Was anyone else in your vehicle?

Ismael: No.

Daniels: Did you leave the Chastant house at the same time?

Ismael: Yes.

Daniels: And where was Laurie Chastant when you left the Chastant house?

Ismael: She was out of the house.

Daniels: Did you see Ms. Chastant?

Ismael: I saw her when she was outside.

Daniels: Mr. Viera, why did you drive Dr. Chastant's truck to Walmart?

Ismael: Because the lady asked me to.

Daniels: What lady?

Ismael: His wife.

Daniels: Dr. Chastant's wife?

Ismael: Yes.

Daniels completed his first round of questioning and Durio took over at this point (referring alternately to Laurie as "Ms." or "Mrs." Chastant).

Durio: When you pled guilty, you said you killed the doctor because you were angry?

Ismael: Yes.

Durio: Was that true?

Ismael: Yes.

Durio: When you went to the barn that morning, did you plan to kill the doctor?

Ismael: No.

Durio: You killed him only because of the argument and the fact that you were angry?

Ismael: Yes, because we argued and because I was pressured.

Durio: What pressure are you referring to?

Ismael: That the lady would hurt me, the child, and my girlfriend.

Durio: After you pled guilty, Mr. Viera, you were sentenced to life in prison, is that correct?

Ismael: Yes.

Durio: And you were sentenced to prison to hard labor, correct?

Ismael: Yes.

Durio: What can be done to you worse than that if you lie?

Daniels: I'm going to object to the question.

Durio: If you are lying today, what can be done about it?

Daniels: Objection.

Ismael: Why should I be lying?

Durio: You said before that you feared that Mrs. Chastant would hurt you or your girlfriend or the child. Do you still fear that?

Ismael: No.

Durio: Where is Nayeli?

Ismael: I do not know.

Durio: Where is Donovan [Ismael's son]?

Ismael: I do not know.

Durio: Was Nayeli pregnant at the time that you killed Dr. Chastant?

Ismael: That's what she told me.

Durio: When did you stop being scared that Mrs. Chastant would do something to Nayeli and Donovan?

Ismael: Since I became a Christian. I have Christ now.

Durio: Were you a Christian when you killed Dr. Chastant?

Ismael: No, but I did attend a Christian church.

Durio: Was Dr. Chastant a Christian when you killed him?

Ismael: I do not know what religion he belonged to.

Durio: What about Laurie Chastant? Was she a Christian when you killed her husband?

Ismael: I do not know.

Durio: Have you ever committed a crime before you killed Dr. Chastant?

Ismael: No.

Durio: How did you get into the United States?

Ismael: Crossing.

Durio: Crossing the border?

Ismael: Yes.

Durio: How did you cross the border?

Ismael: Walking.

Durio: Did you go through the U.S. Customs gate?

Ismael: No.

Durio: Didn't you enter the United States illegally?

Ismael: Illegally, yes.

Durio: Wasn't that a crime? Didn't you commit a crime by remaining in the United States illegally?

Ismael: I do not understand.

Durio: Do you remember a deposition Mr. Daniels and I tried to take at Angola? (Durio was mistaken about the location; it was at the Iberia Parish jail.)

Ismael: Yes.

Durio: Do you remember refusing to testify in that deposition?

Ismael: Yes.

Durio: Why did you refuse to testify in that deposition?

Ismael: Because the lady was there. Because I do not want to see her.

Durio: Isn't it true that you cannot say the lies that you've said today while she's looking at you?

Daniels: Objection.

Ismael: Lies?

Durio: Right, the lies that you told today. Can you say them in front of her?

Daniels: Objection.

Ismael: No, what I'm saying is that I do not want to see her.

Durio: Explain why you can't say these things in front of her.

Daniels: Objection.

Ismael: Because I do not want to see her.

Durio: What can be done to you to make you say those things in front of her?

Ismael: Nothing.

Durio: Isn't that why you refused to testify at the earlier deposition.

Ismael: Yes.

Durio: Okay, I'm not sure I understand the question.

Daniels: You asked it.

Durio: Would you testify to what you've said today in a courtroom where Laurie was present?

Ismael: If you're going to lower my sentence, yes.

Durio: Do you remember telling the police in New Iberia that Laurie paid you to kill Dr. Chastant?

Ismael: Yes.

Durio: Has anyone ever suggested to you that if you testified about Mrs. Chastant, your sentence would be lowered?

Ismael: No.

Durio: What makes you think by testifying that Ms. Chastant paid you to kill Dr. Chastant, you might have your sentence lowered?

Daniels: Objection.

Ismael: I don't know, that's the truth.

Durio: Was Nayeli there when Laurie supposedly paid you to kill Dr. Chastant?

Daniels: Objection.

Ismael: No.

Durio: How did you understand Laurie?

Ismael: Because I understand some English.

Durio: What words did she use when she told you she wanted you to kill her husband?

Ismael: She told me she would give me money if I would kill him.

Durio: What words did she use?

Ismael: You mean you want to hear it in English?

Durio: Yes.

Ismael (in English): I am going to give you this money for kill him.

Durio: Was that before or after you killed him?

Ismael: Before.

Durio: How did you know who Laurie wanted you to kill? What did she call him?

Ismael: My husband.

Durio: And what did you say to her?

Ismael: That I didn't want to.

Durio: She gave you the money anyway?

Ismael: Yes.

Durio: And what did she say after you told her you did not want to?

Ismael: That she would hurt me, my girlfriend and the child.

Durio: Did she say how?

Ismael: No.

Durio: What words did she use?

Ismael: That she was going to hurt me.

Durio: Can you say them in English.

Ismael: I'm going to hurt you, you and your son.

Durio: Did he say it in Spanish or English? Did this man say it in Spanish or English? Are you translating or are you repeating?

Interpreter: Repeating what he's saying.

Durio: I'm going to ask my question again. What words did she use?

Ismael: "I'm going to hurt you, your little boy, and your girlfriend."

Ismael (to interpreter): Excuse me, ma'am. Are you going to keep questioning me or is this going to be for the civil that I was told?

Daniels: It's for the civil.

Durio: It is for the civil and I am going to keep questioning you. Do you understand?

Ismael: I do understand.

Durio: What car did you drive?

Ismael: A red one.

Durio: A red Toyota?

Ismael: Yes.

Durio: Did you drive the Isuzu?

Ismael: Yes.

Durio: The only time you ever drove the doctor's truck was the day you took it to Walmart?

Ismael: Yes.

Durio: Did Nayeli ever drive the doctor's truck?

Ismael: No.

Durio: Did she ever drive the red Toyota?

Ismael: No.

Durio: Did she ever drive the Isuzu truck?

Ismael: No.

Durio: Why did you tell the police that Nayeli drove the Isuzu truck?

Ismael: I don't know, because I don't know what I was thinking.

Durio: Do you remember speaking with a lady, a Spanish-speaking lady by the name of Sergeant Garcia at Iberia Parish Sheriff's Office?

Ismael: I believe so.

Durio: Didn't Sergeant Garcia ask you if you knew where the doctor was?

From that point forward, Ismael suddenly became uncooperative and invoked "I do not remember" or "I don't know" no fewer than thirty-eight times before he again asked the interpreter if the questions were going to continue.

Told that the questions would continue, he replied, "But I feel like you're interrogating me."

Durio: I am.

Ismael: They're asking me about the lady because it's about her money.

Durio: Is that why you're testifying?

Ismael: In other words, this is for some kind of insurance, about the life insurance of the doctor.

Durio: So, what?

Ismael: I have nothing to do with her money.

Durio: What do you know about the money?

Ismael: What I don't understand is what do I have to do about the money?

Durio: Do you want Mrs. Chastant to get the money?

Daniels: Objection, irrelevant.

Ismael: I have nothing to do with her stuff, the lady's stuff.

Durio: Do you want anybody else to get the money?

Daniels: Objection, irrelevant.

Ismael: No, I don't know.

Durio: If you testify the way you have, is it more likely or not that Mrs. Chastant will get the money?

Daniels: Objection, calls for speculation, legal conclusion.

Ismael: I am stressed out. I am tired.

Durio: Do you remember telling Trooper Garcia that you asked your girlfriend, Nayeli, to drive you back to the barn in the Isuzu because your red car's battery had died?

Ismael: I don't know. How much longer is this going to take?

Durio: Do you understand that if you do not allow me to continue my questions, then what you have said may not be admissible in any court? Do you understand that?

Ismael: Yes, but you're repeating and you're repeating the same thing.

Durio: Well, Mr. Daniels is here and if you feel like I am harassing you in any way, I am sure Mr. Daniels will ask the court to stop me, but I do have a right to finish my questions and the judge has said that if you do not allow me to question you and answer my questions…then this deposition…may not be admissible. I'm not suggesting I can force you to testify or that there is any reason for you to testify one way or another, but I am not finished [with] my questions, so I would like to continue.

Ismael: It's fine.

But apparently it was not fine. Under Durio's continued barrage of questions, Viera reverted to his responses of "I don't remember" or "I don't know" another twenty-seven times before saying on four separate occasions, "I don't want to talk anymore."

Durio and Daniels agreed that the deposition should be suspended but not before Durio told Ismael, "That does not mean I am giving up my right to ask questions and Mr. Daniels is not giving up his right to ask questions after me. We are simply suspending the deposition so that we can have time to speak with the judge and we may come back to finish the deposition. Do you understand?

"I understand," Ismael replied, "but I don't want to talk anymore."

With that, the deposition, which began at 9:57 a.m. was suspended at 2:35 p.m., after more than four-and-one-half hours.

It was resumed at 2:20 p.m. on April 11 and would quickly become equally frustrating with Ismael again claiming to not remember or not know answers to questions an additional thirty-one times.

Among Durio's questions that elicited claims of memory lapses were:

- You put your hand on Dr. Chastant's chest to feel for a heartbeat?

- You remember Trooper Garcia asking you about the doctor's cell phone?

- Don't you remember telling him that you had thrown the cell phone out of the window while you were driving his truck to the Walmart?

- Do you remember Trooper Garcia telling you that they had found the doctor's cell phone in your bathroom?

- And that early morning of the 14th, you didn't tell them anything about Laurie Chastant?

- Do you remember telling Trooper Garcia that you moved Dr. Chastant's body by yourself?

- Do you remember telling Trooper Garcia that you drove your red Toyota back to your house?

- Didn't you tell Trooper Garcia that you asked your girlfriend, Nayeli, to drive you back to the barn in the Isuzu truck?

- Didn't you tell Trooper Garcia that you had told Nayeli that you had hit the doctor?

- Didn't you tell Trooper Garcia that Nayeli dropped you at the roadway, that you walked back to the barn, and took Dr. Chastant's truck to Walmart?

- After you talked to Nayeli at the police station, the police questioned you again. Do you remember telling them then that Nayeli did not help you?

- Is it true you then told them you drove your red car back to the house, picked up the Suzuki truck yourself, drove back to the barn, used the truck to dispose of the doctor's body?

- Do you remember ever telling them that you walked back from the house to the barn to get the doctor's truck?

- Do you remember telling one of the policemen that you had more to say?

- Do you remember him (Deputy Toby Hebert) recording his conversation with you?

- Do you remember telling him then, for the first time, that Laurie paid you $1,000 to kill her husband?

- Do you remember when Trooper Garcia came back on the 15th and interviewed you again?

- Do you remember telling Trooper Garcia for the first time on the 15th that Laurie helped you dispose of Dr. Chastant's body?

- Didn't you tell him that Laurie had talked to you about killing Dr. Chastant on December 7th?

- Why did you tell the police that you had taken the Isuzu truck?

- You've always said you killed him because you were angry? Isn't that the only thing in all of your stories that's actually true?

- What did you tell (Trooper Garcia) about the money that Nayeli wired to Mexico on the morning of December 13th?

- About what time did you get to the Walmart with Dr. Chastant's truck?

- Didn't you tell Trooper Garcia that you had gotten there about 9 o'clock?

- Did the policeman tell you that they have a film of you at the Walmart getting out of Dr. Chastant's truck at 9:08 in the morning?

- What was Laurie Chastant's demeanor when she arrived at the barn and saw that her husband was dead?

- Was she crying?

- You told Mr. Daniels that no one had promised you anything, is that correct?

- Isn't it true that you told us before on the 29th, that Mr. Russell Ancelet had come to the prison and talked to you about testifying and mentioned the possibility that your sentence would be lowered? (Ancelet was a private detective retained by Daniels on behalf of the Robert Chastant estate.)

Ismael was not evasive on all questions, however. On several, he appeared to be earnestly trying to answer and those answers were consistent with earlier statements he had made to authorities. And for the first time, he mentioned that Dr. Chastant had attempted to hit him once before.

> Durio: If Laurie talked to you in November and asked you to kill her husband, why did you wait until December 13th?

> Ismael: Because I wasn't going to kill him. We had an argument.

> Durio: Didn't you tell me that Laurie told you that she would hurt you and your wife and your child?

> Ismael: That's right.

> Durio: Did you believe her?

> Ismael: I did, but I wasn't going to do it.

> Durio: If you were scared, she was going to hurt your child or your girl or you, why did you wait so long?

> Ismael: Because I was going to leave them.

> Durio: And why didn't you leave?

> Ismael: I needed some money to leave.

> Durio: Didn't you have $2,000, or actually $2,200?

> Ismael: No.

> Durio: Didn't the police find that in your coat pocket?

> Ismael: No [the $2,200 was found in Dr. Chastant's coat pocket, not Ismael's].

Durio: Where did you leave your red Toyota the day of the murder?

Ismael: At the house.

Durio: Why did you leave it at the house?

Ismael: Because the battery was dead.

Durio: How did you get back to the barn after you left your red car at the house?

Ismael: The lady took me back.

Durio: Laurie Chastant took you back? In her truck?

Ismael: Yes.

Durio: Do you remember telling Trooper Garcia that you refused $800 that Laurie had offered you?

Ismael: Yes.

Durio: Do you remember telling him then that she offered you another $200?

Ismael: Yes.

Durio: Did you know that he was going to hit you on the 13th?

Ismael: No, but a week prior to that he tried to hit me…Maybe that's why he hit me on that day.

Durio: Did Laurie know that Dr. Chastant had struck you?

Ismael: No.

Durio: Hadn't you already told Laurie about that---hadn't Laurie already asked you to kill him?

Ismael: Yes.

Durio: Are you aware---do you understand that Mrs. Chastant was at a doctor's office from before 8 o'clock until about 9:30 while you were killing Dr. Chastant?

Ismael: If that's what she says.

Durio: Are you a professional killer?

Ismael: I've never killed.

Durio: Why would Laurie approach you to kill her husband?

Daniels: Objection.

Ismael: Well, I'm Mexican and if she should have asked someone else, they're not going to do it.

Durio: You think Laurie thought you would kill her husband because you're Mexican?

Daniels: Objection.

Ismael: Yes.

Durio: Why would Laurie pay you in advance to kill her husband?

Daniels: Objection.

Ismael: I don't know.

Durio: Why would you agree to kill someone for only $1,000?

Ismael: I didn't agree.

Durio: Why would Laurie offer you only $1,000 and think you would kill her husband?

Ismael: I don't know.

Durio: If Laurie was smart enough to pay you to kill her husband, why would she be dumb enough to be stuck with you disposing of the body?

Daniels: Objection.

Ismael: So that he would not be seen.

Durio: Isn't this story that you're telling about Laurie just a cover for Nayeli?

Ismael: If that's what you think.

Durio: Do you realize Nayeli is now in Mexico?

Ismael: I don't know.

Durio: You say Laurie drove up to the barn on her own on December 13th, is that correct?

Ismael: Yes.

Durio: And you didn't know she was coming?

Ismael: No.

Durio: And it was right after you had killed Dr. Chastant?

Ismael: Yes.

Durio: And she told you to get plastic bags?

Ismael: Yes.

Durio: And she helped you put him in the back of the Isuzu truck?

Ismael: Yes.

Durio: How had the truck gotten to the barn?

Ismael: She brought it.

Durio: She left her truck at the house?

Ismael: She went to get the car.

Durio: Went to get the truck? The Isuzu?

Ismael: Yes.

Durio: So, she left her truck at the house?

Ismael: Yes.

Durio: She went back to the house and got the Isuzu truck after you had brought your car back?

Ismael: I went to leave the car and she was going in the Isuzu, and then she brought me back.

Durio: So, you drove the red car from the barn to the house?

Ismael: Yes.

Durio: And she drove her truck from the barn to the house, correct?

Ismael: The small car, the Isuzu.

Durio: Did Laurie drive her truck from the barn to the house?

Ismael: She went to get the Isuzu.

Durio: And she drove the Isuzu back?

Ismael: Yes.

Durio: How did you get back from the house to the barn?

Ismael: She brought me in the pickup.

Durio: How did your red car get back to the house?

Ismael: I brought it there.

Durio: How did you get back to the barn from the house?

Ismael: She brought me.

Durio: In the Isuzu truck?

Ismael: The pickup.

Durio: Her pickup?

Ismael: Yes.

Durio: Isn't it true that you couldn't get the Isuzu and the red car back to the house---you couldn't get both of them back to the house without somebody helping, and isn't it true that if you drove Dr. Chastant's truck to the Walmart, you would have had to leave one of the vehicles at the barn?

Daniels: Objection.

Ismael: No, because you do not understand me.

Durio: If you drove Dr. Chastant's truck to the Walmart immediately after you and Laurie disposed of the body, how did your red car get back to the house?

Daniels: Objection.

Ismael: Because I brought it.

Durio: And who brought the Isuzu truck to the barn? Wasn't it you and Nayeli?

Ismael: No, it was me, it was the lady.

At that point, Durio had used up his allotted one hour of questioning and Daniels again took over the questioning for the duration of the deposition:
Daniels: The money that you told us Laurie Chastant paid to you, in what denominations was the money?

Ismael: A hundred.

Daniels: Is there any reason for you to lie about Laurie Chastant's participation in her husband's death?

Durio: Objection to leading.

Ismael: No, there's not a reason.

It represented an anti-climatic ending to hours of questioning Viera.

Tom Aswell

Attorney-Client Privilege Waived

Nancy Dunning, Viera's legal counsel, was a part-time attorney with the Sixteenth Judicial District, Public Defender's Office. She also had her own private practice in which she primarily did succession and some community property work though she is now semi-retired. She had been working for the Public Defender's Office, handling rape and homicide cases for about a year when Ismael became her client the day following Dr. Chastant's murder. Her qualifications, however, predated that by fifteen years, when she was certified by the State Board in 1995 to handle capital cases.

She initially refused to give her deposition because of the attorney-client privilege but when Ismael waived that privilege, she was deposed on May 8, 2013. Attorney Daniels opened the questioning.

She began by explaining that Ismael's last name was Viera Tovar. "He was always Ismael Viera when I was representing him and that's because in Spanish-speaking countries, the individual, the child, takes both the mother's maiden name and the father's surname and they go by the mother's maiden name. So Viera would be his mother's maiden name. Tovar would be his father's name. And so even when he was testifying, he gave his name as Viera." (Author's note: Dunning had this reversed. Viera, his father's surname, comes first.)

Dunning said she was assigned his case on December 14th, immediately after he was arrested on one count of second-degree murder of Dr. Chastant. "The first thing that I did is---at the time, we had one of our secretary/assistants working for us named Rosie Mitchell who was fluent in Spanish. I asked her to translate a letter that I had composed to send to Mr. Viera indicating to him that I would be representing him as soon as the [public defender's] office reopens. That would have been in reference to the Christmas holidays. For some reason, the PDO takes two weeks off at Christmas and New Year's and I was afraid I was going to have trouble getting him an interpreter in the interim."

She said her first meeting with Ismael was on January 4, 2011 and that she had advised him in her letter not to speak to law enforcement officials. But by then, he had already called officers back to tell them that Laurie Chastant had paid him to kill her husband.

Daniels: And in that letter, you advised him not to speak to law enforcement?

Dunning: That's correct.

Daniels; And before we get into that, I just wanted to cover with you very briefly, you have been asked to testify concerning your representation of Mr. Viera in an earlier federal court litigation between Laurie Chastant and various insurance companies?

Dunning: Yes, that's correct.

Daniels: And at that time, my recollection is—and please correct me if I'm wrong—you refused to testify?

Dunning: I appeared for the deposition, but yes, I refused to testify, invoking the attorney-client privilege, because I had no waiver from Mr. Viera to be able to talk about anything that he had talked to me about.

Daniels: Since that time, has Mr. Viera waived his attorney-client privilege?

Dunning: Yes. When he filed for a post-conviction relief application alleging that I was ineffective as his attorney, then that operated as a waiver of the attorney-client privilege. And I would note that you have provided me with a copy of a ruling from Judge Comeaux, who is the judge in this particular case, wherein he finds that the filing of the post-conviction relief application was a complete waiver of Mr. Viera's attorney-client privilege, which therefore, allows me to testify as to any communications that I had with Mr. Viera other than what may have transpired in the grand jury proceeding. That's not in the order you provided me, but based on the conversation between you and I [sic] and my understanding of the grand jury secrecy rule, I can't testify to anything that went on in the grand jury.

Daniels: What, exactly, did Mr. Viera tell you about the incident with Dr. Chastant on your first meeting. And before I get to that, did you advise Mr. Viera that your conversations with him were protected by the attorney-client privilege?

Dunning: Yes, during the course of that meeting, I did tell him not to talk to anyone in jail about our conversations and explained to him the attorney-client privilege, that anything that he told me I could not repeat to anyone, that I would even go to jail if somebody tried to force me to divulge information unless, of course, that privilege had been waived by him.

Daniels: What did Mr. Viera tell you about the murder of Dr. Chastant?

Dunning: He indicated to me that Mrs. Chastant had paid him to kill Dr. Chastant, and that concerning the specific incident in question, he indicated to me that he had met with Dr. Chastant at the barn which was on the property where the family home was located, as well as the pool house or outbuilding that Mr. Viera and his girlfriend and her little boy lived [in]. He met Dr. Chastant out at the barn and Mr. Viera had some items that belonged to Dr. Chastant that he had borrowed from the barn and Dr. Chastant had asked him to return those items and that Dr. Chastant confronted him at the barn and was fussing at him about not returning the items like he told him to, that Dr. Chastant hit him twice in the face and then Mr. Viera picked up the hammer and did hit Dr. Chastant with the hammer.

Daniels: Did Mr. Viera inform you at any point in time during your representation that he had, in fact, been paid by Dr. Chastant's wife, Laurie Chastant, to kill Dr. Chastant?

At that point, her testimony varied sharply with what Viera had said in his depositions in that she described a murder scene at which Laurie Chastant was actually present and witnessed:

Dunning: Yes, he did. He did indicate that to me. He consistently, once he told me Mrs. Chastant had offered him one thousand dollars to kill Dr. Chastant…she had actually paid him the money and he told me at one point specifically…that the reason that he killed Dr. Chastant or that he hit him with intent to kill was because Mrs. Chastant was standing right there at the barn when he was talking with Dr. Chastant, that she had driven up and that when he realized that she was standing there, he felt obligated to follow through with trying to murder Dr. Chastant because of the money that Mrs. Chastant had paid him.

Daniels: You knew, did you not, that when you went to meet with Mr. Viera, that Mr. Viera had already informed the sheriff's department that he was alleging that Ms. Chastant had paid him to kill Dr. Chastant?

Dunning: No, I was not aware of that.

Daniels: You had informed him that anything he told you was strictly confidential, correct?

Dunning: That is correct.

Daniels: In representing someone—in this case, Mr. Viera—who is telling you that he was paid to commit the homicide, did that create any problems with regard to the type of defense that you would present on his behalf?

Dunning: Yes. If I had to defend him on a charge of murder for hire, it would certainly impact the defense. I would certainly have to address that issue but at this point—and I'm talking about January of 2011—at that point in time, my only knowledge about that was based on what Mr. Viera told me and what the prosecutors told me were in the interviews. My concerns about the allegations of murder for hire went more to the issue of what Mr. Viera might be charged with rather than to any defense strategy because, understand that my first visit with him was pre-indictment. He had not yet been formally charged by the district attorney's office. He was what we call a pre-trial detainee, pre-indictment, so I had to discuss with him the impact that that might have on any charge that the grand jury might bring back because murder for hire is one of what we call the aggravators or one of the factors that can trigger a first-degree murder charge which carries mandatory life or a possible death penalty.

Daniels: According to Mr. Viera that he was paid by Mrs. Chastant to kill her husband—the difference between that and that he acted out of rage or retaliation would be the difference between first-degree murder which carries a possible death penalty, and secondary-degree murder, which is life imprisonment, right?

Dunning: That's generally correct, yes, but the issue of rage also would impact on whether there were considerations as to whether or not it might have amounted to manslaughter because he was slapped by Dr. Chastant. The main thrust of my discussions with him prior to the grand jury being convened in March of 2011, was getting him to understand the difference between a first-degree murder and a second-degree murder. There was also another potential factor or aggravator that could have persuaded the grand jury to bring back an indictment for first-degree murder, and that was the allegations that---and Mr. Viera admitted to me and explained to me why he had certain items that belonged to Dr. Chastant.

The state considered the possibility that the fact that Dr. Chastant's phone and his credit card holder were in Mr. Viera's possession. Mr. Viera admitted he had those items, but he explained to me that the reason he had them is that when he was moving the body, they just fell out of his pocket and he just picked them up and put them in his pocket, that he certainly did not attack or try to kill Dr. Chastant to commit any sort of robbery of any kind.

Daniels: Did Mr. Viera give you any information confidentially, as his attorney, concerning Laurie Chastant's involvement in the murder after that murder took place?

Dunning: Yes. He indicated that she actually assisted him in moving the body. Apparently, this encounter transpired right outside in front of the barn. From viewing the crime scene video, which is consistent with what he told me, it was primarily dirt outside the barn. The barn, I don't think, was fully completed and it hadn't been sodded. There wasn't any grass. At any rate, it happened in the dirt. He indicated to me that Mrs. Chastant went to get a little ATV vehicle at the house and bring it back to the site of incident in front of the barn and that she helped him pick up Dr. Chastant's body, put it in the ATV, that Mr. Viera drove the ATV over to a trash pile—and when I say trash, it was primarily discarded building materials and that sort of thing from the building of the barn—in which Mr. Viera hid the body by removing some of the trash, putting the body in and then covering it back up and that while he was doing that, Mrs. Chastant was covering up the blood there that was at the site with dirt from the area.

Daniels: At any point in time prior to the grand jury or subsequent to the grand jury did Mr. Viera attempt to change his recollection or what he told you ultimately about two things—number one, Laurie Chastant paying him to murder her husband, or did he maintain…

Dunning: He never wavered from that.

Daniels: And did he ever waver from the fact that she helped, in some fashion, clean up after the murder occurred?

Dunning: No, he did not.

Daniels: Did you explain to Mr. Viera that because of his insistence that he was paid to kill Dr. Chastant and/or that Laurie Chastant participated afterwards, that that could have the effect of elevating any charges from a second-degree murder to a first-degree murder?

Dunning: Yes, on numerous occasions. In fact, the things that I talked to him most about prior to the convening of the grand jury was just that: his exposure to possibly being charged with first-degree murder and the state seeking the death penalty against him, and the difference between first-degree murder and second-degree murder.

Daniels: And despite that advice to him, his position, you told us a second ago, never wavered from the fact that even though it wasn't in his interest, that he insisted that Laurie Chastant had paid him?

Dunning: I told him that [by] his saying that, he did run the risk of being indicted of first-degree murder. I didn't want to influence any testimony that he might give at the grand jury by telling him not to say something like that or anything like that. I did indicate to him the impact that it might have on the grand jury. The only thing I cautioned about was when he said to me—and he only said this once—that he did it because Mrs. Chastant was standing there. In advising him about whether or not he should consider testifying at the grand jury, I made him aware of the risk that he was taking. But it was his decision to take that risk and testify at the grand jury.

Mr. Viera got what we call a target letter. He was the subject of the investigation or the target of that particular grand jury. The only thing that the prosecutors were taking before the grand jury in relation to Mr. Viera was Mr. Viera. He was the only target. Mrs. Chastant, at that point, was not a target.

Daniels: So, I assume, that being the case, you advised Mr. Viera prior to his grand jury of the fact that he was not obligated to testify?

Dunning: Yes. That's the difference. A target has the right to testify if he or she so chooses but certainly cannot be compelled to testify before a grand jury. That would be a violation of an accused's right against self-incrimination.

Daniels: What was Mr. Viera's demeanor in your meetings with him prior to the grand jury? My recollection was you testified that he seemed aggravated or upset. Do you recall that?

Dunning: He was aggravated in the sense that he was very, very perplexed and very upset that Mrs. Chastant was not being charged for the murder or was not being taken to the grand jury. He thought that if he was being charged with Dr. Chastant's murder, she should be charged, as well, because she paid him to do it.

Daniels: I understand that after the grand jury returned an indictment against him, am I correct in assuming that you continued to represent Mr. Viera up until the time of his plea?

Dunning: I represented Mr. Viera not only up to the time of his plea but through his sentencing, which was not on the same date as the plea. He pled on June 14, 2011 (see Appendix G), but the sentencing was not until July 15th, 2011, although the sentence was mandatory life imprisonment without benefit of parole, probation or suspension of sentence. There was never any question what the sentence was going to be.

Daniels: Did Mr. Viera's position waver at all after his grand jury testimony with regard to Mrs. Chastant's involvement?

Dunning. No, it never wavered. And the tenor of our conversations, once the grand jury handed down an indictment or returned a true bill for second-degree murder, I focused less on the murder for hire and robbery because apparently the grand jury, by handing down the indictment for second-degree murder, they took death off the table.

Daniels: Would it have been possible for the district attorney's office to change an indictment from second-degree murder to first-degree murder after the initial grand jury returned a bill for second-degree murder?

Dunning: Under Louisiana law, no, the prosecutor—the district attorney or his assistants—they could not change it, but they could take the case back to the grand jury and try to obtain an indictment for first-degree murder, yes. He was not out of the woods.

Daniels: As a defense attorney, was it then important for you to get to the point of a plea on an expedited basis?

Dunning: Yes, it was my opinion, based on my experience and knowledge of the law and because he was still at risk, depending on—there was an ongoing investigation into this murder for hire, meaning an ongoing investigation into Mrs. Chastant's possible participation in the murder of her husband. There was a very real possibility that the prosecution, if they found more evidence and felt they had a stronger case than they did when they went to the grand jury in March of 2011, that they could take Mr. Viera back before the grand jury and try to seek …indictment for the first. I felt that was a very real possibility. I felt it was important, under the facts of the case, for him to enter a plea of guilty to second-degree murder as soon as practicable

Daniels: In other words, once he pled, once the pleading was accepted by the court, it's my understanding the court has to accept the plea?

Dunning: That's correct.

Daniels: Okay, once he pled and once the plea is accepted by the court...

Dunning: That would preclude the prosecution from seeking a first-degree indictment from a grand jury.

Daniels: Would it have been your practice to demand in a case like this to leave out any language in the factual basis any allegations concerning the murder for hire?

Dunning: Absolutely, because that would have been totally inappropriate. It would not have been a factual basis for a second-degree murder. It would have been a factual basis for a first-degree murder.

Daniels: The court would have rejected it?

Dunning: Correct. Any court worth its salt would reject a plea to second-degree murder...but the issue of the murder for hire simply just did not come up in this case in terms of the factual basis because the prosecution knew, as well as I did, that it would be totally inappropriate and that the court would not accept the plea with that in there. There was never any conversation, no mention from the prosecution, that there should be any allusion to a murder for hire. There is no indication that Mrs. Chastant may have acted as an accessory after the fact of the murder by helping him cover up the evidence.

Daniels: And that was left out by the DA's office, as well?

Dunning: That is correct.

Daniels: And for reasons you contend, because they wanted to, as you did, the factual basis in this case to fit the plea so that the plea would be accepted by the court?

Dunning: To fit the charge, yes.

Daniels: Were you provided with any evidence by the Iberia Parish Sheriff's Department concerning communications between—on the day of the murder—between Laurie Chastant and Ismael Viera?

Dunning: I was provided with a CD. It contained a list of phone calls that were made from Mrs. Chastant's phone, a list of phone calls that were made from Dr. Chastant's cell phone, and text messages between Mrs. Chastant's cell phone and Dr. Chastant's cell phone during the time that Mr. Viera had Dr. Chastant's cell phone in his possession. (This angle was not pursued any further in Denning's testimony.)

Daniels: In your conversations with Mr. Viera before his grand jury testimony, did he indicate to you that he wanted to testify to the grand jury to tell the grand jury about Ms. Chastant's involvement?

Dunning: Yes. Again, that was a consistent bone of contention with him that she was not, in my words, getting her just desserts. Even the last time I talked to him after he had been sentenced, he still simply could not comprehend why charges were not being filed against her.

Daniels: And Mr. Viera wanted to testi—at least he told you before his grand jury testimony—that he wanted to testify, even though it created a risk to him from the type of charges he could be charged with?

Dunning: That is correct.

Daniels: And you explained to him that he was opening himself up to a first-degree murder charge and that was not in his interest, best interest?

Dunning: I don't know that I told him that wasn't in his interest. I explained to him the risk he was running. Yes, I suppose the long and short of it would have been that I would tell him that it was extremely risky for him to do that. But of course, when you're in those kinds of situation, you've got to be very careful not to run the risk yourself of indicating to your client that he should lie before a grand jury. See, my own feeling was that his explanation about the robbery was very plausible, that the information available both to me and what I understood the prosecution to have at that time made his story about Mrs. Chastant rest solely only on his testimony, that there, at that point, was no independent evidence corroborating what he said.

Daniels: That was back in March?

Dunning: In March of 2011, yes.

Daniels: And in your conversations with the DA's office, did they tell you that the investigation was still ongoing?

Dunning: Yes, I was aware that it was.

Daniels: Has anyone, since that time, told you that the investigation has been, in fact, closed?

Dunning: No.

Daniels: In the many years that you have practiced criminal law...do you have to make at least an internal decision whether or not you believe what your clients are telling you?

Dunning: No. What my job is, is to evaluate the weight and amount of evidence that the state has against my client which, of course, I find out through discovery, and also evaluate the information that my client provides to me, investigate anything that my client tells me that might bear on a defense. My personal belief doesn't factor into it other than based on my experience with juries. I do have to assess whether I think a reasonable person would be more inclined to believe the state's case as opposed to what evidence the defendant might have. That's not to say I don't make my own personal conclusions in some cases, but that I have to not let that factor into the advice I give my client.

Daniels: Since Mr. Viera told you, number one, that Laurie Chastant paid him to murder her husband and that she participated, at least to some extent, in the cleanup afterwards, he never wavered from that position?

Dunning: Never.

Daniels: And that's up through even after the time of his plea?

Dunning: That's correct. Mr. Chevalier [Assistant District Attorney Robert Chevalier], on the date of the plea on June 14, 2011, asked to speak with Mr. Viera after we had entered his plea and Mr. Chevalier did question him again about his contention that Mrs. Chastant participated in the murder, that she actually paid him to murder Dr. Chastant. I guess we were in there about an hour and he still, even during that conversation after he entered his plea, maintained what I've told you here today that he told me.

Daniels: And since that time, he's never changed his testimony with regard to that?

Dunning: Not ever to me.

Daniels concluded his first round of questions for Dunning and Daniel Phillips, of Durio, McGoffin, Stagg & Ackermann, representing Laurie Chastant, took over the questioning.

Phillips: You indicated earlier that Mr. Tovar seemed perplexed that Laurie was not charged in this case?

Dunning: That's correct.

Phillips: What led you to that conclusion?

Dunning: The fact that it was in all of our conversations. In all of my conversations with Mr. Viera, he would always make a comment about her involvement and would ask me each time I talked to him why she was not being charged, and I did spend a good amount of time with him during each visit trying to explain to him that at those points in time, the prosecutors were relying primarily on what he had said about her involvement to law enforcement, meaning the interviews with Frank Garcia and Carmen Garcia, that they were looking for other evidence that might support his contentions. And as time went on, then I had to explain to him about the problem with the timeline based on what he was saying and the time the employees at Mrs. Chastant's doctor said she arrived there on the morning of the incident. But he was preoccupied with it and just could not understand why she hadn't been charged.

Phillips: Did he ever indicate to you any type of reason why he was so concerned that she hadn't been charged?

Dunning: My impression was that it was a basic belief on his part that that was unfair, that if he was going to be charged, she should be charged because she paid him to do it and she was just as guilty as he was, and that was his position.

Phillips: Did he say that to you, or is that…

Dunning: He didn't articulate it in those particular words but, yes, that most definitely was where he was coming from, that it just wasn't right, it wasn't fair.

Phillips: Did anyone from the prosecution discuss with you maybe a potential deal for Mr. Viera's testimony against Laurie?

Dunning: No. We discussed Mr. Viera's contentions which, of course, they were aware of because they had seen the interviews or the interrogations—only to the extent that I was told by the prosecutors, that the state was not in a position to go forward with making Mrs. Chastant a target of grand jury investigation simply on Mr. Viera's word, simply on his testimony. Had they come to me prior to his plea and asked me whether he would testify against her, and that would assume they had corroborating evidence, certainly I would have tried to negotiate a lesser-included plea of manslaughter if they wanted his testimony. But by the time he pled to second-degree murder, they were not interested in having his testimony.

Phillips: You mentioned that there was an underlying thread as to whether Mr. Viera might be using Ms. Chastant as a foil to protect Natalie?

Dunning: Correct

Phillips: Do you know if she was ever charged?

Dunning: To my knowledge, she was not.

With that, Phillips concluded his questions of Dunning and Daniels then asked follow-up questions as her deposition wound down.

Daniels: Mr. Phillips asked you whether or not at any time did the prosecutors offer a deal to Mr. Viera to testify against Laurie Chastant, and they have not?

Dunning: No, they never made any overtures about a deal.

Daniels: Anything that Mr. Viera told you about Laurie Chastant's involvement in her husband's murder didn't come by way or persuasion or encouragement to Mr. Viera based upon some offer on the table from the prosecutor's office?

Dunning: No, it did not.

Daniels: With regard to Natalie, you weren't provided with any evidence that Natalie participated after the fact in Dr. Chastant's murder, were you?

Dunning: No.

Daniels: And you don't know whether any evidence actually exists?

Dunning: No, I did not and do not.

Daniels: And even after his plea, Mr. Viera insisted, number one, that Laurie Chastant had paid to kill her husband, correct?

Dunning: Correct.

Daniels: And that Natalie, his girlfriend, had no involvement?

Dunning: That's correct.

Phillips returned with his own follow-up questions, asking if Viera ever mentioned any type of statements or interviews "in which that he may have made statements that were contrary to the statements that he was making to you as far as Laurie's involvement with the murder?"

Dunning said he never made any such statement to her.

First- and Second-Degree Murder Explained

Attorney Dunning's deposition centered around Ismael Viera's insistence that Laurie Chastant was involved in a conspiracy to murder her husband and, following the murder, participated in an attempt to conceal evidence by helping Ismael hide the body of Dr. Robert Chastant and by covering up the blood at the crime scene. Dunning was consistent in describing her client's steadfast adherence to that claim despite being informed that such a conspiracy, if true, could result in the death penalty for him with the more severe charge of first-degree murder.

Louisiana Law (R.S. 14:30) is specific in defining what constitutes a charge of first-degree murder:

§30. First degree murder
    A. First degree murder is the killing of a human being:

> **(4) When the offender has specific intent to kill or inflict great bodily harm and has offered, has been offered, has given, or has received anything of value for the killing.** (Emphasis added.)

    C. (1) If the district attorney seeks a capital verdict, the offender shall be punished by death or life imprisonment at hard labor without benefit of parole, probation, or suspension of sentence, in accordance with the determination of the jury. The provisions of Code of Criminal Procedure Article 782 relative to cases in which punishment may be capital shall apply.

        (2) If the district attorney does not seek a capital verdict, the offender shall be punished by life imprisonment at hard labor without benefit of parole, probation or suspension of

sentence. The provisions of Code of Criminal Procedure Article 782 relative to cases in which punishment is necessarily confinement at hard labor shall apply.

Daniels attempted again and again to drive home the point that Ismael clung to his claim that he was paid by Laurie and that Laurie helped in trying to hide evidence of the murder as his way of implicating Laurie despite the exposure of his own conviction of first-degree murder.

Though Ismael apparently indicated to Dunning—or Dunning understood him to say at the outset that Laurie Chastant was present at the barn at the actual time of the murder instead of the more consistent story that she drove up shortly afterward. That inconsistency, along with other points, was discussed in an email exchange between attorney Daniels and Dr. Robert Chastant's daughter Michele Chastant Stark on April 22, two weeks before attorney Dunning's deposition.

Michele felt that Ismael was lying about his comprehension of the difference between first- and second-degree murder but she noted that his story was consistent "the entire time." She also felt that attorney Nancy Dunning was simply mistaken in her understanding that Laurie was present at the time of the murder. "Her testimony was the first I had heard of this. I have always understood that Laurie came to the barn after the murder to clean up."

Daniels replied that same day that because Ismael's discussions with his attorney were privileged at the time, "he had no reason to lie and they were against his interest as you pointed out." Moreover, Daniels noted that Dunning negotiated with the DA's office the language of Ismael's plea agreement. "This is important because if you recall, Mr. Durio made the argument about the fact that nowhere in Viera's plea did he mention Laurie's involvement. That's because his lawyer kept it out." [Appendix J]

Dunning was interviewed by the author in February 2021 and reaffirmed that her strategy "was to avoid a first-degree murder charge against Viera. It worked," she said.

Addressing the issue of Viera's claim that Laurie paid him and then helped him in disposing of her husband's body, she said, "My client

[Viera], like other foreigners I've represented, was very poor and not very worldly. He did not have a good sense of time. It was 'before lunch,' 'after lunch,' 'daylight,' 'dark,' never a precise hour or minute," she said. "That posed a problem as far as investigating the wife's involvement.

"The DA did pursue that angle but could not obtain enough corroborating evidence to obtain an indictment."

Dunning, who has had a private practice in Abbeville for thirty years, said Viera had filed for post-conviction relief on the grounds of inadequate representation on her part on the theory that she should have pled his second-degree murder charge down to manslaughter which carried a maximum sentence of forty years. She described Viera's life sentence in light of a lack of any additional evidence of Laurie's participation as "appropriate."

She declined to offer her personal opinion on the validity of Viera's assertion that Laurie paid him to kill Dr. Chastant, but did reiterate her deposition testimony that Viera never vacillated from his contention that Laurie not only paid him, but helped in the attempt to conceal her husband's body.

In defense of Dunning's omissions that were not pursued, such as the cellphone records, it should be noted that public defenders are historically underpaid, understaffed and limited in financial resources with which to pursue evidence and obtain testimony of expert witnesses.

Tom Aswell

"Somebody Was There Helping"

On June 13, 2013, a summary motion hearing was held in U.S. District Court in Lafayette before Judge Richard Haik that produced some curious observations by Haik. The motion was over the propriety of Paul Chastant's use of trust funds to pay his defense attorney. Laurie's attorney, Steven Durio contended that Paul Chastant had no right to use the money for that purpose.

In ruling against Durio, Haik said, "Well, they [the Fifth Circuit Court of Appeal] are going to reverse me on this one, too, then, because I don't think Mr. Paul Chastant did anything inappropriate. I think everything he did, he had to do."

But then, he added, "Do I think your client [Laurie Chastant], after hearing the evidence, had any involvement? The answer to that is no. Okay? I don't. Others may have.

"But certainly, there was enough there that, as a responsible trustee who is responsible for---has a fiduciary responsibility to the trust, he had no choice but to do that. He had no choice. I've read everything you said. You are not going to change my mind. In this case, this guy, Paul Chastant, was the trustee. He had an obligation to defend that trust— especially when he was sued. Yes, he had a countersuit because he said that your client didn't have a right to it. Let me tell you, that was a serious issue. That thing—that situation—and it's not dead yet. This thing could be resurrected to see if somebody else was involved.

"This is a civil trial, not a criminal trial. I don't know what's going to happen with that.

Then he again returned to the issue of Laurie's involvement when he said, "My opinion is, after hearing the evidence, I don't think your client had anything to do with that. I don't. I may be wrong, okay? I don't think I am. *But somebody was there helping—doing something other than the one guy who got convicted* [author's emphasis]. I have my own feelings on who that was, and I don't think it was [Laurie]." [Appendix K]

Thirteen months earlier, on May 23, 2012 (the jury foreperson inadvertently dated the jury verdict May 23, 2010, nearly seven months before Dr. Robert Chastant's murder), a federal jury checked "No" to the single question, "Do you find, from a preponderance of the evidence, that Laurie Ann Futral Chastant participated in the intentional, unjustified killing of her husband, Robert Brown Chastant?" [Appendix L]

That was the basis on which Judge Haik would make his observations more than a year later when issuing his ruling in favor of Paul Chastant in the separate lawsuit filed by Laurie against her former brother-in-law.

But the one thing that must be remembered in that context is that there was no evidence put on to prove her guilt or innocence; it was a civil trial, not criminal. A jury's opinion in a civil trial does not imply either exoneration or guilt in a potential criminal matter. There were many considerations that were not taken into account, some subtle, some of a more conspicuous nature.

- Though Laurie's father, William Futral, claimed only a passing acquaintance with Sheriff Ackal, both Ackal and William Futral are retired Louisiana state troopers, and both worked in Region II at the same time.
- Both began their second careers in 2008—Ackal as sheriff of Iberia Parish, and Futral as a deputy sheriff two parishes away, in St. Landry.
- In 2016, when Ackal and Chief Deputy Gerald Savoy were among eleven officials of the sheriff's department indicted on charges of inmate abuses, Ackal was initially represented by his cousin, the aforementioned U.S. District Judge Richard Haik, by that time retired from the federal bench.
- Laurie Chastant and Dr. Robert Chastant entered into a pre-nuptial agreement prior to their 2004 marriage which specified she would receive only about eighty thousand dollars in the event they should divorce. Within weeks of his death, Laurie filed a claim for more than two million dollars in survivor benefits.

- Several weeks before Dr. Chastant's murder, Laurie discovered while using his personal computer that Dr. Chastant was likely having an affair with a woman, Kristen McClain, of Grand Prairie, Texas.

- Ten days before Dr. Chastant was murdered, on December 3, Laurie's name was signed (she denied it was her signature) to a Consent of Spouse Form waiving any and all rights to Dr. Chastant's defined benefit and profit-sharing plans which would have become effective when funds from the plans were distributed.

- Just prior to Dr. Chastant's murder, Laurie Chastant was said by attorney James Daniels to have become aware that her husband was planning a trip to Dallas to spend the Christmas holidays with Kristen McClain.

- Ismael Viera-Tovar confessed to killing Dr. Chastant with a claw hammer on the morning of December 13, 2010 at the new barn being constructed near the Chastant residence. Viera later claimed that Laurie Chastant had paid him a thousand dollars to kill her husband.

- On December 6, Laurie wrote a six-hundred-dollar check for cash. Four days later, on December 10, she wrote a second check for cash in the amount of four-hundred-dollars. No accounting was ever provided for the purpose of those checks.

- Robert Chastant was killed before he could finalize the paperwork to close the defined benefit and profit-sharing plans which, had the transactions been completed, would have left Laurie with no claim to benefits from either.

- Ismael Viera stood five-foot-six-inches and weighed one hundred sixty pounds. Dr. Chastant stood six-foot-five and weighed one ninety-five. Ismael initially said he carried Dr. Chastant from the scene of the murder to a trash pile behind the barn but later said Laurie Chastant helped him load the body into a mini-truck which transported Dr. Chastant to the trash pile.

- Ismael initially tried to get Nayeli to say she drove him to the barn but when she refused, he admitted she was not involved. It appeared Ismael was trying to protect the identity of the person who drove him back to the barn in the Isuzu utility truck.

- Ismael first told authorities he threw Dr. Chastant's cell phone out the window on his way to Walmart. It was later found in the pool house. Ismael apparently did not want anyone to know who he was texting on Robert Chastant's cell phone the morning of the murder. It was subsequently learned that Viera had sent text messages to Laurie and that she had responded to him.
- Laurie Chastant gave numerous and inconsistent statements regarding her actions on the morning of her husband's murder, first to the Iberia Parish sheriff's homicide detectives, to her in-laws, to Viera's girlfriend, and in her deposition.
- Nayeli told authorities that Laurie Chastant informed her that Dr. Chastant was missing at about 8:00 a.m., an hour before she was actually notified by his office that he had not shown up for work.
- A motion-activated camera that had been installed at the barn and which might have provided valuable information for investigators was removed. Sheriff's Chief Deputy Gerald Savoy testified in his deposition that the camera was never found.
- Dr. Chastant's pickup truck, driven by Ismael to Walmart following the murder, was seized by the sheriff's department for processing. It was kept for more than a year and when attorneys for Paul Chastant were told they could retrieve the vehicle, the missing motion-activated camera was found in the bed of the truck, submerged in water and ruined.
- A rubber floor mat, taken as evidence by investigators, was thought to belong to Laurie's truck. The mat was sent to the Acadiana Crime Lab for processing but there was an extraordinary delay in the crime lab's returning results of its findings.
- Sheriff Ackal is a member of the Acadiana Crime Lab's board of commissioners.
- The mat was initially placed in an outside storage compartment on the Chastants' motor home. Paul Chastant said that Laurie Chastant was insistent on going through the motor home for personal belongings and when given access, went first to the storage compartment. The mat, by that time, had been removed and sent to the crime lab.

- Iberia Parish sheriff's Captain Gerald Savoy, who oversaw the investigation into Dr. Robert Chastant's murder, and Chief of Detectives Adrienne Wells were allowed to give their depositions on December 8, 2011, despite a plea from attorney James Daniels that their testimony could jeopardize the district attorney's ongoing investigation of the murder.
- The investigation by the Iberia Parish Sheriff's Department was sadly inadequate, slipshod and amateurish, revealing a critical lack of urgency in determining if Viera had an accomplice. Sheriff Ackal was uncooperative, refusing to provide information to the FBI. The spate of indictments of Ackal and his deputies that were handed down only a few years later—and the guilty pleas that followed—only served to underscore the chaos that existed in that office.

Finally, there is the personal opinion voiced to attorney Steven Durio by Judge Haik at the conclusion of the trial in the federal lawsuit Laurie Chastant brought against Paul Chastant for his expenditure of trust funds for legal costs. His words are worth a second reading:

"My opinion is, after hearing the evidence," Haik said, "I don't think your client had anything to do with that. I don't. I may be wrong, okay? I don't think I am. *But somebody was there helping—doing something other than the one guy who got convicted.* I have my own feelings on who that was, and I don't think it was your client. [author's emphasis]

We can conclude if Ismael did indeed have an accomplice, it could have been one of only two possibilities: Laurie or Nayeli. Either way, it seems authorities allowed a guilty party to walk.

Laurie, two-million-dollars richer, remarried, protecting her newfound wealth ironically with a pre-nuptial agreement of her own.

Nayeli was allowed to return to Mexico and Viera continues serving his life sentence at the Louisiana State Penitentiary at Angola.

If one of them, Laurie or Nayeli, did help Ismael carry out the murder and transfer of the body to the trash pile in an effort to conceal the crime, then authorities—either the sheriff's office or the district attorney's office, or both—dropped the ball in allowing a guilty person to escape justice that was meted out on an unequal basis.

*Murky waters of Bayou Teche,
which flows through New Iberia.*
Photo by Tom Aswell

Tom Aswell

Epilogue: Money, Matrimony and Misery

A lot of activity occurred in the aftermath of Dr. Robert Chastant's brutal killing, the tragi-comical criminal investigation and the legal battles that followed. In the end, even as Viera began his life sentence in prison, there would be no real investigation into whether or not Laurie played a part in her husband's murder and she would not only come away two million dollars richer, but with a new husband, as well.

On April 12, 2014, before the dust had settled on the final distribution of property from Dr. Robert Chastant's estate, his widow, now thirty-nine, was married to James C. Ingram, III, the son of a prominent Lafayette cardiovascular surgeon.

Eight days earlier, on April 4th, the two signed off on a pre-nuptial marital contract, the second one Laurie would become a party to in a decade. The first, in 2004, was designed to protect the assets of her husband, Dr. Robert Chastant as he entered into his third marriage. The second was to protect her new-found assets derived from her late husband's life insurance policies and his defined benefits and profit-sharing plans as she embarked on her third marriage.

Looking at Laurie's social media page, one would be hard-pressed to know it was her third marriage. Her posts, which appeared to chronicle the nuptials of a starry-eyed debutante as opposed to a veteran of a prior divorce, the death of a second husband and a succession of legal battles, some still unresolved, featured picturesque illustrations of the happy couple's proposal, wedding reception, and honeymoon at St. Thomas, the U.S. Virgin Islands.

Moreover, Laurie did not appear to be the least bit shy in soliciting wedding gifts as if this was her first venture into wedded bliss. Prefacing the wish list itemized on her and her betrothed's gift registry was a brief message that said:

Thank you so much for being part of our special event.

Many people have asked us if there is anything we would like, and to be honest, we already have most of the things we need, but for those who feel the desire, we have set up this special gift registry.

We have chosen this website because it is safe and secure and very convenient.

This website is our first preference of how you can best help us if you like, but please know that what we desire most is your presence (not presents).

We look forward to seeing you at our event.

Love from Laurie Futral and James Ingram.

There followed a list of items that ranged from:

Honeymoon Accommodation: $2,000;
Honeymoon Day Excursions: $500;
Honeymoon Flights: $2,000;
Honeymoon Romantic Dinners: $500;
Rugs: $1,000;
Bed Linen: $100;
Cash: Unlimited.

In late 2014, there was a flurry of activity as a final tabulation of Robert Chastant's estate. The accounting, filed in 16th Judicial District Court in Iberia Parish on September 9, showed $149,500 in business ownership at the time of Dr. Chastant's death, including ownership of his orthodontics practice and his horse farm, Sonriente Stables. Also listed were seven tracts of immovable property, including a time-share unit in Utah, totaling almost $1.6 million, livestock that included nine Peruvian horses, a donkey and a mule valued at $14,950, cash and investments of $141,730, and miscellaneous assets that included furniture, two trucks, a motorhome, mowers, tractors, and trailers valued at $234,972. All told, his assets totaled just a shade under two million dollars against debts of some $2.46 million, including more than $145,000 in legal fees and costs of administering his trust.

On February 13, 2015, Laurie's attorney, Steven Durio, sent a settlement proposal to James Daniels, attorney for Paul Chastant and Robert Chastant's children:

"This letter is an inadmissible settlement offer under Rule 408 on behalf of Laurie Futral Ingram to dismiss the two suits that she has pending against your clients, on the one hand in St. Landry Parish against Paul Chastant, and on the other hand the federal injunction suit against the three children, Robert Chastant, Jr., Michele Chastant Stark and Megan Duval-Chastant Qualls, pending in the federal district court, in exchange for a dismissal of their suits against her, on the one hand by Paul Chastant in Lafayette Parish on behalf of the Succession, and on the other hand by the three children, Robert Chastant, Jr., Michele Chastant Stark and Megan Duval-Chastant Qualls, against Laurie for wrongful death pending in Iberia Parish.

"All dismissals will be with full prejudice and each party will bear its own costs and attorney's fees; except for the dismissals with prejudice, no party will be required to execute any release.

"Please be advised that if this offer is not accepted, we reserve our rights to bring all the foregoing matters to a conclusion and to obtain a judgment against your clients for all loss, damages, costs, attorney's fees, sanctions and other expenses as now outlined in the St. Landry Parish suit against Paul, and to be outlined in similar claims in Lafayette and Iberia Parishes upon conclusion of those matters.

"Jimmy, as you have pointed out, you have two different clients in these various matters, on the one hand, Paul Chastant, and on the other, Robert Chastant, Jr., Michele Chastant Stark and Megan Duval-Chastant Qualls. Please make it clear to both of your two client groups that this offer may not be accepted by either of them without acceptance by the other. Please review this offer with each of your clients and let us have their response as soon as possible. This offer will remain outstanding until 5:00 o'clock p.m. on Friday,

February 20, 2015, and must be accepted in writing, before that time, by all of your clients."

Durio's settlement offer apparently did not appeal to the Chastants because legal proceedings continued until May, when a partial order of dismissal was signed by 16th Judicial District Court Judge Keith Comeaux. The single-page judgment dismissed Robert Chastant, Jr. from the lawsuit against Laurie Chastant. Remaining as plaintiffs were Michele Chastant Stark and Megan Duval-Chastant Qualls. But that case, too, without assistance from the sheriff's department and the district attorney's office in pursuing a criminal investigation, would eventually end with a judgment in Laurie's favor.

On August 25, 2015, nearly five years after her second husband was murdered and sixteen months after she married her third husband, a judgment of dismissal of her lawsuit against Paul Chastant was signed, settling "all issues, claims, demands, reconventional demands, and causes of action."

But as Paul Chastant was quick to point out, he was never notified by authorities that Laurie was officially eliminated as a suspect in her husband's murder.

And, as is invariably the case, not even the two million dollars in survivor benefits could buy happiness. The controversy swirling around Laurie Futral's turbulent life would continue even after the favorable court judgment. Less than two-and-a-half years after her third marriage to James C. Ingram, III, he sued for divorce. The final divorce decree was granted on September 30, 2017, by 16th Judicial District Court in Lafayette (Appendix M).

Appendix

Tom Aswell

MATRIMONIAL AGREEMENT

STATE OF LOUISIANA
PARISH OF IBERIA

BE IT KNOWN that on this **14th** day of **May** , 2004 before me, the undersigned Notary Public, duly commissioned and qualified in and for Iberia Parish, Louisiana and in the presence of the undersigned two competent witnesses, personally came and appeared:

ROBERT BROWN CHASTANT, married first to Sharon Jones Sciancaux from whom he is judicially divorced and then to Susan Cox Chastant, from whom he is also judicially divorced, a domiciliary of Iberia Parish, Louisiana, ("Chastant")and

LAURIE ANNE FUTRAL, married but once and then to David Allen Moore, from whom she is judicially divorced, a domiciliary of Iberia Parish, Louisiana ("Futral")

(hereinafter sometimes collectively referred to as "Appearers" or each individually as "Appearer")

who each declared that:

WHEREAS, Appearers are contemplating marriage to each other in the state of Louisiana; and

WHEREAS, Appearers wish to exclude the Louisiana legal matrimonial regime that would otherwise be applicable to them at the time of their marriage and establish a regime of separation of property;

NOW THEREFORE, effective when and if Appearers marry, it is hereby agreed as follows:

1. Appearers do hereby establish and adopt a regime of separation of property pursuant to the Louisiana Civil Code and formally renounce those provisions of the Louisiana Civil Code which establish a community of acquets and gains between husband and wife.

2. Neither of the Appearers shall have any liability as between themselves and third parties for obligations, debts or liabilities of the other existing at marriage or incurred thereafter.

Appendix A – Page 1 of 3

3. Neither of the Appearers shall have any rights, title or interest in the assets owned by the other at marriage or acquired thereafter.

4. Each Appearer shall remain, as to the other, as well as to third persons, so far as all assets and all liabilities, with the sole exception hereinafter noted, as if not married. The sole exception referred to in the immediate preceding sentence is the solidary obligation of a spouse with the other spouse for necessaries for himself/herself or the family imposed pursuant to Louisiana Civil Code Article 2372.

5. All property and effects of Chastant and Futral are hereby declared to be his/her respective separate property, and each of them does hereby expressly reserve to himself/herself individually the entire administration of his/her respective property and the separate and free enjoyment of each of his/her respective revenues. The fact that either Appearer may assist the other in the administration or management of the property of the other shall not create the presumption of a claim for remuneration in favor of the Appearer assisting the other, but all such services shall be considered and held as gratuitously rendered to each other.

6. All property hereafter acquired in the name of either of the Appearers shall be and remain the separate property of that Appearer in whose name said property is acquired regardless of the manner of acquisition. All property purchased and all proceeds received from any sale of property shall be the separate property of the respective Appearer.

7. All monies earned as salary, commissions, as well as all revenues, products and natural and civil fruits of each Appearer's property shall be his/her respective separate property.

8. Certain, not necessarily all, movable property for the purpose of identification as separate property presently owned by Futral has been itemized and acknowledged by Appearers as belonging to the separate estate of Futral. This list has been initialed by Appearers and copies have been given to each of the Appearers. All other movable property brought into the marriage is owned by Chastant.

9. Each Appearer agrees to contribute to the expenses of their marriage according to his/her respective means.

10. An increase or improvement of the separate property of either Appearer, arising or made during the marriage of the Appearers through the result of the common labor, expense, or industry of the Appearers, shall not create any right to a reward, remuneration, restoration or reimbursement in favor of the Appearer or the legal representatives of the Appearer, to whom the property which has been increased or improved does not belong.

11. This agreement is entered into with the full knowledge on the part of each party as to the extent and value of the patrimony of each party and the rights conferred by law under the legal community property regime, but it is the desire of each party that their respective rights to each other's estate shall be fixed by this agreement,

2

Appendix A – Page 2 of 3

which shall be binding on their respective heirs and legal representatives. Each party admits that they have had the benefit of their own legal counsel and are satisfied with the terms of this agreement.

12. In consideration for entering into this agreement, Appearers agree that if they are divorced from each other within a period of five (5) years of marriage, then Futral shall be entitled to receive the vehicle in which she is driving at that time free of any encumbrance on the vehicle and $10,000 per year for each full year that they were married. The amount due is payable three months after the date the divorce becomes final. The amount due is calculated as of the day the divorce is filed and not the day the divorce becomes final. No interest is payable on any of the above amounts.

13. In consideration for entering into this agreement, Appearers agree that if they are divorced after the fifth anniversary of their marriage, then Futral shall be entitled to receive the vehicle in which she is driving at that time free of any encumbrance on the vehicle and $50,000 cash, plus $30,000 for each full year after the fifth anniversary of the marriage, up to a maximum total cash payment of $200,000, inclusive of the first five years. As an example, if Appearers are divorced after the seventh year, then the total amount received by Futral will be $110,000. The amount due is payable three months after the date the divorce becomes final. The amount due is calculated as of the day the divorce is filed and not the day the divorce becomes final. No interest is payable on any of the above amounts.

14. Appearers agree to execute any and all documents which will be necessary and proper to carry out the terms, provisions and conditions set forth in this Matrimonial Agreement and that the parties shall be completely separate in property.

THUS DONE AND EXECUTED, in multiple originals before the undersigned Notary Public in the presence of the undersigned two competent witnesses on the day, month, and year first written at Iberia Parish, Louisiana.

WITNESSES:

L. M Broussard

Sylvia B Lasalle

Robert Brown Chastant
ROBERT BROWN CHASTANT

Laurie Anne Futral
LAURIE ANNE FUTRAL

NOTARY PUBLIC

Appendix A – Page 3 of 3

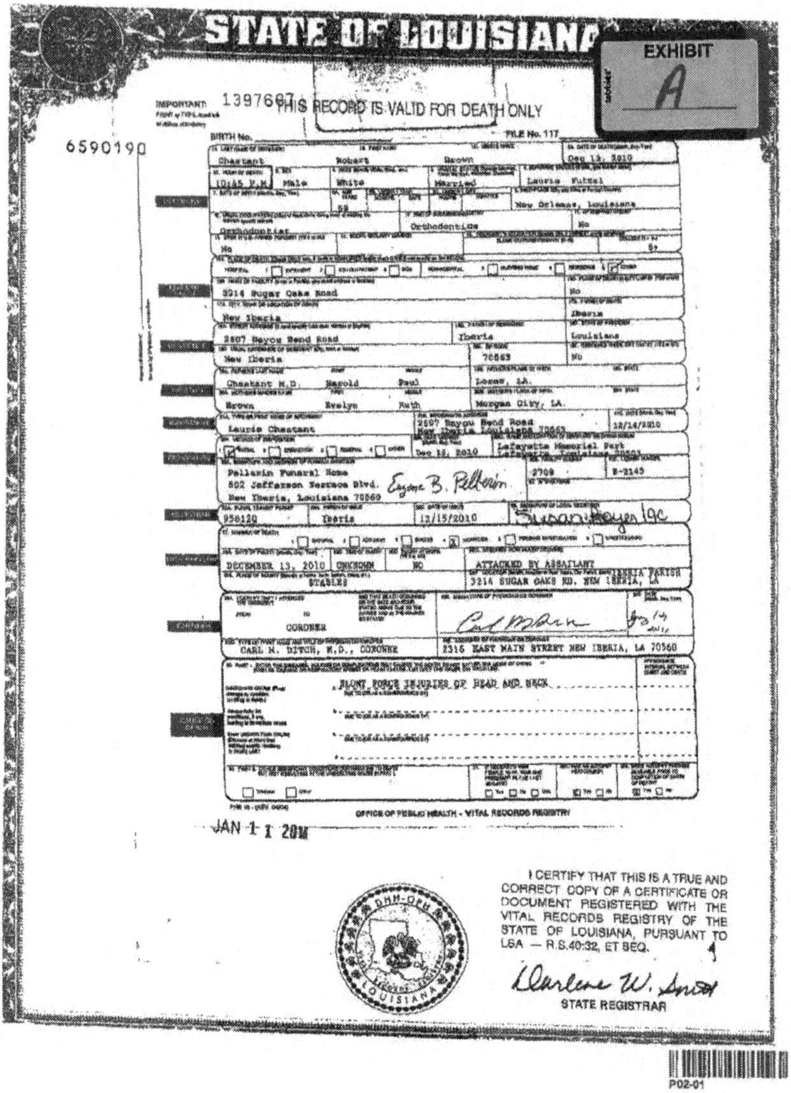

STATE OF LOUISIANA

EXHIBIT A

IMPORTANT 1397687 THIS RECORD IS VALID FOR DEATH ONLY

6590190

BIRTH No. FILE No. 117

Chestant Robert Brown Dec 13, 2010

10:45 P.M. Male White Married Laurie Futsel

58 New Orleans, Louisiana

Orthodontist Orthodontics No

No

3214 Sugar Oaks Road No

New Iberia Iberia

2807 Bayou Bend Road Iberia Louisiana

New Iberia 70563 No

Chestant M.D. Harold Paul Logan, LA.

Brown Evelyn Ruth Morgan City, LA.

Laurie Chestant 2807 Bayou Bend Road New Iberia Louisiana 70563 12/14/2010

Dec 15, 2010 Lafayette Memorial Park Lafayette, Louisiana

Pellerin Funeral Home 2709 B-2143

802 Jefferson Terrace Blvd.

New Iberia, Louisiana 70569

958120 Iberia 12/15/2010

DECEMBER 13, 2010 UNKNOWN NO ATTACKED BY ASSAILANT

STABLES 3214 SUGAR OAKS RD. NEW IBERIA, LA IBERIA PARISH

CORONER

CARL M. DITCH, M.D., CORONER 2316 EAST MAIN STREET NEW IBERIA, LA 70560

BLUNT FORCE INJURIES OF HEAD AND NECK

OFFICE OF PUBLIC HEALTH - VITAL RECORDS REGISTRY

JAN 1 1 2011

I CERTIFY THAT THIS IS A TRUE AND CORRECT COPY OF A CERTIFICATE OR DOCUMENT REGISTERED WITH THE VITAL RECORDS REGISTRY OF THE STATE OF LOUISIANA, PURSUANT TO LSA — R.S.40:32, ET SEQ.

Darlene W. Smith

STATE REGISTRAR

P02-01

Appendix B

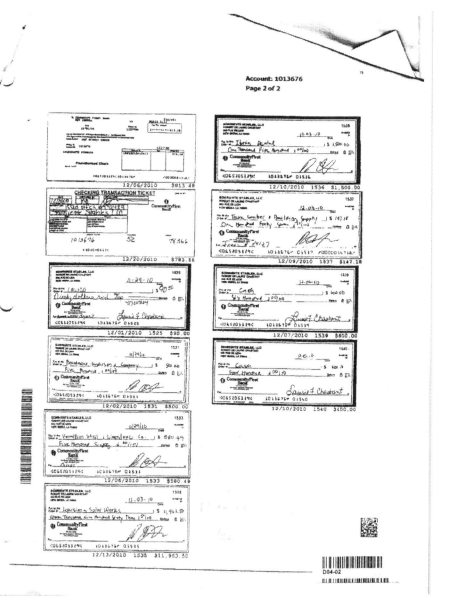

Appendix C

Tom Aswell

UNITED STATES DISTRICT COURT
WESTERN DISTRICT OF LOUISIANA
LAFAYETTE DIVISION

LAURIE ANN FUTRAL CHASTANT	CIVIL ACTION NO. 11-cv-00626
VERSUS	JUDGE HAIK
PRUDENTIAL INSURANCE COMPANY OF AMERICA, ET AL	MAGISTRATE HANNA

CONSENT ORDER

This matter is before the Court on the motion of plaintiff, Laurie Futral Chastant, and defendants, Paul T. Chastant, Independent Executor of the Succession of Robert Brown Chastant, Trustee of the Robert Chastant Inter Vivos 2005 Trust, and Trustee of the Robert Brown Chastant, D.D.S. (A Dental Corporation) Defined Benefit and Profit Sharing Plans ("Trustee"), who advise the Court that they have reached an agreement to be memorialized as a Consent Order; NOW THEREFORE:

IT IS ORDERED that all funds and assets in the Robert Brown Chastant, D.D.S. (A Dental Corporation) Defined Benefit and Profit Sharing Plans (the "Plans"), in the Robert B. Chastant, D.D.S, ADC Defined Benefit Plan Account No. 702-14343-1-6 shall be held in trust therein subject to further orders of this Court, and all such funds will remain as currently invested and not subject to withdrawal except upon further order of this Court.

{L0201070.3}

Page 1 of 3

EXHIBIT
C

Appendix D

IT IS FURTHER ORDERED that Laurie Futral Chastant waives any and all claims to disqualify Paul Chastant as administrator of the Succession and/or trustee of the Children's Trusts or to have James Daniels in any way disqualified as attorney for defendants, Paul T. Chastant, Independent Executor of the Succession of Robert Brown Chastant, Trustee of the Robert Chastant Inter Vivos 2005 Trust, and Trustee of the Robert Brown Chastant, D.D.S. (A Dental Corporation) Defined Benefit and Profit Sharing Plans and further waives any and all claims against Paul Chastant and/or James Daniels, past, present and future, from any and all conflicts of interest, including any and all acts by Paul Chastant in defending this lawsuit and/or acts in settlement of the claims herein, with all parties reserving claims against each other for reimbursement and associated attorney's fees, expenses incurred and costs in the litigation, both past and future which were paid and/or to be incurred by Paul T. Chastant as "Trustee" of the Robert Brown Chastant, D.D.S. (A Dental Corporation) Defined Benefit and Profit Sharing Plans (the "Plans") only to the extent such payments may have been improper under ERISA law or unauthorized by the Plans.

THUS DONE AND SIGNED at Lafayette, Louisiana, on this _17_ day of _April_, 2012.

UNITED STATES DISTRICT JUDGE

Appendix D

Tom Aswell

Participant of the ROBERT B. CHASTANT, DDS, A DENTAL CORPORATION DEFINED BENEFIT
PLAN
Plan EIN: 72-0868551
Plan Number: 003
Robert Chastant

Spouse's Rights
The following page includes a written explanation of the qualified joint and survivor annuity benefit.
If you are married your spouse must consent to this election on the CONSENT OF SPOUSE form,
and his/her consent must be notarized.

It is important for you to know that if you are married and make no election, your benefit will be
paid in the form of the qualified joint and survivor annuity. If you are single and make no election,
your benefit will be paid in the form of a life annuity.

PLEASE INITIAL WHETHER YOU ARE MARRIED:

    ✓ YES, I am married.   NO, I am not married.
My spouse's name is: _Laurie Chastant_
My spouse's Social Security Number is: 439-19-5616
My spouse's date of birth is 12-23-73

Please print clearly.
Dated this 8th day of November , 2010 .

My Social Security Number is: 457-80-7437

My Date of Birth is 12/23/1950

My home mailing address is: 603 Rue de Lion
         Street
    New Iberia   LA   70563
    City   State   Zip Code

My Area Code and Phone number is: 537-367-1271

My E-mail Address is: rb_chustant@yahoo.com

I certify, under penalty of perjury, there is no Domestic Relations Order (DRO) or a Qualified Domestic
Relations Order (QDRO) pending or already in place that affects my benefit in the Plan and there are no
rights to my benefit in this Plan that have been assigned to anyone under a Dissolution of Marriage
Agreement. If there is a DRO, QDRO or Dissolution of Marriage Agreement pending or already in place, I
have attached the Order or Agreement. If, in the future, such Order or Agreement is placed that affects my
benefit in the Plan, I will immediately contact my former employer.

Such Order is made pursuant to State domestic relations law (including a community property law) and
provides for child support, alimony payments or marital property rights to a spouse, former spouse, child or
other dependent.
It is your responsibility to consult with your own lawyer, estate planner or other tax advisor(s) prior
to making any election.

Signature of Participant: _____   Date: 1/8/10

199

Appendix E

FORM 3 - continued
CONSENT OF SPOUSE

Participant of the ROBERT B. CHASTANT, DDS, A DENTAL CORPORATION DEFINED
BENEFIT PLAN
Plan EIN: 72-0868551
Plan Number: 003
Robert Chastant

I declare under penalty of perjury that I: (1) am the spouse of the Participant who is electing to
receive benefits other than in the form of a qualified joint and survivor annuity; (2) am not acting
under duress or undue influence; and (3) understand my right to survivor benefits under the
ROBERT B. CHASTANT, DDS, A DENTAL CORPORATION DEFINED BENEFIT PLAN.

I understand that federal law gives me the right to receive survivor benefits if my spouse dies. I
also understand that if I consent to this waiver Election, I will give up my right to receive the
survivor benefits from the Plan which federal law would give to me automatically and I consent
to this. I also understand that: (1) the effect of this Waiver Election is to cause my right to my
spouse's retirement benefit under the Plan to be paid in a way which may not provide me with
income after my spouse's death; (2) I also consent to this; and, (3) I cannot cancel my consent.

Dated this 3rd day of December, 2010.

Signature of Spouse: *Laurie F. Chastant*

Name of Spouse: Laurie F Chastant
(Please Print)

STATE OF LA (
(Parish)
COUNTY OF Iberia (ss.

BEFORE ME, the undersigned, a Notary Public in and for said State, personally appeared
Laurie F Chastant who executed the above Consent of Spouse as a free and
voluntary act.

IN WITNESS WHEREOF, I have signed my name and affixed my official notarial seal this 3rd
day of December, 2010.

(SEAL)

Judith Vaughn
Notary Public
My commission expires: death

Judith G. Vaughn
NOTARY PUBLIC, Parish of Iberia
Commisison expires at death
Notary ID # 56463

Appendix F

Tom Aswell

Page 3 of 28

STATE OF LOUISIANA : 16TH JUDICIAL DISTRICT

VERSUS DOCKET: 11-0342 : PARISH OF IBERIA

ISMAIEL VIERA-TOVAR
3607 BAYOU BEND RD.
NEW IBERIA, LA 70560 : STATE OF LOUISIANA
Race: H Sex: M DOB: 05/31/1989
SSN: PH:

CERTIFICATE OUTLINING FELONY PLEA AGREEMENT

I. CHARGE:

The defendant, ISMAIEL VIERA-TOVAR, agrees to plead guilty to:

SECOND DEGREE MURDER in violation of LOUISIANA REVISED STATUTE 14:30.1

II. STIPULATED FACTUAL BASIS:

On or about the date alleged in the Bill of Indictment, in the parish of Iberia, the defendant, Ismaiel Viera-Tovar, produced a hammer and struck the victim multiple times in the back of his head and neck area, causing fatal injuries. The attack occurred shortly after a verbal argument between the two, as the victim was walking away from the defendant.

III. SENTENCE:

The Court will set a sentencing hearing to be held at a later date.

_____
Assistant District Attorney

I HEREBY UNDERSTAND and agree to all the above terms and conditions of my plea agreement and conditions of probation. I also understand that this plea agreement contemplates the District Attorney's office will discuss the plea agreement with the victim(s) of said crime, if any, and that this plea agreement may be revoked at any time prior to the entry of my plea of guilty.

EXECUTED this _13th_ day of _June_, 2011.

I, Cecilia Labauve, a previously recognized translator for the 16th Judicial District Court, to the best of my skill and judgment have accurately, completely, and impartially read and translated the above information to Ismaiel Viera-Tovar, in a language that he understands.

_____
Cecilia Labauve

Ismael Viera _____
Defendant   Attorney for Defendant

RECEIVED AND FILED
This ___ day of _June_, 2011
_____
DEPUTY CLERK OF COURT

BY ORDER OF THE COURT
This _14_ day of _June_, 2011
_____
16th JUDICIAL DISTRICT JUDGE

A TRUE COPY
ATTEST: _____ DEPUTY CLERK OF COURT
IBERIA PARISH, LOUISIANA

EXHIBIT
B

Appendix G

- 294 -

Date ▲	Time	To/From	Number	Name	Min:Sec	Additional Info
12/14/2010	02:11 PM	To	337-839-1881		00:05	
12/14/2010	01:27 PM	From	337-380-5791	Prince Sherry	01:48	
12/14/2010	01:06 PM	From	337-739-4402	Rummel Melissa	01:24	
12/14/2010	12:22 PM	From	337-519-6020	Thomas Tere	01:28	
12/14/2010	12:08 PM	From	337-367-8702	IBERIA PARISH	00:27	
12/14/2010	11:37 AM	From	337-365-3277	IBERIA COMM ACT	03:06	
12/14/2010	11:34 AM	From	337-256-3797	Cell Phone LA	01:00	
12/14/2010	11:33 AM	To	337-256-3797		00:32	
12/14/2010	11:32 AM	To	337-519-8595		00:04	
12/14/2010	11:02 AM	To	225-288-5447		09:06	
12/14/2010	10:07 AM	From	337-234-1039	ADVOCATE THE	00:05	
12/14/2010	09:27 AM	From	337-412-5690	Cell Phone LA	00:01	
7/14/2010	09:22 AM	From	337-276-4577	ST JOHN EVANGEL	00:00	
12/14/2010	08:39 AM	From	337-367-1272	Chastant O	00:04	
12/14/2010	08:23 AM	From	662-363-2544	MELTON CHARLES	00:06	

Previous ... 2 3 4 5 6 7 8 9 10 11 12 13 14 15 16 17 18 19 20 Next

Call History

fox your friend in the digital age*

Activity for phone number: 337-560-5841

☐ Print this Page

Call History for the last 30 days

☐ Close this window

All Calls

Call history does not correspond to billing cycles

Date ▲	Time	To/From	Number	Name	Min:Sec	Additional Info
12/09/2010	01:48 PM	From	337-519-6020	Thomas Tere	01:29	
12/09/2010	01:19 PM	From	337-364-3301	IBERIA GASTROEN	00:03	
12/09/2010	12:33 PM	From	337-367-1271	Chastant O	02:33	
12/09/2010	09:19 AM	From	337-367-1210	Chastant O	00:05	
12/08/2010	02:11 PM	To	337-839-1881		00:05	
12/08/2010	10:35 AM	From	337-893-4746	DR R	00:05	
12/08/2010	09:05 AM	From	337-364-0441	IBERIA MED CTR	00:00	
12/07/2010	02:11 PM	To	337-839-1881		00:05	
12/07/2010	01:56 PM	From	337-519-0343	Chasta Robert	00:06	
12/07/2010	11:53 AM	To	337-519-0343		00:02	
12/05/2010	02:11 PM	To	337-839-1881		00:05	
12/05/2010	09:13 AM	From	337-367-1272	Chastant O	00:05	
12/05/2010	02:11 PM	To	337-839-1881		00:05	
12/04/2010	08:33 PM	From	337-781-0200	Cell Phone LA	00:05	
12/04/2010	07:23 PM	To	866-709-2073		00:17	

Previous ... 6 7 8 9 10 11 12 13 14 15 16 17 18 19 20 Next

Appendix H

Tom Aswell

Appendix D

871662
01/06/2011
SCAMP

MOBILITY USAGE
(with cell location)

Dr. Robert Chastant

Run Date: 01/06/2011
Run Time: 13:30:39
Voice Usage For: (337)619-0343
Account Number: 821635961

Item	Conn. Date	Conn. Time	Seizure Time	Originating Number	Terminating Number	Elapsed Time	Number Dialed	IMEI	IMSI
187	12/11/10	01:49P	0:24	13375190343	13373805712	1:29	13373805712	0124260047117	310410344456722
188	12/11/10	01:50P	0:23	13373605712	13375190343	0:06	13375190343		320610344456722
189	12/11/10	09:08P	0:20	16624159871	13375190343	0:00	13375190343	0124260047117	310410344456722
190	12/12/10	05:20P	0:05	13377810200	13375190343	5:17	13375190343	0124260047117	310410344456722
191	12/13/10	07:37A	0:05	13372016408	13375190343	0:37	13375190343	0124260047117	310410344456722
192	12/13/10	08:51A	9:20	13373671196	13375190343	0:08	13375190343	0124260047117	310410344456722
193	12/13/10	09:06A	0:20	13373671196	13375190343	0:09	13375190343	0124260047117	310410344456722
194	12/13/10	09:07A	0:20	13375193854	13375190343	0:00	13375190343	0124260047117	310410344456722
195	12/13/10	09:14A	0:21	13373671210	13375190343	0:00	13375190343	0124260047117	310410344456722
196	12/13/10	09:15A	0:21	13375197998	13375190343	0:04	13375190343	0124260047117	310410344456722
197	12/13/10	09:20A	0:21	13375197998	13375190343	0:12	13375190343	0124260047117	310410344456722
198	12/13/10	09:28A	0:21	13375197998	13375190343	0:07	13375190343	0124260047117	310410344456722
199	12/13/10	09:28A	0:21	13375197998	13375190343	0:03	13375190343	0124260047117	310410344456722
200	12/13/10	09:36A	0:21	13375193854	13375190343	0:00	13375190343	0124260047117	310410344456722
201	12/13/10	09:38A	0:21	13375197998	13375190343	0:13	13375190343	0124260047117	310410344456722
202	12/13/10	09:44A	0:20	13373671210	13375190343	0:00	13375190343	0124260047117	310410344456722
203	12/13/10	10:02A	0:25	13375190343	13375197998	0:06	13375197998	0124260047117	310410344456721
204	12/13/10	10:03A	0:14	13375197998	13375190343	0:04	13375190343	0124260047117	310410344456722
205	12/13/10	10:03A	0:22	13375197998	13375190343	0:07	13375190343	0124260047117	310410344456722
206	12/13/10	10:04A	0:21	13375197998	13375190343	0:06	13375190343	0124260047117	310410344456722
207	12/13/10	10:10A	0:00	13375190343	337560	0:00	337560	0124260047117	310410344456722
208	12/13/10	10:10A	0:14	13375190343	13375605841	0:00	13375605841	0124260047117	310410344456722
209	12/13/10	10:11A	0:06	13375190343	13375605841	0:04	13375605841	0124260047117	310410344456722
210	12/13/10	10:15A	0:22	13375197998	13375190343	0:13	13375190343	0124260047117	310410344456722
211	12/13/10	10:15A	0:08	13375190343	13375197998	0:00	13375197998	0124260047117	310410344456722
212	12/13/10	10:16A	0:01	13375190343	13375197998	0:00	13375197998	0124260047117	310410344456722
213	12/13/10	10:16A	0:01	13375190343	13375197998	0:00	13375197998	0124260047117	310410344456722
214	12/13/10	10:18A	0:22	13375197998	13375190343	1:04	13375190343	0124260047117	310410344456722
215	12/13/10	10:21A	0:22	13375197998	13375190343	0:03	13375190343	0124260047117	310410344456722
216	12/13/10				13375190343	0:26	13375190343	0124260047117	310410344456722
217	12/13/10	11:34A	0:22	13375197998	13375190343	0:21	13375190343	0124260047117	310410344456722
218	12/13/10	11:35A	0:21	13375197998	13375190343	0:09	13375190343	0124260047117	310410344456722
219	12/13/10	11:6BA	0:21	13373678702	13375190343	0:00	13375190343	0124260047117	310410344456722
220	12/13/10	12:21P	0:20	13375793248	13375190343	0:00	13375190343		310410344456722
221	12/13/10	12:37P	0:05	13372782025	13375190343	0:15	13375190343		310410344456722
222	12/13/10	01:41P	0:01	13375190051	13375190343	0:07	13375190343		310410344456722

AT&T Proprietary

AMO

The information contained here is for use by authorized p
not for general distribution.

Appendix I

- 296 -

James L. Daniels

From: James L. Daniels <█████████████████>
Sent: Monday, April 22, 2013 10:38 AM
To: 'Michele Cobb'
Subject: RE: Ismael Viera's testimony

I believe Ms. Dunning's testimony would in itself have been beneficial since Viera's discussions with her were privileged and therefore he had no reason to lie and they were against his interest as you point out. Also, Ms. Dunning testified on page 54 she negotiated with the D.A.'s office the language of the plea agreement. This is important because if you recall Mr. Durio made the argument about the fact that nowhere in Viera's plea did he mention Laurie's involvement. That's because his lawyer kept it out.

James L. Daniels
ATTORNEYS AT LAW

110 E. Kaliste Saloom Road, Suite 210
Lafayette, Louisiana 70508
337-706-8931
337-706-8935 facsimile
www.jdanielslaw.com

From: Michele Cobb [█████████████████]
Sent: Monday, April 22, 2013 10:14 AM
To: James Daniels; █████████████████ Paul Chastant
Subject: Ismael Viera's testimony

Hi Mr. Daniels,

Thank you for providing Ismael's testimony. I was able to read over it this weekend. I remember the judge contacting you to let you know there may be new information available to us in the testimony that might be useful. As I read, there were only a few pieces of information that appeared to be new.

1. Ismael was able to carry on a brief conversation in English without the assistance of an interpreter.
2. His story about Laurie's involvement was consistent the entire time. (I believe that Mrs. Dunning was mistaken about Laurie being present during the actual murder. Her testimony was the first I had heard of this. I have always understood that Laurie came to the barn after the murder to clean up.)
3. He was very angry that Laurie was not in custody.
4. He is still not denying her involvement, regardless of the fact that it possibly could have eliminated murder for hire.
5. The DA told Mrs. Dunning that the case against Laurie was still open at the time of Ismael's sentencing and I believe he said was still an on going investigation to this day.

6. Ismael obviously lied about understanding the difference between 1st and 2nd degree murder, but his story remains the same.

The majority of what I read, was known before the federal trial last summer. Is there anything else that I may have missed that could prove to be helpful or harmful to our case?
Thanks,
Michele Chastant Stark

Appendix J

UNITED STATES DISTRICT COURT
WESTERN DISTRICT OF LOUISIANA
LAFAYETTE-OPELOUSAS DIVISION

LAURIE ANNE FUTRAL,   *   Docket No. 12-2653
                                      *
            Plaintiff,   *
                                      *
VS   *   June 13, 2013
                                      *
PAUL T. CHASTANT,   *
                                      *
            Defendant.   *   Lafayette, Louisiana

REPORTER'S OFFICIAL TRANSCRIPT OF THE MOTION HEARING
BEFORE THE HONORABLE RICHARD T. HAIK,
UNITED STATES DISTRICT JUDGE.

APPEARANCES:

For the Plaintiff: Durio McGoffin, Et Al
                                BY: STEVEN G. DURIO
                                    DANIEL PHILLIPS
                                P.O. Box 51308
                                Lafayette, LA 70505

For the Defendant: Office of James Daniels
                                BY: JAMES L. DANIELS
                                110 E. Kaliste Saloom Rd.
                                Ste. 210
                                Lafayette, LA 70508

REPORTED BY: Mary Thompson, RMR, FCRR
                800 Lafayette Street, Ste. 3105
                Lafayette, Louisiana 70501
                (337)593-5222

13-30856.1128

Appendix K – Page 1 of 4

```
1    position that the interpleader was necessary, because there
2    was a claim that could be asserted that she was complicit in
3    the murder.  And after defeating all of that and getting her
4    money, the Court, nevertheless, awarded the trustee
5    attorneys' fees.
6            And it goes to the Fifth Circuit and the
7    Fifth Circuit reverses and says, wait a minute --
8            THE COURT:  Well, they are going to reverse me on
9    this one, too, then, because I don't think Mr. Paul Chastant
10   did anything inappropriate.  I think everything he did, he
11   had to do.
12           Do I think your client, after hearing the evidence,
13   had any involvement?  The answer to that is no.  Okay?  I
14   don't.  Others may have.
15           But certainly there was enough there that, as a
16   responsible trustee who is responsible for -- has a fiduciary
17   responsibility to the trust, he had no choice but to do that.
18   He had no choice.
19           MR. DURIO:  Your Honor --
20           THE COURT:  Listen, Mr. Durio, I heard the whole
21   trial.
22           MR. DURIO:  I know.
23           THE COURT:  I've read everything you said.  You are
24   not going to change my mind.
25           In this case this guy, Paul Chastant, was the
```

Appendix K – Page 2 of 4

Tom Aswell

```
 1    trustee.  He had an obligation to defend that trust --
 2    especially when he was sued.  Yes, he had a countersuit
 3    because he said that your client didn't have a right to it.
 4    Let me tell you, that was a serious issue.  That thing --
 5    that situation -- and it's not dead yet.  This thing could be
 6    resurrected to see if somebody else was involved.
 7            This was a civil trial, not a criminal trial.  I
 8    don't know what's going to happen with that.  My opinion is,
 9    after hearing the evidence, I don't think your client had
10    anything to do with that.  I don't.  I may be wrong.  Okay?
11    I don't think I am.  But somebody was there helping -- doing
12    something other than the one guy who got convicted.  I have
13    my own feelings on who that was, and I don't think it was
14    your client.
15            But I do think, under the circumstances, a civil
16    jury could have come back and said, yes, we think she was;
17    yes, there was enough there to consider that; yes -- heck,
18    this trial went on for four days, didn't it?
19            MR. DURIO:  Yes, sir.
20            THE COURT:  You know, it was a serious trial, three
21    or four days.
22            But that jury could have come back with a different
23    answer just as easily as they came back with the answer they
24    came with.  And he had an obligation to defend that trust,
25    because if he just capitulated, you know, then there's a
```

Appendix K – Page 3 of 4

```
 1   problem.  Then he would be forfeiting his fiduciary
 2   responsibility.
 3           So I've read everything, Mr. Durio.  I've read
 4   everything you have filed.  I disagree with it.  And I think
 5   that your summary judgment should be denied on behalf of
 6   Ms. Futral, and the summary judgment granted in favor of
 7   Chastant in fact recovering his fees and expenses that he
 8   paid in defense of the underlying lawsuit after the funds
 9   were deposited into the registry of the Court.
10           That's my ruling.  And you certainly can take an
11   appeal, and the Fifth Circuit can do what they want.  I heard
12   the evidence.  I think it would have been improper for
13   Mr. Paul Chastant not to do what he did and contest this
14   matter.  I think then he would have been dodging his
15   fiduciary responsibility.  Plus I think the plan does -- I
16   think it provides for him to do everything that he did.  But
17   even if it didn't, I think he had an obligation to do what he
18   did.
19           Thank you very much.
20           MR. DURIO:  Well, thank you, Your Honor.
21           THE COURT:  I'll sign a formal order upon
22   presentation.
23                           (Proceedings adjourned.)
24
25               * * * *
```

13-30856.1142

Appendix K – Page 4 of 4

Tom Aswell

RECEIVED
USDC W... ...TERN DISTRICT OF LA
TO... L. MOORE, CLERK
DATE ..5⁻/.23./.12.

UNITED STATES DISTRICT COURT
WESTERN DISTRICT OF LOUISIANA
LAFAYETTE DIVISION

LAURIE ANN FUTRAL CHASTANT	CIVIL ACTION NO. 6:11CV626
VERSUS	JUDGE HAIK
PRUDENTIAL INSURANCE CO. OF AMERICA, ET AL	MAGISTRATE JUDGE HANNA

****

JURY VERDICT

****

Do you find, from a preponderance of the evidence, that Laurie Ann Futral

Chastant participated in the intentional, unjustified killing of her husband, Robert

Brown Chastant.

_____YES   ____✓_NO

May 23, 2010
DATE

Keith Edilette
FOREPERSON

EXHIBIT
K

Appendix L

- 302 -

Lafayette Parish Recording Page

Louis J. Perret
Clerk of Court
P.O. Box 2009
Lafayette, LA 70502-2009
(337) 291-6400

First VENDOR   *2017- 5254*

INGRAM, JAMES COVINGTON III

First VENDEE

INGRAM, JAMES COVINGTON III

Index Type : CONVEYANCES   File Number : 2017-00036657

Type of Document : DIVORCE

Recording Pages :   2

Recorded Information

I hereby certify that the attached document was filed for registry and recorded in the Clerk of Court's office for Lafayette Parish, Louisiana

_____
Clerk of Court

On (Recorded Date) : 09/20/2017

At (Recorded Time) : 11:46:35AM

CLERK OF COURT
LOUIS J. PERRET
Parish of Lafayette
I certify that this is a true copy of the attached
document that was filed for registry and
Recorded 09/20/2017 at 11:46:35
File Number 2017-00036657

_____
Deputy Clerk

Doc ID - 040559080002

Appendix M.

Tom Aswell

Biography

Tom Aswell is a veteran of forty years as a newspaper reporter and editor as well as publisher of *LouisianaVoice*, a widely read internet blog about Louisiana politics. He has won numerous awards for breaking news, feature writing and investigative reporting while writing for such publications as the *Ruston Daily Leader* and the *Baton Rouge State-Times*. In 2013, *LouisianaVoice* was named by the *Washington Post* as one of the top 100 political blogs in the nation. His reporting on Louisiana State Police corruption was instrumental in the resignation of the LSP superintendent in 2016.

A native of Ruston, Louisiana, and a graduate of Louisiana Tech University, he is also the author of *Bobby Jindal: His Destiny and Obsession, Louisiana Rocks: The True Genesis of Rock & Roll, Louisiana's Rogue Sheriffs: A Culture of Corruption* and a novel, *Bordello on the Bayou*, a story of political power, lust and treachery.

He also has edited books for two other authors: With Edwards in the *Governor's Mansion: From Angola to Free Man*, by Forest Hammond-Martin, and *Smuggler's End: The Life and Death of Barry Seal*, by Del Hahn.

Aswell is an avid baseball fan, having owned and coached an independent baseball team in Ruston for ten years and lists the Boston Red Sox and Houston Astros as his favorite major league teams. Tom lists Ted Williams, Joe Morgan and Bob Gibson as his all-time favorite players. His greatest baseball thrills are Ted Williams's home run in his very last at-bat in 1960 and Warren Morris's bottom of the ninth-inning two-out, two-run home run that won the 1996 College World Series for LSU.

He and Betty, his wife of more than fifty years, have three daughters and seven grandchildren. Now in semi-retirement, they reside in Denham Springs, Louisiana, with their three dogs.

Made in the USA
Coppell, TX
17 July 2021